WORLD THEATRE
THE BASICS

World Theatre: The Basics presents a well-rounded introduction to non-Western theatre, exploring the history and current practice of theatrical traditions in Asia, Africa, the Middle East, Oceania, the Caribbean, and the non-English-speaking cultures of the Americas. Featuring a selection of case studies and examples from each region, it helps the reader to understand the key issues surrounding world theatre scholarship and global, postcolonial, and transnational performance practices.

An essential read for anyone seeking to learn more about world theatre, *World Theatre: The Basics* provides a clear, accessible roadmap for approaching non-Western theatre.

E. J. Westlake is Associate Professor in the Department of Theatre and Drama and Associate Professor in the Department of English Language and Literature at the University of Michigan. She is a faculty affiliate of the Center for World Performance Studies and is affiliated with the program in Latin American and Caribbean Studies and Romance Languages.

THE BASICS

WORLD THEATRE

THE BASICS

E. J. Westlake

Routledge
Taylor & Francis Group

LONDON AND NEW YORK

First published 2017
by Routledge
2 Park Square, Milton Park, Abingdon, Oxon OX14 4RN

and by Routledge
711 Third Avenue, New York, NY 10017

Routledge is an imprint of the Taylor & Francis Group, an informa business

© 2017 E. J. Westlake

British Library Cataloguing in Publication Data
A catalogue record for this book is available from the British Library

Library of Congress Cataloging in Publication Data
Names: Westlake, E. J., 1965- author.
Title: World theatre / E. J. Westlake.
Other titles: World theater
Description: Milton Park, Abingdon, Oxon; New York, NY : Routledge, 2017. |
Series: The basics
Identifiers: LCCN 2016030354 | ISBN 9781138838048 (hardback) |
ISBN 9781138838055 (pbk.) | ISBN 9781315734729 (ebook)
Subjects: LCSH: Theater—History.
Classification: LCC PN2101. W48 2017 | DDC 792.09—dc23
LC record available at https://lccn.loc.gov/2016030354

ISBN: 978-1-138-83804-8 (hbk)
ISBN: 978-1-138-83805-5 (pbk)
ISBN: 978-1-315-73472-9 (ebk)

Typeset in Bembo
by Keystroke, Neville Lodge, Tettenhall, Wolverhampton

CONTENTS

PREFACE AND ACKNOWLEDGMENTS

When I first considered this project, I was not sure it could be done. The world is a big place and there are innumerable cultures with as many complex and interesting theatrical practices. Any text on "world theatre" could potentially be several volumes. And yet, I was intrigued by the idea of providing a reader with little or no prior knowledge of world theatre with a brief and useful introduction. After polling many of my colleagues about what they thought would be most useful in such a text, I decided right away to omit most discussion of Europe and the United States except when examining ideas that have influenced artists elsewhere in the world and to emphasize the work of artists who are not descendants of Europeans. There are plenty of texts dealing with European and US theatre and many texts on "world theatre" that cover European theatre almost exclusively.

This made the task more manageable, but still daunting. There are no universal principles which tie together all of humankind and, therefore, all of theatre. And so I chose to tie things together loosely (very loosely) through a chronology of the development of recognizable theatrical practice and along routes of human, and therefore cultural, migration – to try to trace the fleeting moments of cultural concretization in a whirlwind of syncretization and change. People have been encountering each other and influencing the ways in which stories are told for millennia.

I want to preface the material in this volume by noting a few choices I have made in the use of certain terms. Most style guides now stress non-sexist terms for all professions. Just as most people no longer use the term "waitress" or "lady doctor," I use the term "actor" to refer to people of *all* genders who perform on stage. Also, I will not refer to people from the United States as "Americans," although this is common practice in Europe. "America" means an entire hemisphere of people and many people in Latin America correctly refer to people in the US as *estadounidense*, or literally "Unitedstatesians." As Mexican performance artist Jesusa Rodríguez notes in her performance as "Freaka Kahlo" in *Arquetipas: A Prehispanic Cabaret* (2004), the two continents have been called "America" by mistake anyway, a European imposition and distortion of history, making the United States doubly devoid of an actual name. In the cabaret, Kahlo holds a contest, "Name Your Country," stating that "When I arrived to New York, I realized that in the beginning: 'NYC' does not mean 'New York City.' It means 'Name Your Country.'"

This project has pushed me out of my comfort zone and into new areas of research. It has been both exhilarating and terrifying. But the support from my colleagues has been overwhelming. I would like to thank colleagues who have read and commented upon those sections which fall under their various areas of expertise: Marjan Moosavi, Evan Winet, Melissa Van Wyk, Leigh Woods, Mbala Nkanga, Emily Wilcox, and Shanti Thirumalai. I also want to thank the team at Routledge for having the vision to initiate this project, especially Talia Rogers who thought of me, Siobhán Poole, Ben Piggot, Iram Satti, and Kate Edwards, and the people in the production department.

I would also like to thank those colleagues on the listserv for the American Society for Theatre Research and on Facebook who weighed in on content: Elly Lien, Beth Cherne, Tim Good, Patricia Moore Zimmer, Mary Shelly, Cathy Lewis, Christianne Myers, Tobin Nellhaus, Luvy Margarita Rappaccioli Navas, J. Ellen Gainor, Susan Kattwinkel, Steve Tillis, John Bell, Jim Al-Shamma, Carol Martin, Sharon Mazer, Kate Wilson, Dan Venning, Arnab Banerji, Kirsten Pullen, Cecil Thomas Ault, Erika T. Lin, Susan B. Finque, John D. Swain, Carol Fisher Sorgenfrei, Richard Schechner, Kathy Foley, Kathleen Worley, Catherine A. Schuler, Farah Yeganeh, Claire Conceison, Wei Feng, Helen E. Moss, Ken Takiguchi, Peter Campbell, Cynthia Ling Lee, Kellen Hoxworth, Daniel Meyer-Dinkgräfe, Gary Williams, Samuel Leiter, Peter Eckersall, and Rossella Ferrari. I would especially like to thank my research assistant for the summer of 2015,

Yuyu Wang, who came to Michigan on a scholarship through the China Scholarship Council from Tsinghua University. She gave her time generously to doing some of the preliminary research on the section on *jīngjù*.

I want to thank my department chair Priscilla Lindsay for her eternal support. Research on this project was partially supported by a block grant from the School of Music, Theatre, and Dance at the University of Michigan. I especially want to thank my supportive and amazing partner Claudia Rene Wier who has spent the last several months encouraging and helping me while somehow at the same time making progress on her dissertation. Let's go ride bikes.

INTRODUCTION: WHAT IS WORLD THEATRE?

The renowned British director Peter Brook famously said, "A man walks across this empty space whilst someone else is watching him, and this is all that is needed for an act of theatre to be engaged" (*The Empty Space* 9). Indeed, most theatre scholars agree that all you need to have "theatre" is (1) an actor, (2) an event, and (3) an audience. As you can well imagine, this covers an enormous amount of activity; and if we say "world" theatre, the project of examining all such activity throughout history and all over the world becomes an impossible task. How then do we talk about "world theatre?"

A century ago, scholars would have defined theatre as a tradition with a play in the form of a written text, performed by trained actors, in a space of a designated theatre. Often the musical forms such as opera were separated out as distinct from the theatre. If you look at textbooks on the theatre from the twentieth century, they might say that theatre evolved from ritual, began as a legitimate form with the Greeks, and was, with few exceptions, a distinctly Western (European and American) form. However, over the last three or four decades, scholars have come to understand the various Eurocentric, and even racist, assumptions underlying this model.

To begin with, the ritual-to-theatre model rests upon a notion of social Darwinism, that is that all societies develop in the same way, from "primitive" to civilized. The model is based on the idea that one could look at present-day "primitive" cultures to understand how all humans behaved several millennia ago. As anthropologists have come to understand that human beings have organized themselves by an infinite range of kinship, subsistence, and belief systems, the idea that there is a universal trajectory is now laughable. The model also suggests that Europe is the "birthplace" of this civilization. And it supposes that European culture and society is the pinnacle of such a trajectory.

The ritual-to-theatre model creates boundaries between disciplines that are artificial and difficult to maintain. On the other hand, there is nothing wrong with a course that covers only European and American theatre as a matter of clarity and brevity. A course in "theatre" certainly could not cover everything. Recognizing that limitation, this text is designed to explore things that might be left out of such a course, and to do so in a way that gives the reader a sense of what the theatre scene might be in the Middle East, Asia, Oceania, Africa, and the Americas. Because the territory of world theatre is enormous, we will explore a few key examples; examples that can be contrasted and compared, but from which no universal ideals should be drawn.

Further delimitation in terms of form will help us focus our attention as well. Peter Brook's definition of theatre covers almost every performative act, that is, every act where someone takes a role for the benefit of an onlooker. However, this definition could apply to political speeches, ice dancing, classroom lectures, or meeting someone in a bar. While the broader idea of performative acts opens up opportunities for further study, this text will stick to a recognizable set of theatre conventions: an intentional narrative, costumes, a designated playing space, and onlookers intentionally engaging in spectatorship. We will cover forms that include spoken or sung text (otherwise we end up including dance), but forms that involve action and interaction on stage known as "blocking" (otherwise we end up including concerts). And we will concern ourselves with what is live rather than mediated, or at least has a significant live element.

Within those boundaries, theatre takes many forms. The makers of theatre have engaged in various forms of theatrical practice over time in many ways. The range of theatrical activity can be as familiar as watching *Death of a Salesman* in a regional theatre such as The Guthrie in Minneapolis. And it can be as strange as watching Karen Finley perform *We Keep Our Victims Ready*, where she reads with an exaggeratedly inflected, almost musical, voice, the inner thoughts of several personae, stopping occasionally to interact with the audience or to smear chocolate frosting on her nude body. Some performances involve the use of puppets or mediatized images. Sometimes there is music, as in a Broadway musical, or opera performance. In realism, actors are asking the audience to suspend their disbelief and to identify with the characters they are portraying. Some forms of theatre are presentational, where actors may play several characters or "step-out of character" (stop acting for a moment) to address the audience directly.

In some cases, a lone playwright has written a dramatic text, and in other cases, a group of people has improvised. The creators of the play might be following a story that is already known to the audience or they might make a story that is completely original. A tradition might call for actors that have extensive training and are paid, or it can be a form created wholly by people in the community who are not theatre artists. Theatre has also had many functions. Makers of theatre have created it to be educational, or to be simple entertainment. Theatre can be transgressive and call for social change, or it can be didactic and normative. Theatre can commemorate past events or imagine a future. Either way, it calls upon the spectators to think, to feel, to reflect, and sometimes, to act.

HUMAN HISTORY

The archaeological record shows that human beings have always migrated. Early humans moved from Africa to Eurasia about 2 million years ago, followed by modern humans about 100,000 years ago. DNA evidence shows the surprising fact that humans continued to migrate back and forth and that migration patterns were never one way. With them, humans took along their language, culture, textiles, beliefs, and eventually, writing. No two groups were alike, and continual contact with other groups of people meant that culture was always dynamically changing.

As some societies that embraced large-scale agriculture developed, so did a more permanent historical record. With a couple of odd exceptions dating earlier, the first form of writing that we know of is Mesopotamian cuneiform in the kingdom of Mesopotamia (in what is now Iraq, Iran, and Syria). Not long after, Egyptians developed hieroglyphics. The Phoenicians modified both scripts, creating something that eventually evolved into Greek, Arabic, Hebrew, and ultimately the Cyrillic and Roman alphabets. Some of the earliest writing in China dates back to about 1200 BCE. The civilizations of the Americas have records of writing in Olmec, Zapotec, and Mayan dating as far back as 900 BCE.

Because so much of human society existed before the rise of written language, and because theatre has often been an oral form and not a written one, there is absolutely no way of knowing what the earliest forms of theatre might have been. One can imagine all of the different ways human beings have engaged in theatrical activity – telling stories, acting out scenes of things that have happened, engaging in pageants, and using objects as characters in dramatic play. And because only certain people were using writing and only for certain things, the earliest written records are extremely limited. Scholars are relatively sure that evidence points to dramatic activity for important royal occasions in Egypt: a stela (or stone) written by Ikhernofret in roughly 1870 BCE suggests that he was a participant in something scholars call the *Abydos Passion Play* at a festival for the god Osiris.

The records we have for the earliest recognizable theatre suggest that different people had special forms of "ritual drama," or dramatic presentations that were part of certain rituals: coronations and burials in particular. There were also plays produced that were part of religious festivals. We have a great deal of information about the Dionysian festivals of Ancient Greece, and we know that competitions were held for the best tragedy: a series of choral odes and dances interspersed with dialogue or song treating stories well known to Greek audiences. The earliest treatise on aesthetics was written about a century after most Greek tragic poetry was written, but this treatise, Aristotle's *The Poetics*, had a profound impact on Western theatre and theatre all over the world.

"QUALITY OF THE SENTIMENT": WHAT IS MEANT BY *AESTHETICS*?

Aesthetics is the underlying set of ideas about art and beauty. It is the philosophy that any culture at any time throughout history has about the observation of art and the critique of art. It comes from the Greek word *aisthētikos*, which means "perceptible" or "material" things. Most of the underlying ideas of any society's sense of aesthetics are taken for granted. But, occasionally, philosophers and artists have taken it upon themselves to define the given aesthetics of their cultures. The earliest texts we have that pertain to theatrical forms are *The Poetics* written by the Greek Aristotle around 335 BCE, the *Nātyasāstra* written by the Indian Bharata Muni between 200 BCE and 200 CE, and the treatises of the Japanese Noh artist Zeami Motokiyo written at the beginning of the fifteenth century CE.

Aristotle (384–322 BCE) was a philosopher and a student of Plato (c.428–c.348 BCE). He wrote about science, the arts, and politics. Much of his work survives because he became the tutor to Alexander the Great and established a library that housed his writings. His work on *The Poetics* reflects his ideas on how people learn about the world through perception. Aristotle did not live during the time of the known writers of classical Greek tragedy, but rather a century later. What he wrote in *The Poetics* was based upon his close reading of these old texts. Based on his observations, he came up with criteria for what makes a good tragedy. *The Poetics* survived in the Eastern part of the European world long after the Western Roman Empire fell, but was not available to Western Europe until the fall of Constantinople in 1453 brought a flood of previously forgotten documents into Italy at the beginning of the Italian Renaissance. Scholars who hadn't given much thought to the "rules" of drama latched onto *The Poetics*, debated Aristotle's meaning, and used their conclusions to establish a template for all of Western drama. It is by this template that the theatre of Europe and the United States is judged, and by extension, by which the aestheticians of these cultures have judged the theatrical traditions of people all over the world.

Aristotle first pondered the reasons human beings create theatre. He felt that human beings desire to continually learn through observation and that our desire to imitate life was innate. He differentiated between forms of drama, noting that comedy was the imitation of low-status characters, and tragedy was the imitation of high-status characters, such as gods, heroes, or royalty. Tragedy, according to Aristotle, had six elements: plot, character, thought, diction, spectacle, and song. Plot was the most important element given that tragedy is the imitation of action, not of people. However, the plot of a drama cannot exist without the spectator's relationship to a certain kind of character, the second element of tragedy. Aristotle believed the aim of tragedy was to effect the proper *catharsis* or purgation of emotion by evoking pity and fear in the spectator. To do so, a tragic hero had to be a person who was basically good, but through some error or weakness has a terrible change in fortune. To have the protagonist be a bad person would not bring this about because the spectator would just feel satisfied at the character's downfall. To have the protagonist be completely good and without flaw would make the spectator feel outrage. But a basically good protagonist who is flawed would be someone with whom the spectator could identify. The protagonist's downfall would evoke pity because the protagonist is basically good and not deserving of such a fate. The spectator would feel terror because, through identification, spectators recognize that such a fate could befall them as well.

Aristotle talks about the protagonist's weakness or flaw as a *hamartia*, which literally means "missing the mark." In other words, the flaw is some kind of excess, for instance overweening pride in the form of *hubris*. This excess was seen as undesirable in Greek cultures and many Greek philosophers talk about a "middle way" or moderation as an admirable quality. The spectator then would wish to be purged of such excess and would then be instructed on the tenets of model citizenship.

Aristotle believed the plot of a tragedy should be of the "proper magnitude," in that a play should not try to cover too much in such a short amount of time. He admired playwrights who focused on one complete action with logically progressing events that served only to further the story. He noted also that the work of the playwright was completely separate from the work of the historian. The job of the historian was to relay events as they happened and in detail. The job of the playwright was to relay what was probable according to universal truths: "how a person of a certain type will on occasion speak or act, according to the law of probability or necessity; and it is this universality at which poetry aims in the names she attaches to the personages." In this way, Aristotle saw tragic poetry as being a higher and more philosophical form than history.

The aesthetics of a culture are inextricably linked with that culture's cosmology, ideology, and cultural norms. Through their tragic drama, the Greeks celebrated their creation of a limited democratic state (only landowning males could participate), their use of a formal judicial process to determine culpability, and overall their ability to reason to make sense of the world. Aristotle believed there was a progression from observation of detail through reason to an understanding of the universal. Aristotle believed reason should be used to choose a "middle way" between extremes. The universal lesson presented through the Greek tragic protagonists is one of failure to find moderation in all things.

Where *The Poetics* deals with the history of classical Greek drama in what might seem to be a detached tone, noting the elements that one might see in the *theatron*, or "seeing place," and judging them according to a system of critical thought, the *Natyasastra* covers the mythic origins of Sanskrit performance and the ways in which its performance of *bhavas*, or "emotions," evokes different kinds of *rasa*, or "tastes." First formulated as a sacred revelation by Bharata Muni sometime between the second century BCE and the second century CE, the *Natyasastra* forms the aesthetic foundation of performance forms (called *natya*, or "drama") in India and those of several other South Asian cultures. According to Richard Schechner, much of the written text of it was lost or fragmented and not really set into a coherent whole until Kashmiri Śaivite Abhinavagupta compiled a copy in the tenth century (28).

Natya is from the Sanskrit word for drama and encompasses many classical Indian dance forms such as *Kathakali* and *Kuchipudi* that have emerged from Sanskrit drama. Performances occur during festivals throughout India, such as Ramlila, the reenactment of the battle between Rama and Ravana. These performances generally deal with stories from the *Mahabharata* or the *Ramayana*, epic tales of Hindi gods and heroes. Forms such as *Kathakali* were originally written to run several hours, often lasting all night. Like many dramatic forms, the performances are comprised of a dramatic narrative, virtuosic dance, and music. Indeed, *"natya"* means all three.

Sastra means "authoritative text." While the written text may seem to be disjointed commentary compiled from several sources, it reflects the continuous oral tradition that has kept the *Natyasastra* at the heart of the various *natya* traditions. Indeed, it is written in the form of a dialogue where several voices commenting on *natya* are apparent. At the beginning of several of the thirty-six chapters, the text takes the form of a conversation: questions from a group of muni, or "sages" about the *veda* (sacred text) of *natya* and Bharata's answers. What eventually becomes the *Natyasastra* are Bharata's responses, compiled and interpolated by generations of scholars.

The *Natyasastra* covers in detail the origin of drama, the dimensions and construction of the theatre building, and outlines the ten types of drama. Chapters also instruct on the proper way to make an offering to the gods of the stage. There are chapters on the hand gestures that are an important part of conveying the text of the story, and on the different movements of the face, limbs, and torso. One chapter deals specifically with the different kinds of gaits a performer uses. The text describes the different character types and corresponding makeup. It also has several chapters on the music that accompanies the dance drama.

At the heart of the *Natyasastra* is an explanation of *rasa*, or the taste that is evoked in the spectator. Bharata notes that the sole purpose of *natya* is its aesthetic: "It is said that the dance is occasioned by no specific need; it has come into use simply because it creates beauty" (68). It exists to bring pleasure to the spectator and to arouse abiding feeling. *Rasa* literally means "taste," viewed as a sensory pleasure manifest from a feast of performance:

> [I]t is said that, as taste (*rasa*) results from a combination of various spices, vegetables and other articles, and as six tastes (*rasa*) are produced by articles such as, raw sugar or spices or vegetables, so the Dominant States (*sthayi bhava*), when they come together with various other States (*bhava*) attain the quality of the Sentiment (i.e. become Sentiment). Now one enquires, "What is the meaning of the word *rasa*?" It is said in reply to this [that *rasa* is so called] because it is capable of being tasted.
>
> (105)

This suggests that you take in the performance through all of your senses and then feel it in your gut. The performance nourishes the audience.

Bharata outlines eight kinds of *rasa* that the performer evokes in the audience. The performer works to perfect the *abhinaya*, or "performance," which is made up of gestures, words, costume and makeup, and the representation of emotion or states. Through the performance, the performer elicits a series of transitory states (such as weariness, agitation, shame, indignation, or fright) to make up a Dominant State (*sthayi bhava*), an abiding emotion, which manifests a corresponding Sentiment or *rasa*. As Schechner notes, the performer may or may not also actually feel the emotion, but such feeling is not necessary so long as it works to create the intended *rasa* (32–33). The eight *sthayi bhava* and corresponding *rasa* are listed here:

Rasa
sringara (erotic)
hasya (comic)
karuna (pathetic)
raudra (furious)
vira (heroic)
bhayanaka (terrible)
bibhasta (odious)
adbhuta (marvelous)

Sthayi bhava
rati (love)
hasa (mirth)
soka (sorrow)
krodha (anger)
utsaha (energy)
bhaya (fear)
jugupsra (disgust)
vismaya (astonishment, wonder)

The relationship between *bhava* and *rasa* is direct. Bharata notes that the relationship between the two is not symbiotic:

> It is apparent that the Sentiments arise from the States and not the States from the Sentiment. . . . The States are so called by experts in drama, for they cause to originate (*sthayi bhava*) the Sentiments in connexion [*sic*] with various modes of dramatic representation. Just as by many articles of various kinds of auxiliary cooked food is [*sic*] brought forth, so the States along with different kinds of Histrionic Representation will cause the Sentiments to originate.
>
> (106–107)

The key in this, however, is that the spectator must be disposed to experiencing the *rasa*, and this requires cultivation. The spectator does not passively accept the state, the spectator must be attuned to the *bhava* being represented: "Just as connoisseur of cooked food (*bhakti*) while eating food which has been prepared from various spices and other articles, taste it [sic], so the learned people taste in their mind the Dominant States" (106). According to Abhinavagupta, the spectator must be cultivated enough to feel the *rasa* to the fullest, and to be lifted, then, to a ninth *rasa* of bliss.

Zeami Motokiyo (1363–1444) wrote several treatises on the art of Noh drama in Japan. He was not attempting to write a definitive public text, rather, he was recording his ideas about the craft of Noh for his successors. But his writing reveals the aesthetic of Noh drama, which grows out of a spiritual view of the performer's craft.

Noh theatre was developed by Zeami's father Kan'ami (1333–1384). Kan'ami ran a theatre company that combined several popular forms of the time including the rhythmic music of *kusemai*, the form of *sarugaku*, and the harvest dances of *dengaku*. The troupe received patronage from the court of shogun Ashikaga Yoshimitsu where they were able to develop the craft now known as Noh. The form incorporates masks, music, and subtle movement on a bare stage as a narrator sings the story being enacted. Zeami wrote his treatises to instruct his successors on the philosophy of Noh, a philosophy based on Shinto, Buddhism, and a combination of Taoist and Confucian thought.

Zeami stated that the purpose of the performing arts was to bring peace and harmony to the hearts of the spectators. This feeling of peace could be brought about by the exceptional beauty of the performer's skill, beauty that is as much of the spirit as it is of the physical movement on stage. A beautiful performance would move people of all classes and thereby bring prosperity and stability to the world.

Fūshikaden (Transmission of Style and the Flower), written in 1402, was the first treatise on drama in Japan. In it, Zeami discusses at length the kind of training necessary at each stage in the life of a Noh artist. Zeami explains two important concepts in Noh theatre: *monomane* (or imitation) and *hana* (or the idea of "flower"). *Monomane* is the imitation in playing the wide range of roles in Noh theatre. Zeami instructs the performer that "[p]laying involves an imitation, in every particular, with nothing left out" (Rimer and Masakazu via Worthen 160). He cautions the performer to know how much he should imitate depending on the kind of character. For instance, a performer could not possibly know the details of the life at court for a ruler. On the other hand, the actions of laborers should be stylized so that their portrayal is not too realistic to be agreeable as a poetic subject. Zeami also writes at length about the idea of *hana*, emphasizing the importance of novelty, but it is novelty within a defined tradition. The flower, Zeami explains, blooms only once in the year, making it novel and beautiful in its time. But it blooms in its proper season. A performer will perform according to the tastes and expectations of the spectator. However, the performance can be infused with novelty:

> even though he changes nothing, he will use anew all his old arts, color the music and his voice in a skillful manner, using a level of concentration he has never felt before, and show exceptional care. If such a successful performance is achieved, those who see it and hear it will find it more novel than usual and they will praise it.
>
> (quoted in Gerould 100)

In this sense, the seeds of the flower are planted in that an actor trains for years to develop skill. The flower then blooms at its appointed time, but amazes in its beauty, the petals of the beauty scattering to the spectators. It is beautiful, but also transient.

In his treatise *Kakyō* (A Mirror Held to the Flower), Zeami further elaborates on the idea of *hana*. Flower is what makes the actor's performance particularly exquisite, or gives it *yugen* or "grace." This is a quality that is not externally apparent, but which excites the audience. An actor can master dance and chant, but still not move the spectator. However, he notes: "there are actors whose voices are not attractive and whose mastery of dancing and singing show defects, yet who are widely thought of as accomplished performers. The reason for this is that both dancing and gesture are external skills. The essentials of our art lie in the spirit. They represent a true enlightenment established through art" (quoted in Worthen 164). An actor cannot be truly great unless the actor, through years of careful training, develops his concentration, originality in his performance, and his spirit.

The theatre aesthetics of any culture arises from that culture's unique philosophy, a sense the people have, performers and spectators alike, of the function of theatre in society, whether that function is to inspire, provoke, affirm, or elevate. What a group of people find enjoyable or desirable will change with social norms and so the examples of theatre we have through time and all over the world are as interesting and varied as every civilization that has existed on Earth. What follows is but a small sample of these unique theatre traditions.

1

THE MIDDLE EAST

The first documented suggestion of a theatrical performance comes from the area commonly called the "Middle East." It is worth noting that the first use of the term "Middle East" was by the India Office in Britain in the nineteenth century. Different cultural groups have different names for the area, although most names refer to this area as "east" in that it is both the eastern part of the Mediterranean and the historically eastern part of the Arab-speaking world. The modern-day nations from Egypt to Iran and the Arabian Peninsula to Turkey are included in this region.

ABYDOS AND THE PROBLEM OF THE HISTORICAL RECORD

Until recently, the account of the *Abydos Passion Play*, or the festival processional ritual of the death, dismemberment, and resurrection of the Egyptian god Osiris, had long been considered by theatre historians to be the first account of a theatrical performance in the historical record. Abydos, or Abdju as it was called, was an important burial site for many of the pharaohs beginning with the first dynasty (sometime between the thirty-fourth and thirtieth centuries BCE). Because of its significance as a burial site, it became a center for the worship of Osiris, the god of the underworld.

Osiris, the mythical ruler of prehistoric Egypt, is the son of the earth god Geb (and some say the sun god Ra) and the sky goddess Nut. He is dismembered by his jealous brother Seth who wants to take the throne from him. Seth scatters his body so that he cannot live in the afterlife. The wife (and also sister) of Osiris, Isis, gathers his remains and reassembles him so that he can live in the underworld. They then conceive a son, Horus, who after violent struggle, reclaims the throne from Seth. The themes of just kingship and coronation, death and resurrection, became ideal material for ceremonies for the burials of rulers, the succession of the throne, and the changing seasons related to the harvest. The latter association was the reason the Abydos procession was performed in conjunction with the annual flooding of the Nile.

While we can imagine that there has been theatrical activity for as long as there have been human beings, we have no record of this activity. And because we can imagine that this theatrical activity has existed, it is tempting to say Abydos is the first event for which we have a concrete artifact, an artifact that seems to be an eyewitness account. This is the reason that this procession has had such great importance in the history of the theatre. Indeed, there are a number of earlier texts of stories and myths that many historians believe were associated with a performance, but we have no record of the performance itself.

However, as Alan Sikes notes in his essay on Abydos, we must use caution when attempting to interpret the text as something "theatrical." The privileging of Abydos as a "passion play" has its roots in the idea that theatre evolved from ritual. Therefore, Abydos, a funerary rite, provided theatre scholars who subscribed to the ritual origin theory with an ideal "missing link" between ritual and theatre. That this has left us with such an open question that continues to be debated makes Ikhernofret's account, and what historians have made of it, worth discussing here.

The account appears on a stela (or stone) and belongs to the man Ikhernofret, a treasurer and "companion of the king" (according to the text) during the rule of Senusret III (reign 1878–1839 BCE). Egyptologist Jan Assmann notes that Ikhernofret's account of the festivities can be divided into four sections: (1) The Procession of Wepwawet (the Opener of the Ways), (2) The "Great Procession" in the *Neshmet*-barque, (3) The Night of the "Battling Horus": the Haker Festival, and (4) the Procession to the Temple of Osiris (227–229).

Most of the text of the stela sounds like any devotional procession:

> I arranged the Great Procession and accompanied the god on his way. I caused the divine barque to sail, and Thoth granted that

the journey went well. I outfitted the barque "Appearing in Maat" of the lord of Abydos with a cabin and put on his crown. How beautiful was his procession to the district of U-poqer! I sanctified the ways of the god to his grave at the peak of U-poqer.

(Assmann 228, note 74)

The sacred boat of Nun was adorned, and on it, Osiris was figuratively taken from the temple to his tomb and then back again. It is similar to the phallic processions from the temple of Dionysus in Athens or saint's day processions where saints are taken from the church, paraded through the town, and then returned. These acts could be called "performative" in that they have many elements of a performing art such as costumes, a text with something of a narrative, and spectators.

Some passages on the stela do indeed sound theatrical and seem to indicate a reenactment of a battle or contest: "I arranged the procession of Wepwawet, when he went to the aid of his father. I beat back those who rebelled against the *neshmet*-barque and subdued the enemies of Osiris" (227), and "I took action for Wennefer on that day of the great battle. I subdued all his enemies on the sand bank of Nedyt" (228). We do not know, however, if these were merely recitations. Assmann suggests that this was a ritual that consisted of recitations accompanied by actions, such as mutilation and burning of figures, or "breaking the red pots," or a ritual slaughter (228). But "action" does not equal "theatre." Assmann adds in his end note that: "Scholars have pictured the beating back of rebels as a ritual drama, referring to Herodotus, who describes a ritual mock battle in Papremis. This seems unthinkable, however, for earlier periods in Egyptian history" (454, note 73). In short, the texts left behind by the ancient Egyptians do not support the idea that Abydos is theatre or even has many of the important elements of theatre.

Ta'ziyeh

With the spread of Islam throughout the Middle East, so too spread *aniconism*, the prohibition of the creation of images of people and any sentient being. While aniconism does not appear specifically in the Qur'an, it is taken up in the *Hadith*, the compiled record of the sayings and actions of the Prophet Muhammed. Islam forbids representations of God, Muhammed, the family of Muhammed, and the prophets, but the Hadith also mentions all humans and animals. With such a religious prohibition, the development of a representational art such as theatre would prove difficult. As with any religion, however, there are differences in interpretation and degree of a prohibition, and in some parts of the Islamic world, many performance forms persist. *Ta'ziyeh* is one such example that has flourished among Shi'ite Muslims.

"*Ta'ziyeh*" means "mourning" or "condolences" in Arabic. It commemorates the martyrdom of Hussein and has a long history in Iran and among Shia Muslims. After the death of Muhammed in 632 CE, a schism developed among Muslims along clan lines. Many Omayyad clan members believed his successor should be elected, which was a long-standing Arab tradition. An opposing clan, the Hashemites, thought that the successor should be someone related to Muhammed. This schism is now between the Sunni and Shia, respectively. The Shia wanted Muhammed's cousin and son-in-law Ali to be caliph, but he and his eldest son were poisoned. The Sunni moved the center of the caliphate to Damascus and the Shia of Kufa enlisted Ali's youngest son Hussein to come to join them against the Sunni. Hussein and his family and his followers, however, were attacked in the desert of Karbala. In 680 CE, the Sunni laid siege to the group, denying them access to water, a sure death sentence in the hot desert. They eventually attacked, cutting the men to pieces with swords and arrows and taking the women and children captive.

Commemoration of this martyrdom has redemptive value in Shia Muslim culture. It is believed that Hussein will intercede on your behalf if you observe and participate in the mourning rituals. In the Safavid dynasty (1500–1736), the mourning of Hussein during the month of Muharram received official support. Chelkowski notes that European visitors to Iran have written about the participants in colorful costumes depicting the death of the martyrs and the events leading up to their martyrdom (33).

These processions gradually evolved into mobile tableaux, each depicting the martyrdom. Some would have battle scenes, while others would show martyrs covered with blood with their limbs chopped off. These tableaux could be compared to English cycle plays or, perhaps, the Spanish *autos sacramentales*, moving through the village with separate scenes from the Bible. The processions would be accompanied by funeral music. At the same time, a form of recitation, taken from a book about the passion of Hussein, developed. These recitations were stationary, but the narration gradually became more dramatic. In the eighteenth century, the two forms were combined into the modern *Ta'ziyeh*. Chelkowski states that the practice of having the protagonists sing their parts while the antagonists merely recite theirs has been in place since the merging of these forms (33). Each scene focuses on individual heroes, including individuals who were martyred before the siege at Karbala. In the nineteenth century, under the rule of Naser al-din Shah of the Qajar dynasty, a permanent modern theatre was built, the Takiya-i-Dawlat. It was during this time that a British envoy collected and published the cycle under the title *The Miracle Play of Hasan and Husain*.

The story of Hussein's martyrdom was ideal for Shia as Rebecca Ansary Pettys notes: "unlike his father Ali, Hussein was not assassinated unexpectedly, but rather embarked on his fateful journey fully aware of the possible consequences. Thus, it was possible to characterize his eventual death as a willing sacrifice which not only gave his martyrdom tragic proportion, but also accorded well with the Shi'yah doctrine of free will" (344). The story is also especially important to the people of Iran for a number of reasons. As Ansary Pettys notes, the schism between Sunni and Shia Muslims was not just a struggle for succession. It was a struggle that inflamed clan rivalry between the Hashemite clan, of which Hussein was a member, and the Omayyad clan (343). More deeply, it was a resistance by Persians to Arab rule.

At the time of the death of Muhammed, the Persian territory of Mesopotamia was still under Sassanid rule, and the Sassanid clan were Zoroastrians. The ruler Khosrow II famously tore up a letter from Muhammed warning him of the consequences of not converting to Islam. In 627 after a long war, the Persians were defeated by the Byzantines, a loss that pushed the Sassanid Empire into decline and chaos. Khosrow II's rivals captured and executed him, leading to a crisis of succession that lasted several years. Eventually, things stabilized under his grandson Yazdegerd III, the last ruler of the Sassanid dynasty. Over the next two decades, the Arabs waged war against the Persians, eventually defeating them in 651.

While the Arabs succeeded in Islamizing the Persians, the Persians remained a distinct people and culture. This is probably in part due to the fact that the Persian language is not just distinct from Arabic, it belongs in a completely different language family. The language survived even after the Omayyad Caliphate made Arabic the official language. This may explain also the persistence of *Ta'ziyeh* and other figural arts despite the Islamic prohibition on figural representation. Another explanation might be the fact that commemorating the death or martyrdom of Persian spiritual figures had a long tradition that predates *Ta'ziyeh* and may have even served as the template for *Ta'ziyeh* performance. Mahani points out that Persians observed the commemoration of the passion of the Zoroastrian god Mitra by acting it out on a platform. More well known is the *Yadgar-i-Zariran* or the *Memorial of Zarir* where Zarir is martyred in battle for converting to Zoroastrianism, much in the way Hussein was martyred. It is believed these mourning rituals gave rise to the tradition of *Ta'ziyeh*. As the mourning ritual predates Islam in Iran, it seems understandable that it would remain an important part of Iranian tradition.

Today, *Ta'ziyeh* is performed throughout Iran, but also in countries with significant communities of Shia Muslims. The actors are sometimes amateurs, but as Beeman and Ghaffari note, there is a professional class of *Ta'ziyeh* actors. Because acting is suspect in the Muslim world, the actors face some stigma in society, but: "this is mitigated by the fact that so much of *Ta'ziyeh* performance deals with the sacred subject of the martyrdom of Imam Hussein. Even so, performers may have to endure occasional quizzical inquiries from friends and relatives about their activities." For this reason, Beeman and Ghaffari explain, actors are generally from families that already support *Ta'ziyeh*.

THE AWAKENING: AL-NAHDA IN THE OTTOMAN EMPIRE

In the nineteenth century, the Ottoman-ruled regions of the Middle East began to undergo a renaissance known as *al-Nahda*. Although it can be said that it began with the invasion of Egypt by Napoleon (1798) and continued to be prompted with other imperialist incursions from Europe, the awakening is more the result of restructuring and reform within the Ottoman Empire itself. This cultural shift opened the way for the development of new literary forms, most notably a secular written drama.

Poetry in the Arab and Persian worlds has had a long and complex history with poetry being an important part of life at court, and storytelling has had an important place in Arab and Persian daily life. But forms such as the novel and drama were developed in places like Turkey, Egypt, and the other Mediterranean countries in the nineteenth century. Some of the earliest writers found inspiration in European, mostly French, literature as students from the Middle East traveled to France and Italy to study science, technology, and military tactics. The short story, on the other hand, was often used to address local social and political issues of the time.

Several writers in Egypt, Syria, and Iran began creating plays that were adaptations of European drama, plays based on stories from the Middle East, and plays that were original stories. One of the first dramatists was Marun al-Naqqash (1817–1855), a businessman from Beirut, then part of Syria. Marun al-Naqqash traveled on business extensively and saw, during one of his trips to Italy, the Italian opera. In 1847, he received permission from the Ottoman authorities to perform an adapted version of Molière's *The Miser* where he cast male friends and family members to play all of the roles (men and women). Marun al-Naqqash also added music to the play. Verse makes up the majority of the text, meant to be sung to the tunes of popular Arabic and French songs. The plot includes two extra acts where the young lovers, in disguise as Turkish officials, punish the miser and take his money. Al-Naqqash also added in a few extra pieces of dialogue, including a lengthy explanation of how the drama promotes good moral behavior and provides warnings about engaging in vice.

Al-Naqqash based his second play *Abu al-Hassan the Fool* (performed in 1849 or 1850) on one of the tales of Scheherazade, a story where a foolish man is made the Caliph for a day, and it is probably the first truly original play in Arabic. Al-Naqqash then received permission to build a theatre by his house and performed another Molière-inspired piece there. After his death, his brother and then his nephew took over the theatre. His nephew Salim Khalil al-Naqqash (1850–1884) also wrote and directed plays and included women in his company of actors. Because he was critical of the government in his journalism, he was forced to leave Syria and go to Egypt.

Another Syrian helped to establish the conventions of modern Arabic drama, Ahmad Abu Khalil al-Qabbani (1941–1902). Al-Qabbani performed in plays written by others, as well as writing his own plays from both European and Arabic stories. Scholars of Arabic literature are relatively sure that al-Qabbani, though learned, did not speak or read any other language, but by then there were translations of European texts readily available and he no doubt saw the plays of Marun and Salim Khalil al-Naqqash. He also studied music and dancing. He performed his first play *Nakir al-Jamil* (1865) and several other events in the home of his grandfather.

Nakir al-Jamil (*The Ungrateful*) involves allegorical characters such as Halim (forgiving), Ghadir (treacherous), and Nasir (supporting). In the drama, Halim, who is the son of the vizier, finds a destitute Ghadir near death in the road. He saves him and makes him his dear companion, freely sharing everything he has. Ghadir resents being indebted to Halim and tries to kill him, but kills the son of the King instead. Ghadir feigns remorse and turns to Halim for help, getting Halim to hide the bloody dagger for him. Ghadir then tells the King that Halim is the murderer, prompting the King to have Halim executed. The King then dreams of Halim's innocence and Ghadir's treachery, whereupon he expresses his wish to bring Halim back from the dead. As it turns out, the executioner accepted a bribe from the vizier to let his son live and so the executioner is able to produce Halim for the King. All ends well as Halim, true to his name, forgives Ghadir. The characters then all praise the Sultan.

Encouraged by Turkish officials who commissioned the actor Iskandar Farah to work with him, al-Qabbani began a theatre in Damascus. Farah and al-Qabbani began staging both original plays and adaptations, and the work of playwrights such as al-Naqqash. The performance of *Abu al-Hassan*, however, sparked a furor among conservatives. Particularly opposed was the Shaykh Said al-Ghabra who, among other things, objected to the portrayal of Harun al-Rashid, the Caliph, in the play. As Muḥammad Muṣṭafá Badawī notes in *Early Arabic Drama*, the original tale is a moral lesson in the difference between our good intentions and what we can actually accomplish. In the play, it is clear that the Caliph wishes merely to amuse himself as he watches the fool, as Caliph for a day, failing miserably at governing. The Shaykh petitioned the Sultan in Istanbul and succeeded in getting al-Qabbani's group shut down. Qabbani then fled to Egypt where he set up a theatre in Cairo.

The plays of al-Qabbani number, according to one source, "about a hundred," another says sixty. He developed some key elements that have become the staple in Arabic theatre. First, al-Qabbani continued the tradition of writing about love and tangled romance, both from the French-inspired plays that were adapted from the tropes of Molière and the Arabic stories that involve love. In some instances, al-Qabbani is referred to as the "Father of melodrama" because of his plays' happy endings. All of his plays end with happiness for the couples and always forgiveness for the treacherous. Most importantly, al-Qabbani solidified and improved the use of music in Arab drama. Indeed, he was musically talented and this is said to be the strongest element of his work.

THE ESTABLISHMENT OF A MODERN THEATRE: SAYYED ALI NASR

With the arrival of the twentieth century, the Middle East was thrown into the turmoil of global tensions. While British, French, and Italian colonization began in northern Africa at the end of the nineteenth century, the Ottoman Empire controlled much of the western Middle East until World War I. The European powers were quick to use the Middle East as a battleground and as a diplomatic bargaining chip with other European powers.

The assassination of Archduke Franz Ferdinand of Austria in 1914 prompted the Austro-Hungarian Empire to invade Serbia. Soon, allies were pulled into the conflict, with Russia coming to the aid of Serbia, and Britain countering the German Empire's invasion of Belgium and Luxembourg. With the Ottoman Empire taking the side of the Germans, the British began using the Arabian Peninsula to take up strategic positions against the Germans. The British initially seemed to offer some hope for people of the Arab world in that they were happy to be free of Ottoman rule and some dreamed of a united Arab state that included the countries from the Mediterranean (the "Levant") and the Arabian Peninsula.

After defeating the Germans and the Ottomans in 1918, however, the British, French, and Russians divided the region and put each new territory under colonial control. The initial agreement, which was later only slightly modified, was put together by the British and French diplomats Mark Sykes and François Georges-Picot during the war. The result of the agreement was that the eastern part of Turkey went to Russia, a part of Turkey, Syria, Beirut, and northern Iraq went to the French, and Jordan, southern Iraq, Kuwait, and part of Saudi Arabia along the Persian Gulf went to Britain. Palestine and Israel were put under international (European) control. The artificial borders established during this time continue to have repercussions in the Middle East, including statements by the Islamic State that their express purpose is to reverse the damage done by the "Sykes–Picot conspiracy." In northern Iran, the British attempted to attack Russia to stem the Russian Revolution of 1917. In return, the Russians briefly annexed land on the south shore of the Caspian Sea.

The upheaval created by foreign powers intervening in the affairs of Middle Eastern peoples was both devastating and life altering. The resistance to European colonialism created unrest and instability. In Iran, the chaos of World War I allowed for the collapse of the Qajar dynasty and the rise of Reza Shah. In some cases, the ensuing climate allowed for the confrontation of social issues, such as the role of women in society, but also created a repressive atmosphere where the government could not be criticized.

One example of this double standard can be found in the work of Sayyed Ali Nasr (1894–1961). Nasr grew up in Kashan, just south of Tehran. He moved to Tehran as a young man to study French and history, after which he became a teacher. He often spent his time writing and translating history books, a reflection of his humanist outlook and his belief that a knowledge of world history was important in understanding one's own future. Nasr believed in working toward a better relationship between the Middle East and Europe, believing in the universal truth of the human condition. When the school where Nasr was teaching closed, he decided to take a job in the government bureaucracy, but was also able to focus on working in the theatre.

According to Nasr, Reza Shah enjoyed the theatre and gave it his unwavering support. While the Shah was brutal in his intolerance of criticism, he was liberal in his ideas about Iranian society. He also began secularizing the Iranian government, having the effect of nearly wiping out religious performances such as the *Ta'ziyeh*, but supporting the secular theatre. With his support, Ali Nasr began the Komedi-e Iran (1921–1930). He also recognized that Iran needed an institution for actor training and created the Honaristan-e Honarpishegi-e Tehran (The Tehran Acting School) in 1939. He invited teachers from all over Iran to teach speech, psychology, and music. He established the Tehran Theatre the following year.

Nasr's sympathies were decidedly pro-government and his one well-known play celebrates the social reforms of Reza Shah. In *Arusi-e Hosseyn Aqa (The Wedding of Hosseyn Aqa)*, written in 1939, Nasr criticizes backwardness and illiteracy. He celebrates education and warns of the dangers of drug addiction. His theatre became a center for like-minded Iranians who embraced social change. As a teacher and director, Nasr invited performers across the ethnic and religious spectrum including Jewish and Armenian performers. He also included women in his company with the support of the Shah, who believed women should be allowed to perform publicly.

World War II brought another occupation by British and Soviet forces, which had the dual effect of loosening censorship while bringing greater influence from European and American theatre. The daughter of George Cram Cook (one of the founders of the Provincetown Playhouse in the United States), Nilla Cram Cook (1908–1982), was the cultural attaché in Tehran during the war. She was put in charge of programming in Tehran from 1943 to 1946 and even attempted to establish a ballet company there. In 1946, possibly because he refused to allow the theatre to become the propaganda arm of the government, Ali Nasr was made the ambassador to India and his assistant, Ahmad Dehghan, took over the theatre.

While the commercial theatre thrived, Tehran was home to experimental groups as well. *Kargah-e nemayesh* (The Theatre Workshop) opened in a rehearsal hall for a ballet school in 1969. The group began by staging the Greek tragedy *Oedipus* (429 BCE) by Sophocles (c.497/6–406/5 BCE) and five short plays by the absurdist writer Samuel Beckett. The theatre lasted for ten years as a flexible space that existed as a laboratory for theatre artists of all kinds to explore new ideas and techniques.

Reza Shah abdicated in favor of his son Mohammed Reza Shah in 1941. Mohammed Reza Shah's government was terribly unstable, leading to the overthrow of the Pahlavi government in 1979. While theatre continued after the Revolution, the new government created an intensely repressive atmosphere, where only plays praising the Revolutionary government were allowed and only after intense censorial scrutiny. A popular version of the events of 1979 is that the *Kargah-e nemayesh* was the first theatre to be closed by extremists, who literally sealed the entrance with bricks and made the space off-limits.

AL-HAKAWATI: THE HOPES OF PALESTINE

Theatre in the Middle East flourished in several countries in the twentieth century, including some of the smaller countries on the Arabian Peninsula such as Bahrain, the United Arab Emirates, and Oman, where wealthy sultans who love the arts have put money into building theatres and concert halls. Theatre also continued under Saddam Hussein in Iraq and in Yemen despite a bitter civil war. Certainly, the most active theatre scene during modern times sprang up in Egypt, initially as an exploration of imported European culture under British colonialism in the nineteenth century, and then in response to it in the twentieth.

One of the first truly original dramatists in Egypt was Tawfiq al-Hakim (1898–1987) who, like many writers of the time, was first inspired to write for the theatre after spending time studying in Paris. He abandoned his doctoral studies at the Sorbonne and returned to Egypt in 1928 to begin his new career. Against a backdrop of farce and melodrama, al-Hakim endeavored to create a serious and intellectual Egyptian drama. Instead of dealing with amusing plots, he wanted to present ideas.

The first play of al-Hakim, *Ahl el-Kahf* (*The People of the Cave*), deals with the story from the Qur'an of the people who seek refuge in a cave from religious persecution only to fall asleep and then awaken after three hundred years. The Qur'anic tale quotes the story from early Christian writing of the Seven Sleepers of Ephesus, Christians who are sealed into a cave by the Roman emperor Decius and awaken during the reign of Theodosius II to a Christianized empire. The tale in the Qur'an stresses that the number of sleepers and the number of years are not relevant to the story and that those are details only God would know. In al-Hakim's play, there are two courtiers and a shepherd with his dog. One of the courtiers has been in love with the Princess and falls asleep with his love unrequited. When the three people awaken after three hundred years they rejoice to discover that Christianity has triumphed. The lovelorn courtier falls for the woman who is now the Princess as she is the descendant of the woman he loved. However, the people of the cave quickly become homesick for the old times that they knew three hundred years earlier.

The People of the Cave had its premiere at the newly formed National Egyptian Group in 1935. The theatre opened with subsidies from the British colonial government to present the European classics, and under the leadership of the poet Khalil Motran (1872–1949), himself a translator of the works of Shakespeare (1564–1616), Pierre Corneille (1606–1684), and Victor Hugo (1802–1885). Al-Hakim sought to explore the problems of modern Egypt through the parable of a people propelled out of the past and into the modern world and the attractiveness of dwelling on the past. Al-Hakim regularly drew on a wide variety of sources, including Greek mythology, the Qur'an, and the *Alf Layla wa-Layla,* or *One Thousand and One Nights,* the collection of folk tales mostly drawn from Arabic and Persian culture dating back more than a millennium.

The return in the Middle East to *One Thousand and One Nights* signals a renewed interest in the region in indigenous folk culture. In Arabic, *hakawati* means "storyteller." The storyteller would travel around to coffee shops and markets to tell stories, often drawn from sources such as *One Thousand and One Nights.* He would set up a small stage and recite these stories using different voices for each character, dramatic gestures, and music. He would encourage the audience to react to the story and to participate. The storyteller sometimes told stories in installments to encourage an audience to return to hear more. It is important to note that this tradition was considered basely popular, something for the illiterate on the street, and not something to be regarded as great literature. As Reuven Snir notes, the collection of *One Thousand and One Nights* did not become canon in the Middle East until it was printed and disseminated throughout Europe as part of the canon of great world literature (60). However, as something wholly indigenous, the idea of the hakawati and the source of *One Thousand and One Nights* provided an apt foundation for anti-colonial nation building. One example where the idea of the popular storyteller has been used for such a project is the case of the *al-Hakawati* company in Palestine.

A group of Palestinian and Israeli artists from Jerusalem founded al-Hakawati in the late 1970s and began working together to create improvisatory theatre that addressed present-day issues. The director was François Abu Salem (1951–2011), the son of a French poet and a Palestinian sculptor. Abu Salem worked in Paris with Ariane Mnouchkine at Le Théâtre du Soleil before returning to East Jerusalem to start his own company with his wife, Jewish writer and costume designer Jackie Lubeck. Using the training he received at

Le Théâtre du Soleil as well as the work of Bertolt Brecht (1898–1956) and Dario Fo (1926–), Abu Salem sought to create theatre that was a blend of participatory and dialectical, European and Palestinian forms. Snir suggests that the improvisational nature of the work was in part a creative response to Israeli censorship.

The group attempted to address the absurdity of life under Israeli occupation, showing grotesque characters on both sides. Most famously, they presented *Alf Layla wa-Layla min Layali Rami al-Hijara (One Thousand and One Nights of a Stone Thrower)*. It was presented just before the First Intifada, the outbreak of violence between Palestinians and Israelis beginning in 1987. In the play, a greedy governor steals the lamp of Ala ad-Din (Aladdin). A Palestinian boy confronts him as a "David" to the oppressor's "Goliath." But then fighting erupts with people on flying carpets firing lasers at each other. Abu Salem typically framed the struggle between occupier and occupied as a struggle also between the past and the present.

While Palestinian and Jewish critics alike hailed the performance, Abu Salem was arrested by Israeli forces. Over the last two decades, the theatre was closed twice by the Israeli Minister of Internal Security: to prevent a literary festival and to prevent a children's puppetry festival. In 2015, because of financial difficulties, it was finally forced to close its doors.

ISRAEL'S HABIMA THEATRE

A diverse range of cultures, languages, and religions make up the Middle East. Although Arabs make up most of the population of the Arabian Peninsula, the Middle East is home to Turks, Kurds, Persians, Copts, Assyrians, Armenians, and many other groups. Muslims, Christians, and Jews have lived in the Middle East for centuries. During the millennia of diaspora, Jewish people were forced to migrate from Israel to countries all over the world. But, as waves of pogroms and expulsions shook Europe, many Jewish people looked to Israel as a place to establish a Jewish homeland. Waves of immigration reached a peak in the twentieth century. Believing this would cause a crisis, the British colonial government of Palestine sought to limit the number of Jewish immigrants it would allow. Rising tensions between the Arab Palestinians and the British, between the Jewish people of then-Palestine and the British, and between the Arabs and the Jews, often erupted in violence.

An attempt by the United Nations to partition Palestine in 1947 was rejected by both Arabs and Jews and war broke out in 1948. After a year of fighting, a temporary border known as the "Green Line" was established and the State of Israel was founded. Israel won a second conflict in 1967 known as the Six Day War and the Green Line essentially became the administrative boundaries between Israel and the occupied territories of the Gaza Strip, the Golan Heights, and the West Bank.

The national theatre of Israel, the Habima Theatre, reflects the creation of the Jewish state. The company began in western Russia (in what is now Poland) under the direction of actor Menachem Gnessin (1882–1952), and teachers Nachum Zemach (1887–1939) and Hanna Rubin-Rovina (1888–1980). In 1918, the company was moved to Moscow and put under the administration of the Moscow Art Theatre. The Jewish theatre struggled with persecution under the Czarist government and continued to struggle under the Soviets. The company's most famous production *The Dybbuk*, under the direction of Yevgeny Vakhtangov (1883–1922), propelled the company to international acclaim. The play portrayed the story of a poor Yeshiva student named Khanan who dies from the love of Leah, the daughter of a wealthy merchant. Because Khanan dabbled in the Kabbalah, the study of Jewish mysticism, he becomes a "dybbuk," a spirit, and possesses Leah on her wedding day. This production, in Hebrew and dealing with Jewish folklore, became an important symbol of Jewish culture.

After touring in the 1920s, the group split, with some members staying in New York and others deciding to immigrate to the British Mandate Palestine. However, as Gad Kaynar notes, the group was not particularly Zionist or dedicated to the creation of a Jewish state:

> they settled in Tel-Aviv, which had already become the worldly, even bourgeois, cultural center of Jewish Palestine, and not in the company's original destination, the national and symbolic center of Jerusalem. Several original members, including the ardently Zionist Zemach, remained in the United States to promote their artistic careers. Several others, who were more committed to the ideals of the Bolshevist Revolution than to Zionism, entertained the idea of returning to the Soviet Union.

(2–3)

The Habima company members wanted to establish a Hebrew-language theatre on specifically Jewish themes, but they also wanted to create theatre that was great art based in an aesthetic that was modernist, avant-garde, and Eastern European.

Over time, Habima Theatre's work evolved as new members grew up in the British Mandate and then traveled abroad to learn about the avant-garde theatre in other countries. The company moved into a permanent space in 1945 and began to do the work of a new generation of playwrights. One such dramatist, Nissim Aloni (1926–1998), studied French and spent a year living in Paris. Aloni moved the company from doing plays about mythical themes and shtetl (village) life, to theatre that addressed contemporary problems in interesting allegorical ways. Habima produced a couple of his plays, including *Akhzar mikol hamelekh* (*Most Cruel of All the Kings*) in 1953 and *Bigdei hamelekh hahadashim* (*The Emperor's New Clothes*) in 1961. In *Most Cruel of All the Kings*, Aloni uses the biblical story of the son of Solomon, Rehoboam, who ignored the pleas of the people, led by Jeroboam, to lighten their tax burden. Instead, he followed the advice of his young peers, increasing their burden and promised to be even crueler than Solomon. Aloni used this as an allegory for the current problems in Israel. In *The Emperor's New Clothes*, Aloni developed the popular parable of the Emperor who foolishly paraded around naked, believing he had purchased the latest, albeit invisible, fashion. Only a young boy was brazen and honest enough to point out the truth. In the play, the boy has grown up to be a cynical opportunist who abandons his girlfriend to marry the Emperor's daughter, since the Emperor has now become ill and will die from walking around with no clothes on. The scorned lover exposes him, and his political aspirations are undone. Aloni formed his own company, the Seasons Theatre in 1963.

After Israel became a state and took control of what are now the occupied territories, the focus of theatre artists in Israel shifted to examining the tense relationship between Jews and Palestinians. Bitter conflict spurred ever more violence in the forms of repression and terrorism. But a few groups took it upon themselves to use art as a way to create a dialogue. One of these companies, the Haifa Theatre, opened in 1961 and continues to employ Jewish and Arab artists. Joshua Sobol, a playwright and the artistic director from 1985 to 1988, said of the situation in Israel:

[W]e accepted more and more the situation of dominating another people.... It's unhealthy for us because it alienates us from our own history and our own experience as a people. Many Israelis feel that they cannot reconcile what happened to their parents, or to the former generations, with what we are now doing.

(interview quoted in Rothstein)

The artists at the Haifa Theatre often stage work that is controversial, leading to protests and occasional censorship. They also occasionally produce plays such as *Waiting for Godot* in Arabic, in order to cultivate an Arabic-speaking audience.

Currently, about half of the plays produced in Israel are original plays in Hebrew, with the other half being plays from other parts of the world. There were two Arab theatres in Israel, but in 2015, the Ministry of Culture suspended funding for the Al-Midan Arab Theatre in Haifa, citing issues with the play *A Parallel Time*. The play is based on the story of Walid Daka, who was serving a life sentence after being convicted of kidnapping and murdering an Israeli soldier. The other group is the Vine Theatre at the Beit Hagefen Arab Jewish Cultural Center.

In the Middle East, theatre has a long history of commemorating important events in the history of the world's oldest civilizations. It has also been used to shape the identity of the modern nations that have formed over the last century, and theatre helps people to deal with the pressing political realities of life in the Middle East. Most recently, a company in Jordan called the Zaal and Khadra began touring a play called *Terrorism at the Door*, an amusing play aimed at young people in order to fight Islamic extremism. They also use performance to raise awareness about health issues, making theatre a force for positive social change in the Middle East.

2

SOUTH AND SOUTHEAST ASIA

Theatre in India dates back to the first century CE with dramatic pieces written in Sanskrit. Most of the plays deal with the stories from the great epics the *Ramayana* and the *Mahabharata*. The introduction to this volume discusses the *Natyasastra* at length, which deals specifically with Sanskrit drama. In it, Bharata describes the training of the actor and the importance of conveying *rasa*, or "taste." From this document, scholars have learned most of what is known about the performance of Sanskrit drama. But we also have a few of the dramatic texts from this time.

Perhaps one of the most famous pieces is the *Abhijnanasakuntalam*, or *The Recognition of Shakuntala*. It was written by a poet named Kalidasa. Scholars know little about the writer and some have guessed that Kalidasa may have lived around the fourth or fifth century CE. Some have suggested that the work attributed to Kalidasa is the work of several authors. Regardless of who this person may have been, the body of work attributed to Kalidasa endures as some of the greatest examples of Sanskrit literature.

The Recognition of Shakuntala takes up the story of Shakuntala, growing up under the care of a sage named Durvasa in a hermitage secluded in the woods. The king Dushyanta sees her one day when he is out hunting. They immediately fall in love and, after a time, are married. He gives her a ring and tells her to come to court to be with him. However, when Shakuntala fails to attend to Durvasa at the hermitage, he puts a curse on Dushyanta so that the king forgets her. Dushyanta will only remember her when he sees the ring, which Shakuntala loses crossing a river. For this reason, Dushyanta doesn't recognize Shakuntala when she arrives. When the ring is finally found, it is too late. It is not until years later that Indra, the God of war, rewards Dushyanta after a battle and he is reunited with Shakuntala.

THE LITTLE CLAY CART: BRAHMINICAL VALUES IN AN ORIGINAL TEXT

Mrichchhakatika (*The Little Clay Cart*), on the other hand, does not take its narrative from the epic stories, but involves instead original characters and an original plot. Written around the same time as *The Recognition of Shakuntala*, *The Little Clay Cart* involves romance, plot twists, mistaken identity, and a wide range of characters. It focuses mostly on the foibles of Chārudatta, a man of the *Brahmin*, or priestly, class who is poor, but only because of his generosity to others. He lives with his wife and his young son. In the first scene, he is talking with his good friend Maitreya. He grieves not for his money, he states, but for the fact that his fickle friends have left him in his poverty. He finishes his offering to the gods and then urges his friend to do the same:

Chārudatta Comrade, I have made my offering to the divinities of the house. Do you too go and offer sacrifice to the Divine Mothers at a place where four roads meet.

Maitreya No!

Chārudatta Why not?

Maitreya Because the gods are not gracious to you even when thus honored. So what is the use of worshiping?

Chārudatta Not so, my friend, not so! This is the constant duty of a householder.

(Sudraka 8–9)

Although he finds himself poor and abandoned, a good Brahmin never neglects his duties to the gods, who are ever aware of spiritual endeavors of the pious.

Indeed, the entire play revolves around the ever-changing fate of any person's life, and the moral imperative to be noble in all things. No one in the course of the play denies the impeccable character of Chārudatta even when it seems he is to be executed for a murder. As one nobleman observes:

A tree of life to them whose sorrows grow,
Beneath its fruit of virtue bending low;

Father to good men; virtue's touchstone he;
The mirror of the learned; and the sea
Where all the tides of character unite;
A righteous man, whom pride could never blight;
A treasure-house, with human virtues stored;
Courtesy's essence, honor's precious hoard.
He doth to life its fullest meaning give,
So good is he; we others breathe, not live.

(20)

His goodness makes him so attractive that he is noticed by the famous courtesan Vasantasenā, who confesses that although she has known many men, she cannot help but love Chārudatta. But her virtuous character is also apparent throughout the play, making the pair deserving of each other.

The love of Vasantasenā for Chārudatta enrages the brother-in-law of the king, Samsthānaka, who is mad with jealousy. Vasantasenā escapes the raging Samsthānaka and hides with Chārudatta, who at first mistakes her for his servant. Comic moments such as these punctuate an otherwise serious meditation on proper Brahminical values. When Maitreya points out Chārudatta's mistake, he apologizes profusely, prompting Vasantasenā to apologize in return for her intrusion. The endless apologies become comic and end only when Maitreya interrupts:

Chārudatta Mistress Vasantasenā, I have unwittingly made myself guilty of an offense; for I greeted as a servant one whom I did not recognize. I bend my neck to ask your pardon.

Vasantasenā It is I who have offended by this unseemly intrusion. I bow my head to seek your forgiveness.

Maitreya Yes, with your pretty bows you two have knocked your heads together, till they look like a couple of rice-fields. I also bow my head like a camel colt's knee and beseech you both to stand up.

(24)

She leaves her jewelry with him for safekeeping, giving them an excuse to see each other again.

A morally instructive interlude follows where a shampooer, fleeing the gambling master to whom he owes money, takes refuge with Vasantasenā. He relays his tale of woe: that he used to serve a virtuous man who was generous and compassionate to a fault, but when the man ran out of money, he could not keep him on as a servant and so he took up shampooing – and gambling. His story moves Vasantasenā and she inquires about the identity of the virtuous man. It is none other than Chārudatta, prompting Vasantasenā to pay the shampooer's debts. In gratitude, the shampooer vows to leave behind worldly concerns and become a Buddhist monk. Humorously, news of an escaped elephant momentarily distracts him from his determination, as he excitedly talks about going to see chaos. But he steels himself, and heads out: "I must hold to my resolution" (18).

The thief Sharvilaka, another Brahmin who has fallen on hard times, breaks into Chārudatta's house. At first, he is appalled and dismayed at Chārudatta's poverty and begins to leave when Maitreya, in his sleep, offers Sharvilaka the box of jewels left by Vasantasenā. By a strange twist of fate, Sharvilaka was looking for valuables in order to buy the freedom of his beloved, who happens to be Vasantasenā's servant Madanikā. Madanikā recognizes the jewels and begs Sharvilaka to pretend like he is just returning them. Vasantasenā overhears all of this and plays along. She then "gives" Madanikā to Sharvilaka, pretending that Chārudatta had decreed that this would be the payment for anyone who had returned the jewels.

The entire plot is then interrupted by political intrigue. King Pālaka has imprisoned a man named Aryaka, who, as it turns out, is the best friend of Sharvilaka. Pālaka heard a prophesy that Aryaka would be king and has arrested him to prevent it from coming true. Sharvilaka, although now married and expected to avoid risks that might make his bride a widow, vows to free Aryaka.

Maitreya arrives with a necklace, the one valuable piece of jewelry left in the household of Chārudatta. Chārudatta has instructed Maitreya to say that Chārudatta has gambled away the jewels and offer the necklace as a meager payment for his sins. Chārudatta does not yet know that Vasantasenā has just seen the jewels, and that she knows full well that Sharvilaka had stolen them. She tells Maitreya to inform Chārudatta that she will stop by that evening. As she readies herself, a storm gathers.

Because Vasantasenā seemed to be hiding something, Maitreya grows suspicious and urges Chārudatta to think better of his feelings for her. He fears that she will come only to demand more money, thinking that the necklace was not worth as much as her jewels. But

Chārudatta tells him that the point is moot since Chārudatta doesn't have enough money to attract a courtesan. When she arrives and asks about the worth of the necklace, Maitreya thinks his suspicions are confirmed, but Vasantasenā says she only asks because she gambled it away, repeating the exact phrase Maitreya used at her residence earlier. Reenacting the same payment for the same sin, Vasantasenā asks Chārudatta to take the gold box full of jewels that had been stolen from his home the night before. The rain pours down and Vasantasenā and Chārudatta go inside.

Vasantasenā sees Chārudatta's son Rohasena playing with his toy cart. Rohasena complains about his toy cart because it is made of clay and not gold. Vasantasenā weeps to think of the child being deprived of the things he wants because of his poverty and so she fills the clay cart with her jewelry so that he can have a gold cart made.

Chārudatta sends an ox cart to pick up Vasantasenā to meet him in the park. A mix-up in cart drivers causes Vasantasenā to get into a cart owned by madly jealous Samsthānaka. The cart meant for her is then boarded by the escaping Aryaka. Everyone involved feels some sense of foreboding. Vasantasenā, Chārudatta, and Aryaka all mention that their eye is twitching, a bad omen. However, Aryaka is delivered to Chārudatta, who helps him to escape the king's men and the mercenaries who are all searching for him. Vasantasenā, unfortunately, finds herself delivered to Samsthānaka. When she rebuffs him again, and violently, he resolves to kill her. He strangles her, covers her body in leaves, and flees the scene. Fortunately, a Buddhist monk wandering by finds her. Happily, she is not dead, merely unconscious. He revives her and guides her to safety. Although she does not recognize him, he is the shampooer she freed from his gambling master and the former servant of Chārudatta. He repays her good karma by saving her.

The next day, a judge mulls his thankless role as someone who is charged with finding the truth in the most difficult of times. The appearance of Samsthānaka prompts him to tell his bailiff that the court is busy, because he knows of the man's evil character. But Samsthānaka insists. He states that he has found the body of Vasantasenā in his garden and that he knows that someone killed her for her money. Knowing that Vasantasenā's mother will tell the court that her daughter went to see Chārudatta, Samsthānaka knows Chārudatta will be implicated. The bailiff brings Chārudatta and even the judge cannot help but be struck by his purity of character. Chārudatta must admit that Vasantasenā was at his home and that she left unnoticed. Maitreya arrives with the jewels, which Samsthānaka swears have been taken from Vasantasenā. Maitreya reminds everyone of Chārudatta's generosity and gentle spirit, but Chārudatta defends himself only half-heartedly because the grief at losing Vasantasenā has overwhelmed him. He also feels guilty for having allowed her to be murdered.

In the final act, Chārudatta laments his fate as he is accompanied by the executioners who are loath to kill the noble man. The proclamation of his goodness by the executioner and Chārudatta's lamentations are long and elaborate. Chārudatta's son arrives with Maitreya and runs to his father. He begs to be executed in his place. Samsthānaka's servant, who knows the true story and witnessed the murder, tries to shout from the tower where he is in chains. But no one can hear him. He throws himself out of the window and lands before the procession to tell his story. The crowd begins to doubt Chārudatta's guilt, but Samsthānaka sees what is happening and makes Chārudatta confess his guilt to the people. He will not, but his silence implies that he is guilty. The executioners hesitate and argue over who should carry out the sentence and impale him, a grisly task, the results of which are described in some detail. And then the fourth and final proclamation is made.

Miraculously, Vasantasenā, led by the grateful monk, arrives in time to save him. The end of the play wraps up rather neatly as Vasantasenā's appearance prompts the executioners to arrest Samsthānaka. Coincidentally, Sharvilaka has just killed King Pālaka and arrives to tell all that the new King Aryaka has stayed Chārudatta's execution. Because Chārudatta had helped Aryaka escape, Aryaka repays him by restoring his fortune and giving him the throne of nearby Kushāvatī. Although the crowd all around him continue to call for the execution of Samsthānaka, Chārudatta refuses to hear it and pardons him. All who aided Aryaka, Chārudatta, and Vasantasenā are rewarded. Chārudatta and Vasantasenā are to be married.

That Chārudatta's wife would have no qualms about the integration of Vasantasenā into the household tells the reader of the play many things. It would not be uncommon for a Brahmin to have many wives at this time, or a wife and a mistress. Also, Chārudatta's wife in the play serves as a reflection of Chārudatta, his virtue in that a virtuous man would naturally choose a virtuous wife. Everyone in his household suffers dutifully, even gratefully, by his inability to provide for them due to his generosity toward others. The character has no name of her own and is simply designated "Wife" in the script. When they are robbed and lose the jewels that belong to Vasantasenā, the wife's only concern is how this will look for Chārudatta. She finds a way to sacrifice for him:

> Better that he were injured in body than in character. For now the people of Ujjayinī will say that my lord committed this crime because of his poverty. [*She looks up and sighs.*] Ah, mighty Fate! The destinies of the poor, uncertain as the water-drops which fall upon a lotus-leaf, seem to thee but playthings. There remains to me this one necklace, which I brought with me from my mother's house. But my lord would be too proud to accept it. Girl, call Maitreya hither.
>
> (54)

She gives the necklace to Maitreya and makes up a story to make him accept it. When Maitreya gives it to Chārudatta, Chārudatta feels ashamed:

Chārudatta What is this?
Maitreya Why, that is the reward you get for marrying such a wife.
Chārudatta What! my wife takes pity on me? Alas, now am I poor indeed!

> When fate so robs him of his all,
> That on her pity he must call,
> The man to woman's state doth fall,
> The woman is the man.

But no, I am not poor. For I have a wife

> Whose love outlasts my wealthy day;
> In thee a friend through good and ill;
> And truth that naught could take away:
> Ah! this the poor man lacketh still.
>
> (55–56)

He rejoices in the fact that he has, at least, an ally in his wife.

Vasantasenā's arrival into his household during the storm prompts a reconciliation where Vasantasenā can return the necklace and express her gratitude to the other members of the household. She says to the maid: "Here, girl, take this pearl necklace. You must go and give it to my lady sister, his good wife. And give her this message: Worthy Chārudatta's virtues have won me, made me his slave, and therefore your slave also. And so I hope that these pearls may adorn your neck" (94). The maid however returns it: "Mistress, his lady wife says that her lord made you a present of it, and it would not be right for her to accept it. And further, that you are to know that her lord and husband is her most excellent adornment" (95). They are united by their mutual love for Chārudatta and express their pride in belonging to such a man. One is to believe the newly integrated family will thrive in their new circumstances.

Sanskrit plays incorporated several framing devices including the use of a prologue, which gave the audience some idea of the play and the issues that were to be addressed. These were sometimes comedic, as the actors would joke about setting up to do the play. In *The Little Clay Cart*, the opening has a prayer and then the director stops the prayer because the audience has settled and is ready for the play. The director then talks about the playwright, a man named Sudraka, who he describes as a noble and wise king. He says that the king emolliated himself, which was customary, at the age of 100 after he saw to it that his son succeeded him. The director then sets the scene, but he notices that there are no actors on the stage: "Why, this stage of ours is empty. I wonder where the actors have gone!" He tells the audience he should be speaking in Prakrit now that he is talking about common things, and not the elevated Sanskrit. He then complains at length about how long he has rehearsed and that he is terribly hungry. He tells the audience that the scene has changed: "Suppose I go home and see whether my good wife has got anything ready or not. Here I am at home. I'll just go in."

Once inside, he sees his wife making elaborate preparations. He tells her he is hungry, but she only teases him:

Director Mistress, I've been practising so long and I'm so hungry that my limbs are as weak as dried-up lotus-stalks. Is there anything to eat in the house or not?

Actress There's everything, sir.

Director Well, what?

Actress For instance—there's rice with sugar, melted butter, curdled milk, rice; and, all together, it makes you a dish fit for heaven. May the gods always be thus gracious to you!

Director All that in our house? or are you joking?

Actress [Aside.] Yes, I will have my joke. [Aloud.] It's in the market-place, sir.

Director [Angrily.] You wretched woman, thus shall your own hope be cut off! And death shall find you out! For my expectations, like a scaffolding, have been raised so high, only to fall again.

Actress Forgive me, sir, forgive me! It was only a joke.

(5)

She explains that it is a fast day in order to pray for a husband in the next life. The director turns to the audience with disbelief:

Director [Wrathfully.] Gentlemen! look at this. She is sacrificing my food to get herself a husband in the next world.

Actress Don't be angry, sir. I am fasting in the hope that you may be my husband in my next birth, too.

He asks who is to officiate at the fast and she tells him it should be a Brahmin of their own kind. He wonders where he will find such a man when he notices Maitreya, the best friend of Chārudatta, coming along. This prompts the exposition from Maitreya about the situation of Chārudatta, and the play begins.

Sanskrit plays also conclude with the lessons to be learned from the drama. In the case of *The Little Clay Cart*, Chārudatta pardons Samsthānaka and instructs the audience that fate is fickle and one must live with continuous change. But all of the Sanskrit plays end happily. The epilogue blesses all:

May cows yield milk and the earth be filled
     with every crop.
May the rains fall on time, and the wind blow
     to gladden all people's hearts.
May living beings rejoice and Brahmins be always honored.
May the virtuous be rich, and the righteous kings
     tame their foes and rule the earth!

(529)

While the plays were written in an elevated Sanskrit, the common characters spoke in a variety of dialects no longer used in modern times. Much of the text was chanted and sung and the performance involved elaborate movement and hand gestures. And so actors had to develop their bodies and voices, commit to meditation and yoga, and eat a special diet. While Sanskrit dramas are no longer presented in the way they were two millennia ago, a derivation of it called *kutiyattam* still survives in Kerala, India.

KUTIYATTAM AND *KATHAKALI*

Sanskrit drama gained in popularity through the millennium and reached the height of its development by the tenth century CE. At this time, a king in Kerala began to develop a new form of dance-drama based on the Sanskrit dramas known as *kutiyattam*, which translates to "combined acting." Kulasekhara Varman supported the new form. He was also a playwright. The changes he made caused a stir among his peers. Kulasekhara preferred lengthy elaboration of certain passages in the drama, an elaboration much abhorred by some critics of theatre at the time. Indeed, one section of a drama would be drawn out and become its own evening's performance, and would even sometimes be drawn out over several days. The performance would have a lengthy introduction of all of the characters and their situations in a *poorvangam* (prologue), the *nirvahanam* (solo acting), and the *kutiyattam* (combined acting).

The form was staged only in certain temples in Kerala as a dedication to the gods there. It was unique in that women appeared on stage and played the women's roles, unlike many forms of the time where men played all the roles. Writers of the form began to use the local contemporary dialect of Malayalam as few people understood Sanskrit anymore. Despite the outcry against these changes, *kutiyattam* endures as a popular performance form today.

Other forms emerged in Kerala, including the popular form of *kathakali*. *Kathakali* developed in the late sixteenth and early seventeenth centuries borrowing many of the conventions of *kutiyattam*, but also other temple dance-drama forms as well, such as the *krishnattam*. The all-male company of dancer-actors train from the time they are children, following a rigorous set of exercises derived from the martial art *kalarippayattu*. It involves physical movement such as jumping and kicking, but also extremely localized exercises for the eyes and other parts of the face and for the hands. Indeed, in addition to the elaborate choreography, the codified hand gestures and eye movements are of great importance for conveying the meaning, the inner state of the character (*bhava*), and therefore the flavor of the moment (*rasa*).

Percussionists and singers accompany the actors. The vocalists sing the narration, but they also sing the lines of dialogue that would be spoken by the characters on stage. *Kathakali* performances begin in the evening and last all night. The performers are on a bare stage, blessed beforehand in an elaborate ritual, and use only a few props. Again, the stories generally come from the epics (the *Ramayana* and *Mahabharata*) and *puranas* (stories older than the epics). They often center on the character of Krishna, one of the manifestations of Vishnu, but unlike the *krishnattam*, all of the stories of the gods are fair game. Scholars imagine that about 500 texts were written during the entire history of *kathakali*, but only a few, thirty to fifty, are performed with any regularity.

The gods and heroes take center stage and make up a classification of characters known as *pacca*, the "green" characters. The actors playing these characters wear elaborate green makeup, which denotes both heroic and pious qualities. Characters who are both heroic and malevolent or arrogant are *kathi*, or "knife," characters. These characters would be like Ravana, the demon king in the *Ramayana*, or Duryodhana, the man in the *Mahabharata* who tricks the Pandavas into a term of exile and then refuses to return the kingdom to them when they return, leading to a bloody battle. These characters also wear green makeup, but with distinctive marks such as red marks on the cheeks, like upturned knives, and white circles on the nose and forehead. *Thadi*, or "beard," characters are not heroic, but simply evil. They are unable to think things through and they act on impulse. "Black" beard characters are capable of some scheming, but "red" beard characters just lash out and destroy. The "white" beard characters have some redeeming qualities, such as the character Hanuman, the Monkey God. Hanuman is revered in Hindu mythology because he came to the aid of Rama in the war against the demon Ravana in the *Ramayana*. The fourth type of character is the *kari* or "black" characters. They are demonic female characters and wear black makeup with white markings. Special animal characters make up the *teppu* type. The final category wear *minukku* makeup, delicate makeup that suggests women characters, Brahmins, and sages.

The conventions of *kathakali* are well established, which is generally the case with any classical art form. While experimentation exists, deviations from convention do not always fare well with connoisseurs and critics. This is the case with the *kathakali* version of Shakespeare's *King Lear* performed by the Annette Leday/Keli Company in 1989. While British audiences were not completely sure how they felt about this adaptation of a British classic, Indian critics expressed ambivalence and disappointment at moments of the story that strayed so far from the rules of *kathakali*. We will take up a more in-depth discussion of such cultural borrowings and lendings in Chapter 8: Collaborations.

PERFORMING OBJECTS: THE *WAYANG KULIT*

Hinduism migrated to Indonesia sometime in the first century CE. When it did, the Indonesians blended it with some beliefs from Buddhism and some elements of the indigenous animism and ancestor worship. While Islam has far surpassed Hindu as the dominant religion, Hinduism in Indonesia today is uniquely monotheistic, as adherents believe all the deities from the Hindu pantheon are manifestations of one supreme being.

It was this spread of a hybrid Hinduism that brought stories from the Indian epics to the people of Indonesia. Here, the presentation of these stories takes a unique turn. The most well-known performance form of Indonesia, in addition to its dance-drama forms, is the *wayang kulit*, the performance of shadow puppets. The use of objects as characters in the theatre raises many questions about the nature of theatre and live performance. In 1999 John Bell wrote a landmark essay on puppetry and "performing objects," a term he notes was first coined by Frank Proschan in 1983. While scholars in disciplines such as folklore and anthropology often write about puppet traditions, Bell states that there had been scant attention paid to performing objects as a field in its own right. While some resist including puppetry when discussing theatre because the characters are not played by live actors, live actors manipulate puppets and masks and other objects. In addition to the countless theatrical traditions that use objects, puppets and masks are becoming an important part of contemporary theatre all over the world. And so a discussion of them cannot be left out of a volume on world theatre.

The word *kulit* means "skin." The word *wayang* literally means "shadow," but the term is used to describe many different forms of theatrical performance that developed over the islands that make up Indonesia. For instance, *wayang wong*, which means "person theatre," denotes several dance-drama forms that use the stories from *wayang kulit*. The *wayang golek* means "doll theatre," and it is a form of puppet theatre that uses three-dimensional puppets instead of shadow puppets. The practice of using shadow puppets may have been imported from India, particularly a form known as *Ravana Chhaya* from the eastern coastal state of Odisha. Similar techniques can be found in shadow puppetry throughout Asia, from China to Turkey, and some scholars suggest people have shared these traditions throughout the region. The *Ravana Chhaya* told the story of Ravana from the *Ramayana* and involved shadow puppets made of deer skin. The *wayang kulit* puppets are made from water buffalo hides and are mounted on sticks made of bamboo, or more commonly from water buffalo horn. They are elaborately painted and many have articulated limbs that can be moved. Many of the characters and stories are from the Indian epics, but the *wayang kulit* employs indigenous characters and even Persian heroes as well. Also, the *kayon*, or "tree of life," appears during times of transition or to represent natural forces. It is a large leaf-shaped puppet that represents time, natural forces, or beings for which there is no puppet.

The *punakawan*, or clown servant characters, in Javanese *wayang* are indigenous to Java. The clown characters serve to upset the order and to offer social protest. The clown character Semar has three sons: Gareng, Petruk, and Bagong. According to Jan Mrázek, the clown scenes in Javanese *wayang* represent a rupture in the structure of the performance. He observes that the clowns are alone on the screen and the usual positions according to status are ignored. While the noble characters speak in high dialects that are often inaccessible to the audience, the clown characters speak in the common dialect, using slang and coarse language. The music for these characters no longer follows the strict meter used for the rest of the performance (44). Scholars have many theories about the origins of the clown characters, but some suggest that the clowns represent indigenous deities that have been demoted since the arrival of Hinduism/Buddhism and then, later, Islam.

The first recorded instance of *wayang* in Java dates back to 840 CE in a note by King Lokapala where he states that the performers presented a *wayang* performance. A later inscription from 907 by King Balitung states that Galigi presented a *wayang*. We have more detail in this second inscription. It states that for a dedication of the land for a monastery, Galigi performed the story of young Bima, one of the Pandava ("Pandawa" in Indonesian) brothers from the *Mahabharata*. There were also dances, songs, and clowning.

One artist manipulates the puppets, the *dalang*, and that person is also the narrator, director, and conductor of the *gamelan*, the musical ensemble which accompanies the performance. The *dalang* must memorize a vast number of stories and has a lot of control over the tone and pace of the performance. The *dalang* sits behind a cotton screen that is lit from behind with all of the puppets. The *dalang* conducts the *gamelan* with auditory cues, usually by tapping a metal plate with his or her feet or by hitting with a mallet the wooden chest that is used for storing the puppets. Traditionally, performances lasted all night, often for up to nine hours. In modern times, the *wayang kulit* might accompany something like a corporate anniversary party, in which case the performance would be very short. The *dalang* works the entire time without a break. It is customary for the *dalang* not to eat during the performance.

Generally, the art of the *dalang* stays within *wayang* families, and the young men take an apprenticeship when they reach the age of 13. The apprenticeship would involve being the "stagehand" for the *dalang*, including setting up and "striking," or taking down, the set. The apprentice may also be a musician in the *gamelan* or assist with the puppets during the performance. The apprenticeship would involve learning the art of puppetry and narration, but also involve the spiritual aspects of the ritual that accompanies the *wayang*.

Usually, the profession of *dalang* has been reserved for men, but a very few women are working as *dalang* today. Scholar Jennifer Goodlander, who has trained as a *dalang* herself, discusses this phenomenon and the difficulties women *dalangs* have faced in a 2012 article in *Asian Theatre Journal*. As Goodlander observes:

> Until recently, the *dalang* has always been male, but now a handful of women in Bali are studying and performing as *dalang*. This

innovation comes not without controversy because many people in Balinese society question women's ability to undertake the difficult physical and spiritual tasks of a *dalang* and whether this type of performance is even appropriate for a woman.

(55)

Goodlander notes that a few women have become *dalang* since 1975 precisely because of the opening of several schools for the arts. In Indonesia, women are seen as having a duty to the domestic sphere, and so the profession continues to be almost exclusively male.

Wayang kulit continues to be popular in Java and Bali, but also in Lombok, Madura, Sumatra, and Borneo. Bali continues to have a predominantly Hindu population and the Hindu cosmology persists in the *wayang* of Bali. In the fifteenth century, Islam came to Java, but the *wayang* traditions thrived in Java as well. The Muslim *dalang* adapted many of the stories of the *wayang*, but they still reflect local values. Ghulam-Sarwar Yousof notes:

> Thus while the principal characters of the *Mahabharata* and *Ramayana* originate in the pair of Hindu epics, they no longer fully represent Hindu or even Indian values. Neither, it may be added, do they represent Islamic values as enshrined in the shari'ah. These values are manifested, rather, through mysticism. All literalism is thus transcended into universalism with a strong dose of indigenous cultural values.

(87)

The *wayang kulit* represents a unique blend of the cultures that make up the islands of Indonesia. The art varies from community to community and changes with cultural trends.

Today, there are modern versions of *wayang* and broadcasts of performance on television. *Dalang* continue to innovate. Occasionally, Javanese *wayang* have included pop singers and electronic music along with the *gamelan*. Some have included more than one screen and more than one *dalang*. Of these innovations Jan Mrázek states: "Many people see innovation and *wayang's* popularity today as positive developments. Many other people, including many perform-ers (even some of those who incorporate radical innovation into their performances), claim that *wayang* is 'falling apart' or 'broken' (*bubrah, rusak*), that it prostitutes itself as it seeks popularity, and only serves the tastes of the present." But Mrázek argues that this is how *wayang* remains a vibrant and dynamic form in Javanese culture:

> [I]t looks and faces now in one direction, now in another, and its face constantly changes expression in response to its changing inner state and in response to what it is facing and with what it is being faced, at the same time that it tries to keep up appearances.... In short, it is alive, it vibrates with life, it has both life's inconstancy and its persistence

(39)

RATNA SARUMPAET: THEATRE AND SOCIAL JUSTICE IN INDONESIA

The Portuguese arrived in Indonesia in the sixteenth century and then the Dutch in the seventeenth century. Both powers were anxious to dominate the spice trade and Indonesia had vast resources in nutmeg and clove plants which are native to the area. For many years, the Dutch East India Company occupied Batavia, a colony situated on Java on land that is now part of Jakarta. The Dutch government took over when the company collapsed in 1889, establishing the Dutch East Indies, which included much of Indonesia, as a full colony. Colonial administrators violently crushed any revolt by the Indonesian people. World War II and a brutal occupation by the Japanese destabilized colonial rule enough that, after a long and bitter struggle, Indonesia gained independence.

In 1950, Indonesia entered a period of parliamentary democracy with Sukarno as president. The excessive factionalism made for a rough beginning as secular nationalists, Islamists, and Communists vied for control. People who had benefited from colonial and Japanese occupation were eager to secure their positions and resisted change. As factional fighting broke out, Sukarno declared martial law and began to expel Dutch and ethnic Chinese from the country and purge the military of dissidents. In 1959, he instituted what he called a "Guided Democracy," designed to bring balance between the military, Islamist, and Communist groups.

Indonesians referred to Sukarno as the great *dalang* because he manipulated the government to bring balance and some stability to chaotic political forces. But Sukarno also consolidated power. He disbanded the parliament and created instead the Provisional People's Consultative Assembly under his control. He had military opponents imprisoned and dissolved rival political parties. He also made himself "President for Life" in 1963. As the economy began to collapse, tensions between rival groups worsened and Major General Suharto took command of the military. The kidnap and murder of six generals resulted in the massacre of thousands of people in 1965 and Suharto became "president" the following year, through what has been called a "soft coup." Suharto became president through a presidential directive, referred to by Indonesians as the *Supersemar*, alluding to the triumph of the clown character Semar.

Suharto brought back foreign investment, which brought economic growth, but mostly to his own enrichment and the benefit of a few. But a student-led democracy movement in the late 1990s led by Megawati Sukarnoputri, the daughter of Sukarno, brought international pressure for Suharto's government to make reforms. When Suharto was "elected" president by the parliament for the seventh time, protests erupted and Suharto was forced to resign. Elections in 1999 brought in a democratic government.

Ratna Sarumpaet (1949–) was born in North Sumatra, Indonesia, to a Christian family. She went to Jakarta in the late 1960s to study architecture. However, she changed direction when she witnessed *Karsidah Barzanji*, a dramatic adaptation of Islamic verse by political theatre artist and poet W. S. Rendra. Sarumpaet formed her own company *Satu Merah Panggung* (One Red Stage) in 1973 and married Achmad Fahmy Alhady the following year. It was then that she converted to Islam. Alhady was violently abusive. Sarumpaet left the theatre for film and television until after her divorce in 1989. She returned to the theatre with a focus on women's issues.

Marsinah: A Song from the Underworld and Marsinah Accuses

In 1993, a group of workers at a watch factory went on strike. The Regency Governor had ordered that wages be raised, and the company refused to comply. A 25-year-old woman by the name of Marsinah helped to organize the strike and was one of the negotiators. While the company agreed to the workers' demands, several of the representatives were ordered to a military command office where they were forced to resign. Marsinah was not summoned and went to look for her coworkers after her shift. After visiting a couple of friends that evening, she disappeared. Her body was found three days later in a hut not far from the factory. The medical examiner declared that she had been beaten, tortured, and raped and died from internal injuries.

News of Marsinah's death galvanized the student and worker protest movements. And it had a profound impact on Ratna Sarumpaet. Barbara Hatley explains Sarumpaet's keen interest in Marsinah's story:

> Ratna, who played the part of the Marsinah figure in the play, speaks passionately of her obsession by Marsinah's story, bringing together her own long-term concerns with the oppression of women and with social injustice more generally. These are issues she sees as integrally linked, inasmuch as Indonesia's authoritarian, hierarchical socio-political system, historically and in the present day, is male-created and male-dominated, encoding and celebrating male values. Ratna herself feels a strong personal identification with Marsinah through the suffering and violence of her own marriage – "I am Marsinah," she frequently states.
>
> ("Women in Contemporary Indonesian Theatre" 597)

But Hatley also points out that Sarumpaet feels uneasy with the label of "feminist" or the charge that her plays should bring social change for women.

Sarumpaet wrote *Marsinah: Nyanyian dari Bawah Tanah* (*Marsinah: A Song from the Underworld*) in 1994. She and her small company performed it several times in Java at the end of that year. She states that the two newsmagazine sponsors of the play were shut down by the government before the play could get off the ground. The Indonesian Legal Rights Institute suddenly withdrew an offer to fund the final performance in Jakarta without explanation. But Sarumpaet managed to mobilize women writers and activists to pool together the resources they needed.

In 1991, Sarumpaet had performed her adaptation of Sophocles' *Antigone* (441 BCE) based on the version by French playwright

Jean Anouilh (1910–1987), a 1943 version that makes clear parallels between Antigone's plight and that of those involved in the French Resistance to the Nazi Occupation. In Sophocles' play, Antigone defies her uncle, now the ruler of Thebes after the exile of Oedipus. Sarumpaet used the play to criticize the harshly patriarchal *batak* culture of northern Sumatra, the culture of her heritage. Sarumpaet's admiration for Antigone's defiance from her rocky tomb, and Sarumpaet's visits to the tomb of her own recently deceased father stirred Sarumpaet's imagination. She decided to configure her presentation of Marsinah to be a conversation among the dead.

The play begins with a row of spirits with their backs to the audience. A young woman can be heard crying throughout the action of the play. A debate between a woman, denoted in the script as "X," and a Judge takes up most of the play, with a few other scenes interspersed. A Mother passes through occasionally, describing her children, representing the mother of all of Indonesia. A woman emerges from the factory where she works and collapses. A guard harasses and nearly assaults her when the other women of the factory beat him nearly to death. The woman they rescue later hangs herself. In the end, X has a protracted argument with a man, a representative of industry and progress, about his responsibility toward the people who have been harmed by development. In the end, she questions, but again finds, her faith.

Through the argument with the Judge, Sarumpaet examines the responsibility of the legal system in protecting human rights. X confronts the Judge and asks her if she has ever ruled on behalf of interests that were truly just or treated human beings as human. The Judge is defensive: "if you talk about the national image, about investment, about the international economy, then you should realise that the problem is not limited to what the legal system might possibly achieve. Who makes the rules? Who signs the decrees? I'm only a Judge" (25). X refuses to allow the Judge to absolve herself as the Judge refuses to accept responsibility.

X must confront the man who represents progress in Indonesia as well. While the man keeps saying he understands the poor, he also blames them for not being as resourceful as he has been. X reminds him that the cards were always stacked in his favor and that he has willfully exploited his fellow Indonesians' progress to satisfy the "lusts of a few" (35). For this, he calls her "backward" and accuses her of being against the economic development of Indonesia. X explains: "For most people who live in this country, your concept of development, with its lofty ideals, ends up being no more than rape" (36). Villages have been plowed over, the environment has been poisoned, and people are starving.

Sarumpaet later adapted the full play into a one-woman show entitled *Marsinah Menggugat* (*Marsinah Accuses*) — the title a riff on Sukarno's defiant statement against the Dutch colonizers as "Indonesia Accuses" — which she performed herself. In the published version of the monologue (and it seems that there are a few variations over the course of the performances by Sarumpaet as the piece continued to evolve), Sarumpaet channels the spirit of the murdered woman Marsinah. Evan Winet states that she performed in front of portraits of Marsinah, and images of her were circulated in programs for the audience ("Between Umat and Rakyat" 62).

As "voices of the past" fade at the start of the performance, Marsinah drops to the floor in despair: "I see so many blood-stained hands ... I see how greed can be perpetuated, how capitalists can keep raking in profits, Managers and those in power continue to laugh and chat over every drop of my sweat." Sarumpaet grounds the story of Marsinah within the system of corrupt capitalism of late twentieth-century Indonesia, a system that destroys the people who seek to change it: "But if a lowly worker like me dares open her mouth to demand a pay raise? She'll be killed" (*Marsinah Accuses* 393). On the other hand, she notes, her death is being used to bring justice for workers in a "sick society" (394).

The voices begin again. Marsinah is startled, but affirms that she is not afraid. What follows is a harrowing account of Marsinah's life before she was murdered and then the murder itself. She describes a life of poverty and hard work and a life under the shadow of violence. But then that life was taken from her: "I scratched out a living for a mouthful of rice there, always stumbling, hounded by your bullying and threats. I was tortured there ... I was raped there, brutally murdered ... You killed me. You tore from me the right to live ... What sort of society did you think I'd call it? What sort of society?"

Marsinah describes the attack from her point of view, as if she were able to speak from the grave. She describes being grabbed off the street, forced into a car, and then removed from the car and dragged for several yards. As she is beaten and tortured, she states, she was "abused with streams of filthy words during every torture that followed." Sarumpaet creates an affective experience for the audience as they feel Marsinah's desperation as the attack becomes more brutal. Sarumpaet conveys the acute sense of panic and unmediated fear, especially as she describes the physical violence of her body being lifted and smashed down until she cannot move and her attackers violating her with something that breaks her pubic bone.

Her account of the last moments elicits a feeling of unparalleled horror:

> The blood was black and dirty,
> Really dirty
> It covered my belly
> Covered my inner thighs.
> It was spattered on the floor,
> All over the door, on the table legs
> Everywhere
> Those were the last moments
> I was able to feel something.
> Something too painful.
> Something so terrifying
> So brutal
> God, no one deserves to suffer like that.

(396)

After taking her audience through Marsinah's unfiltered experience, her final appeal is for justice in a situation where justice was never served.

Sarumpaet was arrested in 1998 for gathering with a small group and singing the Indonesian national anthem. The prosecutors discussed charging her and several others with crimes that carried sentences of several years. International pressure, levied in large part by the International Centre for Women Playwrights, forced the prosecution to back down and indict her on a lesser charge. The judge sentenced her to 70 days, a term which she had already served awaiting trial, and so she was released. Not long after, Suharto resigned. Sarumpaet continued to write political plays such as her 2004 *Anak-Anak Kegelapan* (*Children of Darkness*), which focused on the children of the victims of the Communist purges of 1965.

While the plays of Sarumpaet are political and the protagonists are women, Evan Winet points out that Muslim faith recurs as a central theme in much of her work: "[T]he Islamic identity of her protagonists is consequential. In all of Sarumpaet's plays about Marsinah, this character challenges and ultimately seeks solace in Allah, ... In these plays, as in much Islamic literature, Allah is a mystery though also the ultimate source of justice in a highly corrupt world" ("Between Umat and Rakyat" 61). The final scene in *Marsinah: A Song from the Underworld* shows an archetypal struggle with faith in the face of oppression and suffering. While the chorus recites Qur'anic verses throughout the play, the Mother urges X to remember God. X rejects her plea: "Which God, Mother? Not a day passed without me bowing down before Him. From hour to hour I followed in His footsteps, until I thought I really understood His ways. Understood His omnipotence, His boundless love. But what did I get?" (*A Song from the Underworld* 42). But Heaven intervenes and helps her emerge from the darkness. A bright light brings the love of God into her heart and she is then at peace: "Purify me, O Allah. Wrap me in a fresh shroud, and lay me in the place Your hand shows me" (45). For Sarumpaet, Islam acts as the foundation to her activism, and the knowledge that all will face divine judgment underscores her plea for justice. Sarumpaet continues to write, act, and nurture women theatre makers in Indonesia.

3

EAST ASIA

JĪNGJÙ: BEIJING OPERA

In the nineteenth century, a British diplomat named Thomas Francis Wade created a system for writing Chinese words using the Roman alphabet, a process known as "Romanization." Herbert Giles, also a British diplomat, modified the system a generation later. The "Wade–Giles" Romanization system was used for a hundred years, and even after the People's Republic of China adopted the Hanyu Pinyin system in the 1950s, Europe and the Americas continued using Wade–Giles. Under Wade–Giles, the capital of China was known as "Peking." The Chinese-speaking world has now widely adopted Pinyin as the International Organization for Standardization. Therefore, it is now correct to say "Beijing." There may be times, however, where sources you read and sources quoted here may use the old style. When we say "Peking Opera" and "Beijing Opera," we are talking about the same thing.

In simplified Chinese, the name is 京剧, which in pinyin Romanization is *Jīngjù*. This literally translates to the "Opera of the Capital." 剧 literally translates to "theatrical work." In fact, the name in Taiwan is 國劇, or *guójù*, which translates to "national theatre." The form did not originate in Beijing, however.

Jīngjù came to Beijing from the southern province of Anhui for the eightieth birthday of the Qianlong Emperor in 1790. The Qianlong Emperor, number six in the line of the Manchurian rulers, reigned over a particularly prosperous time for the Qing Dynasty. Four troupes came from the province to perform at court, but the performances became popular when groups started to perform for the public. Performing troupes also came from the province just to the west of Anhui, the province of Hubei, and influenced the development of the form in Beijing. The Hubei troupes performed Han Opera. Several other regional forms affected the development of *Jīngjù*.

Jīngjù performances involve some spoken text, singing, gestures, and acrobatics. The performers appear on a mostly bare stage with only a few set pieces, if any, such as a table or a gate. *Jīngjù* uses *Xīpí* (西皮) and *Èr huáng* (二黄) styles of music, originally the music of the Han Opera. The movement and singing are stylized and the speech is in an archaic Mandarin dialect. The performers wear elaborate headdresses and costumes with long sleeves much like they wore in the Qing Dynasty (1644–1911). All of the adult male characters have beards. Generally, the makeup and costume denotes social status and tells the spectator something about the personality of the character.

As in many professions, students of *Jīngjù* had to apprentice to a master. The student would have to pay the master, generally by accumulating debt that was to be paid off through performance earnings in the first years of work. Students would train in acrobatics first, and then learn the singing. As Hu Hung-yen (Hú Hóngyàn, 胡鴻燕) noted in an interview in *Educational Theatre Journal* in 1974:

> But before an actor learns to sing, he is first trained in acrobatic skills. Thus not only will an actor on stage have a clear and a good voice, but every movement of his hands, head, and body will be full of charm. Only then will the audience be enchanted. For this to occur, the audience must see not only the actor's performance but they must sense the thoroughness of his training.
>
> (Chang, Mitchell, and Yeu 184)

She goes on to note that connoisseurs would understand right away the quality of the performance, but also the type of character being portrayed. But she believed that anyone should be able to judge an actor's performance.

Initially, all the actors were men as the Qianlong Emperor had forbidden women to perform in Beijing during the eighteenth century. Women began to perform sporadically in *Jīngjù* at the end of the nineteenth century. All-women companies appeared in Shanghai at the turn of the century and the ban on women performers was officially lifted at the start of the Republic in 1911. The leaders of the Republic believed in gender equality. Today, men continue to play women's roles and some women perform men's roles. However, cross-gender casting does not imply any parody. Actors train for the role they would execute best.

Roles are divided into several categories. The male (Shēng, 生) roles include the cultivated adult man, the young man, and the fighting man. The young man character has a high voice that sometimes breaks (like the changing voice of an adolescent). The fighting man would be an actor that is good at stage combat and acrobatics. There are several types of female roles (Dàn, 旦.), but the main ones are the noble woman, the young woman, the fighting woman, and the elderly woman. Several male actors made their careers playing *dàn* roles. The work of Méi Lánfāng (梅蘭芳, 1904–1961) received so much acclaim that his style came to be emulated and known as the "Mei School." He traveled throughout Asia, Europe, and the United States and had a profound influence on the ideas of Konstantin Stanislavski and Bertolt Brecht. The additional roles are the Painted Face (Jìng, 净) roles, recognizable by the color of their elaborate face paint, and the Clown (Chǒu, 丑) roles. Only the Jìng and Chǒu roles have extremely stylized face paint.

The face paint of the Jìng roles tells the spectator about the personality of the character and even tells the spectator exactly who the character is. The color denotes personality traits: red is a heroic warrior, white is a scheming villain, black is a strong and occasionally rough personality. Red, white, and black were the original colors, but other colors were added, such as purple for serenity and yellow for intelligence. Certain objects or patterns will indicate a specific person. A white spot on the nose bridge indicates a Chǒu role, the clown. However, no two face paint patterns are exactly the same. The actor puts unique touches into the patterns of that character's specific makeup.

The clown roles must be incredibly skilled at acrobatics and improvisation and they must be able to make many of their physical feats look easy, as if they happened accidentally. An example of the clown would be Sūn Wùkōng (孫悟空), the Monkey King from *Jīngjù* performances based on *Xīyóu jì* (*Journey to the West*, 西遊記). Scholars believe the novel *Journey to the West* dates back to the sixteenth century and was written by Wú Chéng'ēn. The novel takes its story from historical events: the travels of the monk Xuánzàng to India in the seventh century to receive the Dharma at Nalanda, a Buddhist school in northeast India. In the novel, Xuánzàng recruits many disciples, including Sūn Wùkōng.

Some scholars believe that the character of Sūn Wùkōng evolved out of both Chinese folk tales and the stories of Hanuman from India. The Monkey King wreaks havoc wherever he goes. He embodies the trickster, further complicated by the fact that some of his mischief ends up giving him more power. For instance, he gets into the Lǎozǐ's pills of longevity and steals and eats the peaches of immortality. Although he is initially invited to Heaven by the Jade Emperor, he discovers that his job as Protector of the Horses is the lowest job in Heaven. The heavenly forces are unable to placate him and he begins to cause chaos.

One popular *Jīngjù* work that features Sūn Wùkōng is *Shíbā luóhàn dòu wùkōng* (*Eighteen Luohans Fight the Monkey King*, 十八羅漢鬥悟空). A company from Beijing chose this among about a half-dozen pieces to bring to the United States after China and the US normalized relations after 1979. Beijing and New York became sister cities, and the visit was highly celebrated. In *Eighteen Luohans Fight the Monkey King*, Lǎozǐ decides to destroy Wùkōng for his trickery. Lord Lǎozǐ has his Luohans throw him into a furnace. A "Luóhàn" is the Chinese word for Arhat, or a Buddhist monk who has reached the highest stage of enlightenment just short of becoming a Buddha. The Luohans lock Sūn Wùkōng in the furnace for forty-nine days. When they try to speak to the Monkey King spirit, however, the very much alive Monkey King speaks from inside the furnace. He busts it open and demands to be let out. Instead of cremating him, the furnace has tempered him and made him stronger. It has given him gold eyes that can see great distances. He twirls his staff, which can change size and weighs several tons. The eighteen Luohans try to subdue him, but he is victorious after a glorious battle and returns to his home on *Huāguǒ Shān* (花果山), the Flowers and Fruit Mountain.

Some of the most popular *Jīngjù* involve the *qīng yī* (青衣), or the "noble woman" roles. Adapted from a novel written in the early seventeenth century, the play *Yù Táng Chūn* (玉堂春) is a favorite among *Jīngjù* audiences. The courtesan Sū Sān (苏三) meets and falls in love with Wáng Jīnlóng (王金龙), a young student studying for his civil service exams. When Wáng runs out of money, he is barred from the brothel. However, Sū gives him her savings and urges him to return to take his exams.

After he leaves, Sū is sold to be the concubine of a rich merchant. She lives unhappily in the household of the merchant, and her despair drives her to attempt suicide. Because Sū discovers that the merchant's wife is having an affair with a young man, the wife attempts to poison her. The plan backfires, however, because the merchant ends up eating the noodles instead. After he dies, his wife frames Sū for the murder. The magistrate sentences Sū Sān to death and she is taken to the court in the provincial capital to have her case reviewed. It turns out that the official that asked to have the case reviewed is none other than Wáng Jīnlóng. He did so well on his exams, he has become an important official in the capital. When he sees that the accused is his beloved, he vows to discover the truth. Finally, at the climactic trial, the maid confesses, and Sū is set free. She and Wáng can now be together.

Jīngjù reached the height of popularity in the beginning of the twentieth century. Xu Chengbei notes that in the 1930s there were at least ten theatres in what was then the small city of Beijing. Additionally, some actors, including the legendary Méi Lánfāng (梅蘭芳), began to branch out to create new kinds of theatre, *Jīngjù* on modern themes. These plays were set in the present day and involved contemporary costume and settings. These were not popular variations, but they laid the groundwork for *Jīngjù* after the Revolution.

After the fall of the Republic and the beginning of the People's Republic in 1949, cultural activities were considered to be part of the revolutionary project. During the first seventeen years of the People's Republic, *Jīngjù* received large state subsidies, and many new plays were written, while many old plays were revised to correspond with the new revolutionary values. With the Cultural Revolution (from 1966 to 1976) came a strict ban on traditional Jīngjù. The wife of Chairman Máo Zédōng (毛泽东), Jiāng Qīng (江青), instituted a practice of only staging *Yàngbǎnxì* (样板戏), or "model plays." These Revolutionary Operas focused on the plight of ordinary people such as workers and people engaged in the struggle for the Revolution. The ideas of Máo took center stage and the ending was always the triumph of Communism. The operas were disseminated via live performances, film, radio, comic books, music records, and calendars.

Hóng Dēng Jì (The Red Lantern, 红灯记) is set during the Second Sino-Japanese War. It features the story of three generations working toward bringing about the Revolution. The father of the Lǐ family, Lǐ Yùhé (李玉和) is arrested. A simple railroad worker, he had a special assignment to pass along important information to the Party by telegram. Unfortunately, one of his comrades turns him in, choosing instead to become a traitor to the Party rather than be prosecuted himself. The Japanese agents come to the Lǐ household, but Lǐ's mother refuses to give up the telegram the agents are seeking. Grandma Lǐ (李奶奶) realizes she must reveal the truth to Lǐ's daughter Tiěméi (李铁梅). The agents become frustrated with the family's steadfast resistance and order the family executed. While Lǐ and his mother are killed, Tiěméi survives. She passes along the important telegram and joins the Party.

Following the end of the Cultural Revolution in 1976, traditional *Jīngjù* operas were revived in the People's Republic, and they remain a vital part of the performing arts world in the twenty-first century. Starting in the 1980s, intercultural adaptations of *Jīngjù* also became popular. The leading school for training *Jīngjù* performers today is the National Academy of Chinese Theatre Arts (中国戏曲学院, est. 1950), which is located in Beijing.

Jīngjù also thrives in Taiwan. Taiwan was colonized by the Chinese in the seventeenth century following Spanish and Dutch colonization. European colonists had subjugated the indigenous population on the island and imported Chinese laborers from Fujian province. Ethnic Chinese continued to migrate to Taiwan through the eighteenth and nineteenth centuries. At the end of the nineteenth century, with the First Sino-Japanese War, China ceded Taiwan to the Empire of Japan. Taiwan remained under Japanese rule until the end of World War II in 1945.

When Taiwan became part of the Republic of China, there was great unrest. The people of Taiwan were used to being separate from China and economic instability made matters worse. Although most of the people in Taiwan were now ethnically Chinese, they had lived under Japanese rule for decades. As more people migrated from mainland China to the island, the people already on the island considered themselves to be "native Taiwanese" and the people from the mainland to be outsiders.

In 1947–1949, conflict on the mainland between the Chinese Nationalists and the Communist Party became a full-fledged civil war. Defeated on the mainland in 1949, Chiang Kai-shek (蔣中正), the leader of the Chinese Nationalists, or the Kuomingtan (Guómíndǎng in Pinyin, 中國國民黨), moved the Republic of China government to Taiwan. Since this time, the status of Taiwan has been complicated and the source of much tension. The Chinese of the People's Republic of China consider Taiwan to be part of China and look forward to the day Taiwan will be reintegrated with the mainland. In the twentieth century, most Taiwanese also looked forward to that day, but to the day when the Communists would finally be defeated and the Kuomingtang restored to power. Increasingly, the memory of being part of China is fading, and more people see Taiwan as an independent nation.

The Chinese nationalists brought many cultural practices with them when they fled mainland China. This includes the practice of traditional *Jīngjù*, referred to as *guójù* in Taiwan. Establishing government-funded *guójù* was an important part of asserting Chinese Nationalist dominance over Taiwan. As Nancy A. Guy points out:

> The Nationalists believed that their recovery of the mainland depended on maintaining their citizens' desire to return home, and Peking opera was considered a powerful force in working toward this end. . . . The sound of Peking opera evoked memories of a nostalgic past that in turn reaffirmed identity with the mainland and perpetuated a desire to return home.
>
> (91)

To that end, the Kuomingtang refused to support and even suppressed performance forms, such as Gezai (Gēzǐxì, 歌仔戏), that had evolved on the island over several hundred years. Beginning in the 1990s, the people of Taiwan have begun to question the idea that *guójù* is actually Taiwan's "national theatre," and the Gezai opera has continued to be hugely popular.

NOH, KABUKI, BUNRAKU: CLASSICAL AND POPULAR JAPANESE THEATRE

Chinese language and culture had a significant impact on the Japanese throughout the first millennium. Before the introduction of Chinese writing, or *kanji* (漢字), Japan had no written language of its own. By the beginning of the seventh century CE, the Japanese had a regular diplomatic relationship with China and with Korea, which was also heavily influenced by Chinese writing and culture. Through interaction and migration, religion, music, and literature spread throughout East Asia. When Chinese Buddhism, Confucianism, and Taoism came to Japan, they existed together alongside older Japanese Shinto thought and beliefs.

As I mentioned in the Introduction, Japanese *noh* theatre was developed by Kan'ami (1333–1384) in the fourteenth century. Yuzaki (later changed to Kanze), Kan'ami's theatre company, combined several popular forms including the music of *kusemai*, the form of *sarugaku*, and the harvest dances of *dengaku*. Yuzaki came to the court of the shogun and performed for the then-17-year-old Ashikaga Yoshimitsu. Yoshimitsu was so taken with the performance, he became a patron of the company. It was there that Kan'ami and Zeami were able to develop *noh*. Eventually, during the Edo Period (1603–1868) the Tokugawa shogunate regulated and refined *noh* into what it is today. The shogun consolidated *noh* training schools and *noh* troupes, and certain practices became standard. For many centuries, only men could become *noh* actors. However, some women have entered the profession since the beginning of the twentieth century.

The *noh* stage represents a Shinto shrine and is a bare stage surrounded by four pillars. There are two extensions, one along the back for the musicians (*atoza*), and one along the side for the singers (*jiutaiza*). The actors enter from a bridge known as the *hashigakari*, a bridge that figuratively connects the supernatural world with the mundane. Each pillar (*bashira*) on the stage has significance: the pillar associated with the primary character (*shitebashira*), the pillar associated with the secondary character (*wakibashira*), the flute pillar (*fuebashira*), and the sighting pillar (*metsukebashira*).

Over time as *noh* has developed, the costumes have become more codified and elaborate. The costume will tell the spectator what kind of character is being embodied by the actor, whether the character is male or female, high or low class, a warrior or a demon. While costumes may have been more stylized to directly represent different kinds of people, they are more or less based on the beautiful and expensive robes the samurai gave to actors as gifts. The outer robe (*shozoku*) is woven of a thick silk with elaborate embroidery. Actors wear an inner robe and trousers, and a special kind of sock (*tabi*) that enables the actor to glide easily across the stage. *Noh* is often called "the art of walking" because this subtle sliding of the feet (*suriashi*) is such an important element of the performance.

With some exceptions, *noh* actors wear wooden masks (*omote*). Each character has a special kind of mask with a subtle expression. The masks show the inner state of each character, whether the character is troubled, mysterious, naive, dignified, jealous, or has some supernatural power. A character may change masks, such as the actor in the play *The Lady Aoi* who changes from the *deigan* mask, the mask of a woman who is turning evil through her repressed jealousy, to the *hannya* mask, when the woman is transformed into a vengeful demon. *Noh* uses few stage properties. Mostly, actors use a single fan which will often represent other objects such as swords or walking sticks. A few set pieces may be used only to indicate location.

The Tokugawa shogunate also determined what program a day of *noh* entertainment would follow. Under these guidelines, *noh* plays fall into five categories: god plays (*waki*), warrior plays (*shura no*), women plays (*kazuramono*), miscellaneous plays, and ending plays (*kiri no*). The evening would first begin with a blessing (*okina*). The god plays are then called "*waki*" plays because they are companion pieces to the blessing, just as the *waki* actor is the companion character to the main, or "*shite*," character. The warrior plays usually deal with a warrior character who has ended up in "*asura*," an afterlife of eternal warfare. The women plays feature noble or old women and often include a graceful dance. Several plays make up the fourth miscellaneous category, but many of them are madness plays (*monogurui no*), which feature characters driven mad by grief. The ending plays are fast-paced and involve supernatural characters and sometimes signs of good fortune for pious characters. *Noh* can further be divided into real world (*genzai*) and fantasy (*mugen*) plays. Fantasy *noh* begins realistically, the first act follows the *waki* character arriving at some place that has special meaning, such as a battleground or a legendary temple, and meeting the *shite* character who seems to be a normal human being. However, in the second act, the *shite* character appears in its true form, such as a demon or ghost, and performs a dance that tells the true story. This apparition usually happens in a dream or a vision that the *waki* has, and it vanishes, often when the sun rises.

The original *sarugaku* form was comic. Its great popularity sprang in part from the acrobatics and dancing, but also from its satirical humor. This humorous side of *sarugaku* developed into the *kyōgen* pieces that continue to be an important part of *noh*. The characters of the *kyōgen* pieces are common people: monks, thieves, farmers, and the blind. There are also funny plays about bumbling sons-in-law, clever wives, and undependable husbands. The characters are always good-hearted and often fortunate people who tell funny stories full of clever wit. Before the Edo Period, the humor was a good deal bawdier, but the refinements of the Tokugawa shogunate smoothed over the coarseness of *kyōgen*.

The combined forms of *noh* and *kyōgen* are written in an archaic language not understood by anyone but the most educated in the *noh* form. However, the *noh* theatre continues to be popular. The movement is slow, emphasizing the thoughtful musings of the main characters. The stories are designed to help the spectator reflect on the transitory nature of existence and the connection of human beings to the divine. But *noh* was also designed to uphold a particular social order. During the shogunate, the social ideal was that women were obedient to men, peasants were obedient to feudal lords, and lords were obedient to the shogun. Tragedy strikes when the hierarchy of feudal society is upset, and in the course of the play, order must be restored.

During the Edo Period, *kabuki* first appeared as a form of dance performed mainly by women. According to popular legend, the founder of *kabuki* was the performer, Izumo no Okuni (c.1572–?), who danced first as a priestess at the Izumo Shinto shrine. Okuni originally danced as a way to raise money for the shrine. She incorporated folk dance and bawdy humor into her act and soon became popular in Kyoto. She eventually left the Izumo shrine and formed a troupe of dancers. However, soon other groups of women formed, many of them in brothels, and *kabuki* began to receive some negative attention. Although this story is apocryphal, we do know that a performer named "Okuni" existed. Likely, there were many women already doing the same kind of dance performance.

Before long, the shogunate banned the all-women *kabuki* troupes in 1629, leaving troupes that were made up of adolescent boys. However, this turned out to be equally problematic. Audiences also found the boys to be attractive and the performances were still full of bawdy humor. Often the performances continued to be offered in situations where the boys were prostitutes and available to the spectator. Banning women had done little to stop the sexual nature of or the sex trade associated with the performance. The shogunate banned all *onnagata* (female) roles to prevent cross-dressing in 1642. Boys were banned from *kabuki* in 1652. Mostly, the bans proved to be ineffective and troupes persisted. Eventually, troupes were made up of adult men only and *onnagata* roles were restored. Like *noh*, women did not perform in *kabuki* again until the twentieth century. From this time on, *kabuki* became immensely popular, partly due to its accessible themes (love, honor, heroism), comedy, acrobatics, and spectacle. But being the form of common people, it was subject to continuous regulation.

Kabuki emerged as a highly physical performance form and *kabuki* actors were known for being able to adapt any new material for the stage. This emphasis on the performance meant that the stage needed to serve the actors and their abilities. The first *kabuki* theatre used what was essentially a *noh* theatre stage. However, companies adapted and changed the performance space regularly. As Earle Ernst noted:

> This gradual process was greatly aided by the fires which period-ically and frequently destroyed not only theatre buildings but also large sections of Japanese cities. The *Kabuki*, consequently, was never encumbered with a permanent form of theatre build-ing. The vigilant government made regulations concerning the auditorium, but it made none about the acting areas. Architectural changes in the playing areas were the result of a single consider-ation, that of permitting the actor to move toward and through the audience.
>
> (206)

In the eighteenth century, the *hashigakari* continued to be widened, but as the theatres became larger, the *hashigakari* was no longer ade-quate. After 1724, *kabuki* theatres began to include the *hanamichi*, or "flower path," a bridge that extends out into the audience. Important scenes are often played out on the *hanamichi*. The *kabuki* performers consider the weakest part of the *hanamichi* to be the part in the back of the audience. The strongest part of the *hanamichi* is what is called the *shichisan*, or the "seven-three" position. This is the spot seven-tenths on the way to the stage. When actors arrive at this point, they may pause to show their great skill.

Technological advances in the eighteenth century meant further elaborations of the *kabuki* stage. A *mawari-butai*, a revolving stage first developed in the puppet theatre *bunraku*, became part of the *kabuki* stage and several trap doors were added. Spectators enjoyed watching actors suddenly disappear and reappear, sometimes transformed. In the early nineteenth century, a second rotating stage was added inside the first and could be rotated in the opposite direction. By the mid-nineteenth century, *kabuki* theatres used wires to fly actors (although poles had been used much earlier). Gas and then electric lighting used from the end of the nineteenth century added even more to the spectacle.

Kabuki actors apply their own makeup, beginning with total whiteface makeup called *oshiroi*. They then add lines to accentuate their facial expressions. The makeup for the *aragoto*, or "rough style," *kabuki* is the most exaggerated. *Aragoto kabuki* features bold heroes battling the forces of evil. The warrior characters have red and black lines to create a kind of "glaring" look. Villains and demons have blue or purple lines. *Wagoto kabuki* ("soft style") features more realistic-looking makeup and regular human beings.

The puppet theatre *bunraku* developed later than *kabuki*, but because of the overlap between the two art forms, you cannot really discuss one without the other. *Bunraku*, originally known as *ningyō jōruri*, began around the turn of the seventeenth century. Artists began to perform various puppet versions of the dramatic and musical storytelling form of *jōruri* together with music of the *shamisen*, the stringed instrument that accompanies *bunraku* and *kabuki* today. When the Takemoto-za theatre opened in Osaka in 1684, it ushered in the golden era of what we now call *bunraku*. In the mid-eighteenth century, puppet artists made several advancements. The puppeteer could now move several features of the face and the hands of the puppet. The single puppeteer was replaced with three working together – the master puppeteer operating the head and right hand, the apprentices operating the left hand and feet.

There are two kinds of *kabuki* and *bunraku* plays: *jidaimono* (history plays) and *sewamono* (domestic plays). In *kabuki*, there are also *shosagoto* (dance plays). Because, like *noh*, *kabuki* involves a full day of entertainment, different kinds of *kabuki* plays may make up a program. A *kabuki* actor may specialize in the *shosagoto*, which often involves dance without narrative, quick changes, and sometimes a series of solo dances of different characters by one dancer. A special dance floor (*shosa-butai*) is laid over the *kabuki* stage for *shosagoto* to allow for the stylized dance movement. The *sewamono* are often about lovers who are unable to be together and decide to commit suicide so that they can be together in the afterlife.

The first professional playwright, Chikamatsu Monzaemon (1653–1724), established many of the conventions of both *bunraku* and *kabuki*. In a play Chikamatsu originally wrote for *bunraku*, *Sonezaki Shinjū* (*The Love Suicides of Sonezaki*, 1703), a young merchant Tokubei has fallen in love with a prostitute Ohatsu. However, his uncle and master has decided Tokubei should marry his wife's niece. For the marriage, the uncle pays a handsome amount of money to Tokubei's stepmother as a dowry. When Tokubei refuses, the uncle demands Tokubei return the money to him. Tokubei retrieves the money, but temporarily loans it to his friend Koheiji who turns out to be untrustworthy and refuses to pay him back. While Tokubei relays this story to Ohatsu, Koheiji enters the brothel. Tokubei hides under Ohatsu's robes while Koheiji brags about stealing the money. He also shares his glee at the fact that Tokubei will be exiled, leaving Ohatsu to be claimed by Koheiji. Tokubei and Ohatsu decide they must commit suicide together. They sneak out of the brothel and head into the woods. By a dying pine tree, they slash their throats.

In the *jidaimono*, every element of the performance is highly stylized, including the dramatic exits of the actors. The actor may perform a series of movements (*kata*) followed by a moment of freezing in a dramatic pose (*mie*) to represent high emotion. This *mie*, if expertly executed, can draw wild applause from the audience. Writers have developed hybrid versions that mix *sewamono* and *jidaimono* (*jidai-sewa mono*) to combine historical stories with themes of love and family.

Because the shogunate placed a ban on portraying current political events, *jidaimono* often disguised current events, giving characters pseudonyms and placing events further back into the past. The most well-known example is the story of Akō Vendetta. It was written first into a *bunraku* piece by Chikamatsu called *Goban Taiheiki* (*Chronicle of Great Peace on a Chessboard*, 1706) and it was then adapted by several writers for both the *bunraku* and *kabuki* stages. One of the most well-known versions, *Kanadehon Chūshingura* (*The Treasury of Loyal Retainers*) was written by Takeda Izumo, Miyoshi Shōraku, and Namiki Senryū for the puppet stage in 1748 and then adapted for *kabuki* immediately after.

The actual events happened in the years 1701 and 1702, but the play is set in the fourteenth century. In the historical account, the *koke*, or the master of ceremonies for Edo Castle, Kira Yoshinaka, was training the daimyo Asano Naganori for a visit by the Emperor's envoys. Evidently there was some dispute about the kinds of gifts or bribes the young Asano was supposed to pay Kira and Kira began to publicly insult him. Asano attacked Kira with his sword but then was ordered to commit ritual suicide, or *seppuku*. His land was confiscated, and his retainers now without a master became *rōnin*, or masterless samurai. The *rōnin* spent the next year plotting revenge. They broke into Kira's estate and killed him and were, in turn, ordered to commit *seppuku* for their crime. The graves of the 47 *rōnin* at Sengaku-ji are among the most visited graves in the world. Indeed, the story of intense loyalty had great appeal to the Japanese and has been wildly popular in live performance and in film to this day.

In the *kabuki* version created by Nakamura Matagoro II and James R. Brandon, Lord Enya Hangan and his 47 samurai are at the court of Moronao, the chief counselor of the shogun. While there, Moronao professes his desire to Enya's wife, Kaoyo. Later, she has her husband deliver a letter to him rejecting his advances, which humiliates and angers Moronao. Moronao taunts Enya and continues taunting him until he cannot take it any longer. Enya draws his sword and strikes Moronao on the forehead and tries to kill him. However, his retainers hold him back.

Drawing a sword in the palace is a capital crime, and so Enya is sentenced to death by *seppuku*. Furthermore, the shogun will confiscate his estate and Enya's samurai will be *rōnin*. When the sentence is carried out, Enya's chief retainer Yuranosuke arrives. He stays with Enya as he commits the ritual suicide and hears his final words. Enya begins to say the word "revenge," but catches himself and says "remember me" instead. But Yuranosuke understands.

A year has gone by, and the retainers have moved on. They secretly conspire to seek revenge for their dead master. Okaru, who is the wife of the retainer Kanpei, has sold herself to a brothel to help raise money. Yuranosuke pretends to waste his time at the brothel in order to feign disinterest in revenge. One night, his son brings him a letter, spelling out the revenge plan. Curious, and convinced the letter is some harmless love letter, Okaru spies on Yuranosuke as he reads it. Yuranosuke sees Okaru and asks her to come down from her room. He makes several seemingly drunken suggestive jokes and offers to buy her contract if she lives with him for three days. Confused by his sudden amorousness, but happy at the prospect of freedom, she agrees.

As she waits, Okaru's brother Heiemon, who is also one of Enya's retainers, arrives. Okaru is ashamed that she is a prostitute, but Heiemon tells her that he is proud of her for raising money for the plot. Okaru excitedly tells him that Yuranosuke intends to buy out her contract and that she will be able to return home soon. Heiemon becomes angry at Yuranosuke, assuming that this means he is just enjoying himself at the brothel and is not committed to the revenge plot at all. Okaru tells Heiemon that he has it all wrong and tells him about the letter she saw Yuranosuke reading.

Heiemon, however, realizes what Yuranosuke truly intends. He tells Okaru that it is clear that Yuranosuke has no intention of freeing her. In fact, Yuranosuke saw Okaru spying on him and is worried that she will give away the plot. Yuranosuke intends to kill Okaru to protect the information in the letter. Heiemon also relays the news to her that her father had been killed accidentally by her husband Kanpei and that Kanpei committed *seppuku* not long afterwards. Okaru is devastated.

Heiemon decides that it would be best if he killed his sister himself. He is a low-ranking retainer, and he believes that it would demonstrate his loyalty to the others. Okaru, now stricken with grief, agrees. Thankfully, Yuranosuke overhears all of this and, convinced of the loyalty of both, stops Heiemon from killing Okaru. He takes Heiemon's sword and puts in in Okaru's hand. He then guides Okaru's hand to thrust the sword into the floor, the hiding place of Moronao's spy, who had been hiding in there the entire time. The final scene is the spectacular battle of the retainers invading the house of Moronao and beheading him.

In the twenty-first century, *bunraku* and *kabuki* both remain popular. While both forms rely on the classical repertoire, artists of both forms have attempted to experiment with new plays with mixed results. Artists have staged plays using material from new novels or from foreign stories such as *La Traviata* and *Hamlet*. *Bunraku* and *kabuki* receive some support from the government as they are regarded as important traditions despite the growing interest in contemporary performance forms and new media.

JAPANESE CONTEMPORARY THEATRE: CLASSIC FRAGMENTS AND INTERNATIONAL COLLABORATIONS

The twentieth century proved to be a tumultuous time for East Asia. With the rise of communism, first in Russia and then in China, and the beginning of the Cold War between pro-communist regimes and pro-capitalist states, newly formed tensions between Chinese, Japanese, and Korean people reached boiling point. With the end of the Tokugawa shogunate and the restoration of the Meiji Emperor, Japan became a powerful economic and military force. Japan occupied Korea and Taiwan, and, in 1931, invaded China. Escalations of tensions brought about the Japanese invasion of French Indochina (what is now Vietnam, Cambodia, and Laos) as well. The Pacific War of World War II was long and bloody. The culmination of the conflict was the dropping of atomic bombs on the cities of Hiroshima and Nagasaki by the United States, killing between 100,000 and 200,000 people.

After the Japanese defeat in World War II, Japan was occupied by the United States. Because Korea was occupied by Japan and Koreans forced to fight for the Japanese, the allies occupied Korea as well. The forces of the United Kingdom, United States, Soviet Union, and China partitioned Korea leaving the area north of the 38th parallel to be administered by the Soviets and the area south of it to be administered by the United States. Korea soon became contested territory in the Cold War, however, and the Korean War began in 1950. When fighting ended in 1953, the country was permanently divided between north and south. Tensions remain high between North and South Korea as they do between the People's Republic of China and Taiwan (discussed earlier).

Butoh: coping with grief

After World War II, the Japanese began to heal from the painful aftermath and confront rapid change under foreign occupation. It was in this context of collective grief that Hijikata Tatsumi created the performance art *butoh*. Performance scholars describe the 1959 premiere of Hijikata's piece *Kinjiki* (*Forbidden Colors*) as a revolution in the dance world. The piece, based on a novel by Yukio Mishima, began in blackout. A small beam of light revealed a dancer, Ohno Yoshito, standing downstage. There was no sound. Hijikata appeared behind the dancer and gave him a white hen, which the dancer placed between his legs. Ohno and Hijikata pursued each other. After a while, all the audience could hear was the heavy breathing of the two men and a male voice whispering "Je t'aime." The performance stirred enormous controversy both because of the gay male sexuality and what many people thought, mistakenly, was the killing of the hen.

Butoh's original name was *Ankoku-Butoh*, which translates to "dance of darkness." Hijikata hoped to subvert traditional ideas of grace and beauty in performance in a dance scene that was dominated by the conventions of *noh* and the influence of European forms of dance. A distinct feature of *butoh* performance is to paint the body completely white as a way to indicate anonymity and strip away all that people perceive of the performer based on their prescribed identity. The movement is often slow and extremely controlled. *Butoh* uses grotesque images and taboo subjects, focusing on sections of Japanese society that are marginalized – the homeless, drug addicts, sex workers, and LGBT people. As Vicki Sanders described: "Blemishes on the nation's powdered white cheek, they became Hijikata's metaphor for all that was rejected by Japan's classical definition of beauty" (148). While Hijikata and the originators of *butoh* sought to reject the oppressiveness of tradition, Sanders points out that *butoh* is still firmly rooted in Japanese aesthetic and thought, mostly through its meditation on transience, its use of emptiness, and its spiritual dimension rooted in Buddhism.

Setagaya Public Theatre

The Setagaya Public Theatre has two important missions. One is to bring cultural life to the community in which it resides through free performances and activities for the public, and the second is to bring together fragments of culture to create a unique repertoire. The company uses fragments that are both Japanese and foreign in its work, often to startling effect.

The Setagaya Public Theatre opened in 1997. In 2002, they appointed Nomura Mansai as the artistic director, bringing together traditional performance with the avant-garde. Nomura comes from a family of *kyōgen* performers. He is considered to be the Intangible Cultural Property *Nohgaku*, the tradition of *noh* and *kyōgen* performance practice that has been passed down for generations. Nomura began acting at the age of 3 and has continued to work on stage. As a boy, he had a small role in the film *Ran* (1985), Akira Kurosawa's (1910–1998) adaptation of *King Lear* (1606) by Shakespeare. Over the last few years, Nomura has appeared in a variety of adaptations of Shakespeare for the *noh* stage, including *Machigai no Kyogen* ("Kyogen of Errors"), *Kuninusubito*, a Japanese adaptation of *Richard III*, and an adaptation of *Macbeth*. He has created other modern *noh* and *kyōgen* works, some based on foreign texts and some based on Japanese stories.

For *Macbeth*, Nomura created a piece that involved only five actors playing the parts of Macbeth, Lady Macbeth, and the three witches. By distilling the cast to five basic characters, Nomura hoped to explore each character more fully. The text focuses on the aspirations and anxieties of Lord and Lady Macbeth and delves into their internal conflicts. The distillation also shows the influence of *noh* and *kyōgen*, the minimalism and economy of character and theme. Nomura played the role of Macbeth.

In *Kuninusubito*, Nomura used a combination of *kyōgen* actors and actors from *Shingeki*, "Japanese New Theatre." *Shingeki* was started by *kabuki* actors at the beginning of the twentieth century. These actors wanted to break out of the strictures of *kabuki* and incorporate more European styles into their productions, such as realism. The music in Nomura's production was *kabuki* music. One woman, Kayoko Shiraishi, played all of the women in the play. Nomura played the title role of Richard III. In fact, he often directs work and acts in it at the same time. For him, this means he will continually change and improve the production:

> This is because in Kyogen there is no director and the performing style is one in which you face the audience and communicate with them to shape your performance and staging, and I wanted to use that style of actor–audience relationship in this production of *Kuninusubito*. When creating a theater work, it can be very

important to have the ability to work impulsively and intuitively, but at the same time I feel that it is necessary to have the time to let it mature through interaction with the audience.

(Performing Arts Network Japan "Artist Interview")

Indeed the Setagaya Public Theatre will keep running something in repertory for a number of years. *Macbeth* has been performed since 2011. And over time, the director and the actors adjust the piece based on the reception, but with their own insights as well.

OCEANIA

The term "Oceania" generally means the region of the tropical Pacific that includes Australia, Micronesia, Melanesia (which includes Papua New Guinea and Fiji), and Polynesia (which includes Aotearoa/New Zealand). People settled the Australian continent more than 45,000 years ago, making the Australian Aboriginal population the second-oldest population on Earth. Geneticists believe the Australians began migrating from Africa through Asia about 75,000 years ago, and split off from Eurasian people before Europeans and Asians split off from each other. Papuans settled the islands of Oceania 3,500 to 4,000 years ago. Polynesians settled Aotearoa/New Zealand in the thirteenth century CE, and waves of European immigrants began coming to the area in the eighteenth and nineteenth centuries. Today, the diverse cultures and the colonial history are woven into ancient tradition in the art, music, and theatre of Oceania.

FIJI: TA, RUA, FOLU

People began settling the islands that make up Fiji 3,500 years ago from the neighboring islands. Fiji belongs to a grouping of cultures known as Melanesia, which has as its westernmost point Papua New Guinea and spreads east with Fiji as the point furthest east. The people of Melanesia share a genetic connection to the group of people who migrated to Australia and are called "Austronesian" people. They are distinct from the Polynesians who appear, according to genetic evidence, to have moved through the area quickly to settle the islands further east. Pottery from early Polynesian people predates the arrival of Melanesians on Fiji, but no one knows how many, if any, of the Polynesian people stayed and how much they may have influenced early Fiji culture.

European explorers began to take an interest in Fiji, first for the sandalwood that grew there, and then, when that was depleted, for the sea cucumber that could be caught in the surrounding waters. The introduction of muskets to Fiji helped to intensify fighting between clans. On the island of Bau, Ratu Tanoa Visawaqa became the first *Vunivalu*, meaning "high chief" or "war lord," in 1829 after his brother Ratu Naulivou Ramatenikutu died. Struggle against rival clans led to Ratu Tanoa's exile, but his son Ratu Seru Cakobau helped to reinstate him. In 1852, Cakobau became Vunivalu. Not long after, he claimed all of Fiji as his kingdom, a claim that was rejected by other chiefs. He dominated western Fiji, but was only able to subdue the eastern part of Fiji with an alliance with the chief of Tonga, Ma'afu. The Tongans had converted to Christianity, and Cakobau converted in 1854. This brought the influence of the Methodist Church to Fiji.

Fiji had a fragile and unstable unity, and many chiefs continued to reject Cakobau's claim to authority. The United States did recognize Cakobau. This recognition, however, meant that the United States held Cakobau responsible for a $44,000 debt. This had arisen because, in 1849, the house of the US Consul living in Fiji, John Brown Williams, was hit by a cannonball and burned. The cannon fire was part of a celebration on the island. Fire also destroyed Williams's store on a separate occasion, and Fijians looted the store. The US Navy sent Commander Edward B. Boutwell to collect compensation of $5,000 from the Fijians. But over time more claims by more US citizens caused the amount to reach almost $44,000. Boutwell commanded Cakobau to pay three installments of $15,000.

In 1862, Cakobau offered to cede Fiji to the United Kingdom in exchange for payment of the debt. But the UK did not recognize Cakobau's authority and declined. In an attempt to pay the debt, Cakobau sold some land to the Polynesia Company, a group of capitalists from Melbourne. But the ongoing chaos and violence forced the UK to look at Cakobau's offer anew and, in 1874, Fiji became a British colony.

Colonization had a profound effect on Fiji. The British invited the Australian company Colonial Sugar Refining to establish sugar plantations on the islands. Fijians continued to own the land, but indentured laborers from India were brought in. While many Indians settled in Fiji after their contract was fulfilled, most could not buy land as so little was available. This created separate and distinct classes based along ethnic lines, with Fijian landowners, Indian laborers, and European merchants and administrators. Because of the unequal conditions for Indians, agitators organized labor strikes. During World War II, when Fiji was occupied by the Allied Forces, Indians refused to serve, citing their status as second-class citizens. After the war, the military force that remained in place was made up almost exclusively of Fijians.

As constitutional reforms were put into place, the British drew up political parties according to ethnicity and gave Fijian chiefs extensive veto power in the government. In 1970, when Fiji achieved independence from the UK, the Alliance Party won the first election and held power until April 1987. It was then that a coalition between the National Federation Party (predominantly Indian) and the Labour Party (led by a Fijian Timoci Bavadra) won the elections. Bavadra became the prime minister, but this victory put a majority of Indians in the legislature, something which many Fijians could not abide. The following month, a lieutenant colonel named Sitiveni Rabuka led a coup and had Bavadra jailed. The military government nullified the new constitution of Fiji. By 1993, many Indians had left Fiji and Rabuka became the prime minister. Rabuka softened his position during the 1990s and agreed to a new constitution that reserved a certain percentage of legislative seats for ethnic Fijians. However, the office of prime minister could be held by a Fijian of any ethnicity. In 1999, Indian Mahendra Chaudhry won the election, only to be removed the following year. An interim government was established with Laisenia Qarase appointed as interim prime minister. Another election was held, but Qarase beat Chaudhry in a contested race.

Qarase wanted to resolve the problems of the past and proposed a program of reconciliation: compensating coup victims and pardoning the perpetrators. Tensions arising from this program led to yet another coup by the military in 2007. A new constitution was written in 2013, but the same military leaders who led the coup were elected to government the following year. The ethnic tensions and political instability, much of which was created by the legacy of colonialism, continue to fuel the production of culture in Fiji. Artists such as native Fijian Vilsoni Hereniko (1954–) create dramatic works to facilitate a discourse to define a Fijian identity and envision a Fijian future.

Vilsoni Hereniko – The Monster

Vilsoni Hereniko comes from the island of Rotuma, a small island far-flung from the rest of Fiji. Life on Rotuma and the mythology of the island are featured in Hereniko's feature film *Pear ta ma 'on maf* (*The Land Has Eyes*, 2004). In the film, which used almost exclusively Rotuman actors, a young Viki witnesses the injustice of her father Hapati being falsely accused of stealing coconuts from Koroa, the neighbor. Because Hapati does not speak English, he must rely on Poto the interpreter, who is colluding with Koroa to cheat Hapati out of his land. Poto tells the magistrate that Hapati confesses to stealing, and the magistrate fines Hapati ten pounds. This will likely mean that the family will lose their land. Hapati has told Viki about the Warrior Woman, the progenitor of the Rotuman people. Her tenacity in the face of adversity and her belief that there is divine justice serves as an inspiration to Viki. Hapati quotes the Warrior Woman: "The land has eyes, the land has teeth, and knows the truth." Viki notices that Hapati has been showing signs of illness, and indeed he dies during the course of the film. But Hapati pleads with Viki to succeed in life and to do well in her studies so that she is not a victim to injustice, and indeed she wins a chance to study in Fiji proper. Viki is strong, like the Warrior Woman, and her desire for knowledge, to learn English and to study beyond what she can learn on Rotuma, are not at odds with her identity as a native Rotuman. In fact, Hereniko shows her desire to reach forward into the future does not mean a rejection of her past and who she is.

Hereniko earned his doctorate at the University of the South Pacific in Fiji and was studying there when the 1987 coup occurred. The coup was a rupture in Fijian politics, as the Alliance Party had been elected without incident since Fiji gained independence. The political situation seemed stable and the people of Fiji seemed to trust the political process. However, class and racial tension simmered underneath the surface, and the divisions created by colonization reached breaking point when ethnic Indians were elected to office. That many Fijians only trusted the political process so long as native Fijians were in charge became all too clear.

The plot of *The Monster*, which Hereniko wrote in response to the coup, involves two allegorical characters, a Fijian beggar and an Indian beggar. The two fight over a basket of food. The Fijian, named "Ta," which means "One," found the basket first and claims this as her reason for getting the basket. The Indian, named "Rua," which means "Two," states that they must abide by the rules that they had agreed upon. Rua claims that Ta should remember her because Ta brought Rua to the island to begin with, but Ta says she does not remember her. When Ta suggests Rua return from whence she came, Rua states that she has no place to which she can return.

Ta complies with Rua's demand for following the rules, but because the contests are physical, Rua continually loses due to an injured leg. As they try to come up with ways to settle their dispute, Rua decides they should toss a coin, but Ta calls both "heads or tails." When Rua tries to call "heads," Ta claims she has already called it. Rua threatens to appeal to the audience, something Ta fears because it means giving control of the decision to someone else. Ta relents and allows Rua to choose "heads." Rua wins the toss. As Rua takes the basket, she is surrounded by dancers who menace her while she tries to eat. They are spirits in masks, wearing dry banana leaves and carrying war clubs. Eventually, the dancers disappear. Rua appeals to Ta, who refuses her help.

Eventually, Folu, which means "Three," finds them and says she has been looking for them. Folu claims she used to live with them, but in the way that Ta does not remember Rua, neither of them remember Folu. Folu says she has a message for them to take care of each other, at which point Ta and Rua chase Folu away. Ta and Rua begin to argue over the basket and "the rules" again. This escalates until Ta jumps on Rua and they leave the basket to fight each other. However, as they are fighting, a gigantic monster that is "ugly, multi-coloured and horrible" appears. Ta and Rua must fight for their lives, but they eventually succeed in defeating the monster. They are changed by their mutual action:

Ta I feel different.
Rua Something's changed in me. I don't understand.
Ta Neither do I. (Pause) We have killed the monster!

(They look at each other fondly and shake hands. Then, they pick up the basket of food, place it between them and feed each other).

(190)

The allegory shows the struggle between ethnic Fijians and Indians for control, one group feeling that they should have control because of being there first, and the other group relying on the rules of governance agreed upon by all when they achieved independence. The third character represents former colonial powers, feebly attempting to order the other two to work together. Once they face their true foe – political instability, violence, and poverty – the two indeed must join forces.

Although the military imposed a ban on artistic expression after the coup, the company went ahead with the production at the University of the South Pacific anyway. Soldiers posted on campus, even those who saw the production, had little, if any, experience attending the theatre and no experience with something so allegorical. Evidently, the allusions to the struggle for power, the elections, and the coup did not register as overtly political.

Hereniko's message was full of optimism that such mutual interest would win out. Diana Looser notes that Hereniko was able to see things from a different perspective. She notes that the Rotumans are:

> a Polynesian ethnic minority from an island incorporated as part of Fiji under the aegis of British colonialism. As an indigenous citizen of Fiji but with a different viewpoint—not ethnic Fijian, diasporic Indian, or colonial British—Hereniko was perhaps uniquely positioned to perform an immediate evaluation of the coup conflict.
>
> (Looser 203)

Hereniko, himself, says as much:

> As a Rotuman playwright living in Fiji, these two opposing positions seemed misguided. It was too simplistic to think merely in terms of one race against another; it seemed more a question of quests for control and power. Yes, race may have had something to do with it, but it was just one of the many factors at play. Who knows, perhaps it was just a mask worn to hide more private and personal ambitions.
>
> ("Interview" 191)

As a Rotuman, Hereniko viewed the ethnic tensions at play as part of a false rhetoric that hid the personal ambitions of those who used it. The Monster is a metaphor for allowing one's judgment to be clouded by racist ideology and abandoning mutual goals.

Hereniko says that some criticized the idealistic ending of *The Monster*. One colleague who had been harassed by the military felt that the Monster symbolized Rabuka and that the Monster should be killed. Hereniko, however, felt that the idealism was necessary, that theatre should serve as more than a simple mirror of real life. It should "act as a pointer," he notes, "to other paths that might lead to harmony, otherwise, why should anyone go to the theater?" (193)

AUSTRALIA: DREAMING THE FUTURE

After the first people settled Australia, they remained relatively isolated from other groups of people. No one really knows why the migration happened when it did, what route the people took, or why no one else migrated to Australia later on. The only known contact Australians had with the outside world came through trade with fishermen from Indonesia. The fishermen traded modern goods such as cloth, tobacco, and alcohol for use of the waters off the northern coast. This contact began in the eighteenth century and possibly as early as the seventeenth century. But by the time outsiders made contact, the Australian people had settled the whole of Australia in 250 distinct nations speaking at least that many indigenous languages.

European explorers showed some curiosity about, but little serious interest in, Australia until James Cook claimed the east coast for Britain in 1770. With the looming independence of the United States, Britain had run out of options for the transportation of convicts, and Australia seemed ideal. Britain sent the first ship of convicts to Botany Bay in 1788. The original group of European settlers decided that Botany Bay was unsuitable so they moved the colony to Port Jackson and founded the city of Sydney.

Given the fact that no one asked the indigenous population their permission to settle there, the colony was off to a rocky start. Some people welcomed the foreigners, but other groups resisted. Conflict broke out sporadically. And European microbes wiped out tens of thousands of people. Open conflict between white Australians and Aboriginal Australians died down in the early twentieth century, but racial tension continued to exist.

By the mid-nineteenth century, Australians successfully lobbied for voting rights. Women and Aboriginal people could vote in some limited circumstances and in some places. The women's suffrage movement was successful in gaining the right of women to vote and, in many cases, run for office by the end of the nineteenth century. Indigenous voting rights were not fully secured until 1967. Australia officially gained independence from Britain after World War I. However, Australians did not actually ratify their independence until years later, in 1942. Even then, Australians did not exercise their independence until 1986 when all formal colonial ties to the United Kingdom were severed.

The territories of Australia became a federation in 1901, and the general will to become one distinct nation accompanied a new nationalism in the arts. White Australians began to write a uniquely Australian literature and music. Up until then, only foreign plays, mostly British, had been performed on the continent. Vaudeville and blackface minstrel companies also flourished. Australian writers began to craft a real body of Australian drama early in the twentieth century.

In 1954, the establishment of the Australian Elizabethan Theatre Trust resulted in dozens of theatres opening and germinating new work, including the Union Theatre Repertory Company in Melbourne, the Elizabethan Theatre (formerly The Majestic) in Sydney, the Marionette Theatre of Australia in Sydney, and the Australian Theatre of the Deaf in Victoria. In 1955, Ray Lawler, after some moderate success as a playwright, penned *Summer of the Seventeenth Doll*, a tightly constructed work of realism looking into the lives of six characters in Melbourne. The Trust sponsored a national and international tour of the play, which sparked new interest in Australian culture.

The only representations of Aboriginal people appeared in plays written by white Australians, usually as comedic or mythical. Composer John Antill attempted to incorporate elements of Aboriginal music into his ballet *Corroboree* in the 1940s. In 1954, Antill teamed up with choreographer Rex Reid and dancers of the National Theatre Ballet Company to stage the dance with the Sydney Symphony Orchestra. Antill said he had seen a "Corroboree," the white Australian word for a variety of Aboriginal gatherings for song, dance, and sport. Reid attempted to incorporate elements of traditional ceremony into a formal, contemporary ballet. However, the piece represents a gross distortion and monolithic ideal of Aboriginal culture.

In the twentieth century, Aboriginal Australian playwrights began to experiment with combining Aboriginal culture with European performance forms. Several playwrights used theatre as a medium to bring Aboriginal stories to the stage and to address contemporary issues facing Aboriginal people. Kevin Gilbert (1933–1993) staged perhaps the first example of critically acclaimed indigenous theatre in 1968 with *The Cherry Pickers*. Gilbert's parents, a Wiradjuri woman and white man, died when Gilbert was a boy. He escaped an orphanage and grew up in camps of extended family in New South Wales. He performed mostly migrant labor until 1957, when he went to prison for shooting his wife during an argument. In prison, Gilbert began writing, and wrote *The Cherry Pickers* based on his experiences as a migrant worker. Gilbert's writing was revolutionary in that he wrote in the Aboriginal-English dialect. The play was given a reading that year and then fully staged in Nindethana Theatre in Melbourne in 1971.

Robert Merritt's *The Cake Man* was staged at the Black Theatre Arts and Culture Centre in Redfern in 1975. The play focuses on life on a New South Wales Aboriginal mission. The family of Sweet William, his wife Ruby, and their son Pumpkin Head live on the mission and dream of a better life, a life that seems out of reach. Allegorically, they also await the arrival of "The Cake Man," a divine being who delivers cake to Aboriginal children and, by extension, the same opportunities as white children. Evil men have blinded the Cake Man, however, and he has been unable to find the Aboriginal children. The director Bob Maza brought in some non-indigenous people to work on the show, which stirred some controversy in the Centre in Redfern, but Maza was committed to the idea that collaboration among talented people from diverse backgrounds was good for the Centre. Some of the indigenous artists feared the perception that indigenous artists cannot do anything on their own.

Jack Davis – all to remember

The next writer of great significance comes from Western Australia instead of the southeast. Jack Davis (1917–2000) grew up in Yarloop, not far from the coast, and was a Noongar Australian. Davis led various cultural organizations and wrote poetry. After studying drama, he began to write for the stage. His first major success grew out of the reaction to the 150th anniversary of Europeans arriving in Western Australia. According to Maryrose Casey, Davis was appalled at the promotional material, which depicted the tabula rasa of Australia being "discovered" by Europeans. It left off any mention of the Aboriginal People or their history. Andrew Ross, the director of the Youth Theatre for the National Theatre of Perth commissioned Davis to write a Theatre-in-Education (TIE) piece that told the story of the indigenous people during colonization. Davis wrote *Kullark*, which was produced in 1979.

Kullark tells the story of the Noongar people starting with the first encounter of Europeans and the resistance and murder of the Noongar resistance leader Yagan. It weaves the present day in with the past, showing how colonialism has affected different generations. The play includes a young man in 1979 struggling with the justice system as well as his father's disappointment at the continued racism he experienced after he fought in World War II. It also weaves in stories from Davis's family history. Davis felt that it was imperative that he show not just the history of the Noongar people, but the Noongar people as being in the present. The text was multilingual – written in standard English, Western Australian Aboriginal English, and Noongar. The reaction of the Western Australian public was astounding. It continued running for years.

Encouraged by the success of *Kullark*, Davis teamed up with Andrew Ross again on the reworking of one of his earlier plays into what is now known as *The Dreamers* (1982). They formed the Swan River Stage Company and began working on staging the play. Davis himself played the main role of Uncle Worru, who has come to stay with his family in the last few months of his life. He arrives at the home of his niece Dolly, her husband Roy, and her three children, Peter, Meena, and Shane. Her cousin Eli also stays with them. Uncle Worru relays stories from the past:

Peter Aw right, Pop, but you gotta tell us another yarn now.
Uncle Worru Aw right, yeah.
[*He stops suddenly.*]
Eli Yeah, come on, Pop.

Uncle Worru By rights I shouldn' be tellin' you fellas this.

[*Pointing to Roy*] Aw right for 'im.

Roy It's all right Unc.

Uncle Worru All right. Well, you know that Christmas tree, that's the *moodgah*, that's the *Nyoongah* name.

Peter Yeah?

Uncle Worru Well, when our people was *noych*, their *kunya* – that's what *Wetjala* call soul, *unna*?

Roy Yeah, that's right, Uncle.

Uncle Worru Well their *kunya* would go and stay in the *moodgah* tree, some time for a l-o-o-ng time, an' when the *moodgah* flowers were gone, summertime, their *kunya* would leave the *moodgah* an' go to Watjerup. That way, over the sea, Watjerup, thaty way, *boh-oh*.

[*He gestures westward. His audience is mesmerised.*]

Peter Where's Watjerup, Popeye?

Uncle Worru Kia, Watjerup, that's what *Wetjalas* call Rottnest. An' if you go Mogumber old settlement, lotta *moodgah* up there 'cause, 'cause that be *Nyoongah* country for lo-o-ong time. An' them *moodgah* they strong, they kill other tree if they grow near them, *bantji, muttlegahruk, tjarraly, kudden*, kill 'em, finish, 'cause *kunyas* make him strong an' only *boolya* man can go there near the *moodgah*, cause the *boolya* man is strong too, like that tree; an' 'e can drink water an' take 'oney from the *moodgah*. Anybody else, that's *warrah*, they could be finish, *unna*?

[*An eerie silence overcomes them. PETER shudders and jumps up.*]

Peter Come on, this is gettin' too morbid. Let's have some bloody music.

[*They relax and pour drinks. PETER turns the radio on and begins to dance drunkenly.*]

Uncle Worru

[*laughing*] Ah, you don't call that dancin', do you?

(24–25)

The stories are variously received and ignored by family members. On one hand, they want a connection to tradition, but they also struggle with crushing poverty and hopelessness. The men cannot hold a job and spend whatever money they can beg from strangers or steal from Dolly to buy alcohol. Peter gets into fights and by the second act is in jail from being in a stolen car. Meena, who has been doing well in school, begins to lose interest in studies and becomes sexually active with a boy her mother dislikes.

Davis's story could easily be read as a lament for a dying culture. A tribal family walks across the stage at various times, first singing, then in chains, then in period clothes that don't keep them warm enough in the winter. Dolly ends the first act with a lament:

> You have turned our land into a desolate place.
> We stumble along with a half white mind.
> Where are we? What are we? Not a recognised race.
> There is a desert ahead and a desert behind.

The daily realities of this "desert" are grim, with " benches, our beds in the park" and an appeal to the effects of drinking methylated spirits to relieve the pain:

> White lady methylate,
> Keep us warm and from crying,
> Hold back the hate
> And hasten the dying.
> The tribes are all gone,
> The spears are all broken.

(64)

The effects of alcohol and drugs on families have been devastating, breaking up traditional community and kinship ties.

To the children, heritage is an abstraction. In an early scene, Shane asks Meena a series of questions about capitals of the United Kingdom. Meena teases him when he asks for the capital of London for not knowing that London *is* the capital. Her own homework consists of a report on Aborigines:

Meena I just worked out something amazing: you know how Aborigines have been in Australia for at least forty thousand years, right?

Roy So they reckon.

Meena And if there was three hundred thousand here when Captain Cook came, that means that . . . that . . . hm, hang on, hang on . . .

Shane Come on, what's the big news then?

Meena Shut up you . . . listen . . . forty thousand years plus, three hundred thousand people, that means that over twelve million

Aborigines have lived and died in Australia before the white man
came.

Roy Dinkum?

Shane Oh boy, they must've shot a lotta 'roos and ate a lotta
dampers.

Meena They didn't shoot them.

Shane I know! Three dampers a day for forty thousand years, how
many's that, Pop?

Roy I dunno, better ask your mother.

Dolly Me, I wouldn't have a clue.

Meena You don't count it up like that, slowly. Anyway, flour is white
man's food. Aborigines used grass seeds.

[*Reading from a book*] Jam seeds, wattle seeds, and –

Dolly

[*removing the damper from the oven*] OK. Who wants a feed instead of
just talkin' about it?

On one hand, the scene shows children alienated from their culture,
particularly Shane who struggles to learn the capitals of the colonizer.
Davis doubly removes Shane when he includes Shane's response
about food. The "dampers" he refers to are an Australian bread
made from wheat by a quick, sometimes unleavened, method used
by white settlers. The momentary interest in Aboriginal history is
disrupted by Dolly's announcement that the food she has prepared,
kangaroo stew and damper, is ready to be eaten. However, Davis
portrays a family occupying both the traditional world and the world
of today.

Eventually, Uncle Worru loses touch with reality, and the audience sees the stories acted out as if they are invading the present.
Uncle Worru believes he sees people who are long dead and gets lost
in memory. At first, Dolly blames this on drunkenness, but begins to
realize his life is slipping away. In essence, he begins to connect with
dreaming, both literally in his sleep and spiritually in his transition to
the state before and after life.

A traditional dancer moves to sound of the didjerridu to symbolize
the connection between the present hardship and the traditions of
the past. His dances reflect the state of mind of Uncle Worru, acting
out his dreams of his youth, lighting the fire to keep warm in the
winter, and then as a "featherfoot," a *Tjenna guppi*, the "executioner"

in Aboriginal custom. Uncle Worru makes it clear that he does not want to return to the hospital. He asks his niece to take him to a Noongar doctor in Pinjarra. She explains this to her sister's son Robert who has given her a ride home in his car and has offered to try to help get Peter out of jail on work release:

Dolly He reckons he wants to go to Pinjarra next week.

Robert What for?

Dolly He wants to see the *boolya* man.

Robert Don't worry Auntie, I'll drive you down there.

Eli Waste of fuckin' petrol money, if you ask me.

Robert I'll be paying for the petrol, not you.

Eli Why don't you take him up here where you been takin' him for the last four or five years?

Dolly They'll only keep him there. You know how he hates hospitals.

Eli I still reckon he's better off in hospital than someone mumblin' a lot of blackfella bullshit over him.

Robert Can't you see the old bloke believes in it? It's not going to do him any harm. It's faith healing, purely a case of mind over matter, auto-suggestion. Call it what you like.

Eli You call it what you like, I call it bullshit.

Dolly [*to Eli.*] Pipe down, you.

Roy [*laughing*] Let 'em go, let 'em go.

Robert Now you take the Bible, the story of Noah's Ark. It would have been physically impossible for Noah to transport every species of animal on earth for forty days and forty nights.

Roy Oh, that's my nephew. You're solid, neph'. Keep goin', keep goin'.

Robert [*pointing at Eli.*] And to prove it even more –

Eli [*knocking his hand*] Don't you fuckin' point at me.

[*He twists Robert's finger.*]

Robert [*stepping back*] To prove it even more, Noah would have had to have a staff of thousands to feed all those animals and look after them.

Eli Yeah, well you listen, you think you know everything. What about them big boats come into Fremantle? They take thousands of sheeps and take 'em to other countries. If those fellas can do it, Noah coulda done it.

Robert The point is because thousands of people for thousands of years have believed in the story of Noah's Ark, they believe through faith. You see what I mean, Auntie?

Dolly [*uncertainly*] Yeah.

Roy Well, I don't.

Eli He's talkin' out of his *kwon*. If it's in the Bible it's bloody true.

Robert Listen coz, belief in the Bible is based on faith, not fact.

[*He points, Eli grabs his finger and twists it hard.*] Hey! Cut it out.

Eli I told you not to point, didn't I?

[*Twisting it viciously*] Didn't I?

(90–92)

Eli's jealousy of Robert continues to create dramatic tension. Robert has done well for himself in a white world: he has a good job as a legal officer and drives a nice car. Dolly tells Meena that she wishes she would find someone like him. The contrast between Robert and Eli is stark.

Eli lives from social welfare check to social welfare check. Occasionally, he begs for money and runs a con pretending to be blind. He enters the stage wearing an eye patch, explaining "me and old patchy had a good day." But Eli expresses contempt for other Noongar:

[S]ome of them *Nyoongahs* spotted me. There they was: 'Give me fifty cents, brother', 'Give me a dollar, nephew', 'Give me fifty cents, uncle'; and you know none of them black bastards are related to me. That's true. Pop, I never seen blackfellas like 'em, they real bloody dinkum out and out bludgers. Can't stand the bastards.

(58)

Davis's characters are complex, not wholly immersed in or cut off from Noongar culture. Eli resents Robert's success in white culture. But, where Robert supports the idea of Uncle Worru seeking out a Noongar doctor, Eli rejects it and Robert's assertion that it is no less believable than the Bible.

The passing of Uncle Worru, at the end of the play, marks a passage through colonial time. His death severs the family's connection to a rich past, but while they move from it, they simultaneously move toward it. Dolly's final tribute traces this line:

> Stark and white the hospital ward
> In the morning sunlight gleaming,
> But you are back in the *moodgah* now
> Back on the path of your Dreaming.
> I looked at him, then back through the years,
> Then knew what I had to remember:
> A young man, straight as wattle spears
> And a kangaroo hunt in September.
>   [. . .]
> We camped that night on a bed of reeds
> With a million stars a-gleaming.
> He told me the tales of *Nyoongah* deeds
> When the world first woke from dreaming.
> He sang me a song, I clapped my hands,
> He fashioned a needle of bone.
> He drew designs in the river sands,
> He sharpened his spear on a stone.
> I will let you dream – dream on old friend
> Of a child and a man in September,
> Of hills and stars and the river's bend;
> Alas, that is all to remember.

(112)

Davis continued writing and working for Aboriginal rights until his death in 2000.

Into the twenty-first century – "make the story of your future, son"

Critics often cite the opening of Jimmy Chi's (1943–) musical *Bran Nue Dae* (1990) as a watershed moment for Aboriginal theatre. Chi became a musician after a psychological breakdown in Perth while he was studying to become an engineer. He performed with his band Kuckles, and eventually began working on a musical about his experiences as a multiracial Australian (he has Chinese, Japanese, Scottish, and Bardi Aboriginal heritage), traveling from his home in

Broome to the big city of Perth and returning home again. The musical was directed by Andrew Ross, a non-Aboriginal man who had worked with Jack Davis and many other indigenous artists.

In the play, the Aboriginal boy Willie prepares to return to Catholic school. He promises his sweetheart Rosie that he'll be back for her. Once in the school, he finds the religious dogma and strict discipline oppressive and runs away after being punished for taking food from the commissary. On the streets of Perth, he meets an old Aboriginal man named Uncle Tadpole who resolves to help him get home to Broome, over 2,000 kilometers to the north. Tadpole pretends to be struck by a Volkswagen bus and coerces the two hippies inside, Marijuana Annie and Slippery, to take them. Along the way, the police discover Annie's marijuana plants in the bus and put everyone in jail. They are released the next morning and continue on to Broome.

Reaching home, Willie has come full circle. The journey takes on spiritual dimensions as a rite of passage, including the night in jail, something experienced disproportionately by Aboriginal Australians. Willie recognizes that he is in danger in the jail: he knows Aboriginal people are victims of violence and that he could be killed there. When they are released, Willie declares, "I'm a man, now." Finally, Willie is reunited with Rosie and with his mother, but also with the priest who presides over his school in Perth, Father Benedictus. It turns out that Willie's mother and Benedictus are the parents of Slippery and that Tadpole is actually Willie's father. The final celebration and the song "Bran Nue Dae" weave together evangelical Christian ideas of being reborn with the demand for political change. Of this hybridity, Helen Gilbert states:

> Overall, *Bran Nue Dae*'s governing conception of Aboriginality suggests a culture fully cognizant of its rich historical past but struggling constantly not to be confined to that past. . . . conceptions of Aboriginality based solely on racial origins are not only untenable (given many Aboriginal people's lack of knowledge about their ancestry because of colonial assimilation policies) but also unhelpful. It is, paradoxically, the dynamism of hybridized Aboriginal identities, both rural and urban, traditional and contemporary, that best ensures the survival of the culture.
>
> (322)

Bran Nue Dae created an opening for Australians to examine long-held prejudices and old stereotypes. The use of the musical theatre form and musical styles ranging from Aboriginal music, to country music, and reggae, mixed with biting political commentary and humor allowed a variety of ways the play and its themes could be accessed. The success of *Bran Nue Dae* influenced other musicals by Aboriginal authors such as *Funerals and Circuses* (1992) by Roger Bennett and *The Sunshine Club* (1999) by Wesley Enoch.

After the establishment in 1973 of the Aboriginal Arts Board, several indigenous companies formed, including the National Black Theatre (open from 1974 to 1977) in Sydney, headed by Bob Maza, and Yirra Yaakin (started in 1993) in Perth, Kooemba Jdarra (also 1993, now closed) in Brisbane, and Ilbijerri Theatre Company (formed in 1990) in Melbourne. These companies have nurtured a whole generation of new directors and dramatists, and Aboriginal theatre has become an important cultural institution for Aboriginal people and for Australia as a whole. Two important artists to come out of this vibrant theatre movement are Jane Harrison and Wesley Enoch.

Jane Harrison (1960–), who is Muruwari, wrote *Stolen* in 1998. The Ilbijerri Theatre presented it for the first time at the Melbourne International Arts Festival. *Stolen* deals with the story of five Aboriginal children who were removed from their families as part of a series of legislative acts at the end of the nineteenth and beginning of the twentieth centuries. White Australian lawmakers argued that mixed-race children needed to be removed from Aboriginal homes for their own protection. What they needed protection *from* varied from policy to policy, but many white Australians argued that mixed-race children would be rejected from Aboriginal communities and would have a better life in white society. Many white Australians also believed Aboriginal culture would die out and that it would be better to help children assimilate as quickly as possible. But no due process existed for the families. Authorities did not have to prove neglect and, in many cases, they did not really keep accurate records. No one is certain how many children were removed, but it is probably between 55,000 and 100,000 children between 1910 and the 1970s. Children were placed in institutions, forced into domestic service or labor, or placed with white foster families. *Stolen* follows the five children as they become adults and struggle with substance abuse, mental illness, alienation, and suicide.

Wesley Enoch (1969–) headed Kooemba Jdarra and Ilbijerri and also worked with Queensland Theatre, Sydney Theatre Company, and the Belvoir Street Theatre. He was born on Minjeeribah (Stradbroke Island) and grew up in Brisbane. He is of Noonuccal Nuugi descent from the Quandmooka people. Enoch has directed many plays by Aboriginal writers, including the plays by Kevin Gilbert and Jack Davis. And he has given many Western classics an Aboriginal mise-en-scène.

Enoch's own play *The Story of the Miracles at Cookie's Table* (2007) won critical acclaim after its premiere at the Griffin Theatre in Sydney. It featured Leah Purcell, an actor who has gone on to work in film and television. Purcell had a big break in 1993 when she was cast as Marijuana Annie in *Bran Nue Dae*. Enoch's play focuses on the struggle between a hard-drinking woman, also named "Annie," and her son Nathan for a family heirloom. Cookie, Annie's great grandmother was born under a tree. The people of the island believe if you are born under a tree, you are forever connected to that tree and you draw strength from it. Because Cookie is connected to the tree, she feels it when it is cut down and she must follow it to the mill where it is made into a table and then to the estate where it comes to rest. Cookie becomes the cook in the estate and passes the table down to her daughter Kawana, who passes it down to her daughter Faith, who is Annie's mother.

Annie returns to claim the table, but she encounters her estranged son, who has been raised by Faith. They both feel they have claim to the table and to the family history. Nathan, who left life on the island to work for the government in Sydney, feels bitter that his mother left him and wants to know who his father is. Annie refuses to tell him. As the play moves back and forth through time, the audience learns that Annie's relationship to Faith was contentious. Eventually, Annie reveals that she was raped when she was 13 and that the rapist was Nathan's father. She tells Nathan anything but the truth, that she didn't remember who the father was and that she was wild. Enoch frames the play with storytelling, the story of the table, the story of Faith returning to the island after her husband died, the stories Faith's sisters have told Nathan about the family history, and the story of Nathan's father. In the end, Annie tells Nathan he needs to make his own story:

> I'll tell you everything but you got to work out what you really want the story to be. The story of the future. Those old girls [Faith's sisters] weren't telling you what the true stories were, they were telling you what they wanted them to be. The stories are about marking out the horizon, about getting the sun to rise another day. You got to make the story of your future, son. Not let the story of the past lead you. Go on. You tell it how you want it to be. You tell me how the future is and I will tell you everything you want to know. Go on.
>
> (53)

Nathan and his mother create a story together about burying the table in the family cemetery and of a tree growing from it, a large tree that holds the island and her people together. History and tradition hold the family together, but they must continue to shape the future.

In the twenty-first century, a few Aboriginal artists combined the elements of traditional storytelling with the contemporary form of the solo auto-ethnographic performance. Tammy Anderson, who grew up in Tasmania, created her autobiographical piece *I Don't Wanna Play House* in 2001, and then toured it for several years. The original performance included a band, but she then toured only the solo performance. Anderson pieces together stories from her harrowing and traumatic childhood. In an interview on the Australian Broadcasting Station in Goulburn Murray, Anderson noted: "My dad is aboriginal and was swallowed up in the system, and didn't come back home to his family after an accident in jail and was gripped by alcohol" (Jess). Anderson's mother saw a string of violent men after that, and Anderson had to care for her and for the other children. She performs the piece to raise awareness about domestic violence and child abuse.

AOTEAROA/NEW ZEALAND: TAKI RUA

"Aotearoa" is the Māori word for the country known in English as "New Zealand." Māori and English are both official languages of Aotearoa/New Zealand, and so the country has come to be called by both names. While the English word comes from the Dutch naming the country after a state in the Netherlands (Zeeland, meaning literally "sea land"), no one knows for certain the exact meaning or origin of Aotearoa. It is often translated to mean "land of the long white cloud."

Polynesians began settling Aotearoa/New Zealand in the late thirteenth century and continued into the fourteenth century. Over the centuries, Māori culture expanded through the north and south islands and several distinct *iwi*, or tribal units, developed. The *iwi* are made up of several smaller subtribes and clans. Europeans began to arrive in the eighteenth century, including various traders, whalers, and missionaries, and people from Britain began to create settlements. Many Māori traded with the Europeans and the acquisition of muskets upset the balance of power among the different *iwi*. Several powerful companies, including the New Zealand Company (representing capitalists from Britain) and the Nanto-Bordelaise Company (from France), began aggressively colonizing Aotearoa/New Zealand for their own interests. This often involved questionable purchases of Māori land.

In response, the British government began negotiating with the Māori to cede Aotearoa/New Zealand to the British Crown. The Treaty of Waitangi was drafted and signed by the British representative Captain William Hobson and several Māori chiefs. Hobson worked to insure that copies were signed by as many Māori leaders as possible. While the treaty made Māori people citizens equal to British citizens, the terms of the treaty were unclear and have remained a point of contention between Māori and Pākehā (non-Māori) people since.

The influx of Europeans increased exponentially, which put a strain on Māori landownership. Some Māori sold their land. In many instances, however, land was taken, either because there was some confusion about ownership, or because open hostilities between British and Māori would result in confiscation. As land losses uprooted many Māori and as industrialization accelerated, Māori people migrated to urban areas. By the mid-twentieth century, the Māori population shifted dramatically from rural to urban spaces. In the city, the Māori had to deal with poverty, substance abuse, and crime. Racism, which had been dormant until then, became apparent and tension between Māori and Pākehā escalated.

Largely in response to racism and to some of the social problems from urbanization, Māori leaders began to organize and to emphasize the importance of Māori language and culture. With the Maori Affairs Amendment Act 1967, which concerned more government involvement in administering Māori landownership, Māori began to call for a review of the original Treaty of Waitangi, mounting public protests on Waitangi Day each year. Finally, a Waitangi Tribunal was established in 1975. After years of review, the Tribunal concluded that the Māori had not intended to give up their sovereignty. Māori and Pākehā continue to work for resolution.

Out of the renewed effort to preserve and promote Māori culture, Māori theatre emerged. Several companies formed in the late 1960s through the 1980s, beginning with the Māori Theatre Trust in 1966. The Trust formed after a tour of *Porgy and Bess* that had, with the exception of two actors brought in from New York, an all Māori cast. In 1972, Harry Dansey (1920–1979), a Māori writer and journalist, wrote *Te raukura (The Feathers of the Albatross)*. *Te raukura* was about the Taranaki village of Parihaka and their struggle to keep their land in 1879. The population of the village was already swollen with Māori who had had their land confiscated by the British when white settlers began pushing for the land there as well. The Māori began a campaign of passive resistance and would plow land settlers had taken and blockade roads. In response, the government jailed or expelled the villagers and the town was looted. The play opened at the Mercury Theatre in Auckland with George Henare, one of the prominent members of the Māori Theatre Trust, playing the role of Te Whiti, the leader of the village and of the nonviolent protest movement there.

Most of the companies that followed sprang up in Wellington as part of political activism, such as the Te Ika a Maui in 1976, and Maranga Mai in 1979. Rangimoana Taylor's Te Ohu Whakaari toured schools to educate youth about Māori history in 1983. And in 1989, Jim Moriarty left Te Ika a Maui and formed the Te Rakau Hua O Te Wao Tapu Trust to do community-based theatre in prisons and with at-risk youth. Several companies and collectives sought to treat theatre like a *marae*, a Māori word for communal gathering or meeting place. It can also mean the act of being hospitable or generous. In this sense, spectators are invited to partake in a communal gathering. They remove their shoes and are welcomed with a chant. The spectator is an active participant in the event.

The Depot theatre began producing plays in 1983. Initially, The Depot focused on producing new work by New Zealanders and included classic plays by Europeans like Shakespeare and Chekhov in the repertory. The company had an inclusive vision of New Zealand plays and was made up of both Māori and Pākehā artists. In 1990, the members of the group renamed the theatre Taki Rua and dedicated themselves to producing Māori plays. The last European play produced at Taki Rua was Chekhov's *The Three Sisters* in 1997. The company has since been a laboratory for new Māori playwrights including Briar Grace-Smith (1966–) and Hone Kouka (1968–). Taki Rua produced Briar-Grace Smith's first major play *Nga Pou Wahine* in 1995. Te Atekura, a young woman, makes a journey of self-discovery through family stories of her ancestors. The roles of five characters are played by one actor. In 2015, the company revived the play with a creative team of women as a tribute to the women artists of Aotearoa/New Zealand.

Hone Kouka staged his first major play *Nga Tangata Toa: The Warrior People* at Taki Rua in 1994. Kouka based his characters and themes on Henrik Ibsen's *The Vikings at Helgeland* (1857) and set the play in 1919. He felt the Nordic myth's themes of honor and revenge easily translated into Māori themes of *mana* and *utu* as a Māori soldier returns from fighting for the British in World War I. Kouka followed *Nga Tangata Toa* with a trilogy of plays: *Waiora* (1996), *Homefires* (1998), and *The Prophet* (2003). The trilogy marks the migration of Māori people to the city. As Kouka notes:

> *Waiora* was about the urban migration of Maori, those of us who left home, *Home Fires* is about those who stayed behind and ensured lots of the stories about the past were remembered. You had to leave to gain strength but after one generation you realise there's lots of strength back home as well and you need both. You have to keep the home fires burning or the stories will die.
>
> (Interview quoted in Herrick)

The Prophet is a play about a family gathering to unveil the headstone of a member who has committed suicide. The young cousins of the boy who has died have all returned from school. They meet up on the basketball court during the few days they are home. The third play, then, deals with the current generation, their alienation and confusion, their hope, and how they envision the future.

5

SUB-SAHARAN AFRICA

Humankind originated in Africa. Paleoanthropologists and archaeologists discovered the oldest human fossils in Africa. Different species of hominids evolved in Africa, including modern humans, and then migrated elsewhere. Today, a wide variety of climate zones, languages, and cultures make up this second-largest continent. The Sahara Desert, at nearly a million square kilometers, occupies nearly all of the land in northern Africa, and it also divides the states that are part of the Mediterranean and the Arab worlds from the other regions. Sub-Saharan Africa is made up of the Sahel (the arid southern edge of the Sahara), tropical savannah (including the Eastern Miombo woodlands and Serengeti), tropical rainforest, and the Kalahari Basin. Sub-Saharan Africa is home to over a thousand languages.

Historical anthropologists have attempted to piece together some of the earliest events in the history of Sub-Saharan Africa, a difficult task since most African languages were oral languages and there are few written artifacts. We do know, however, about a few key events. One of the earliest events is what is called the Bantu Expansion, which began around 1000 BCE and continued until about 300 CE. The Bantu grouping of languages includes several widely spoken modern African languages, including Swahili, Shona, and Zulu. Bantu languages are part of the Niger–Congo family of languages, the largest language group in Africa. The Bantu people migrated from western Africa from what is now Niger and Cameroon, headed east to what is now Kenya and Tanzania, and headed south to the Kalahari Desert and what is now Botswana, Namibia, and South Africa.

Several kingdoms arose from the Bantu migration, beginning in the eleventh century with the Great Zimbabwe, a stone fortification created without mortar by the Shona people who descended from the Bantu. The Kingdom of Mutapa expanded from the Great Zimbabwe down into the rest of southern Africa beginning in the mid-fifteenth century and lasting until well into the seventeenth century. In central Africa, the Luba Kingdom consolidated its power (1585–1889), and also gave rise to the Lunda Kingdom.

The Bantu in the east encountered Arab and Persian people and Bantu inflected with Arabic words became Swahili. The robust trade gave rise to the Swahili city-states along the coast in the fifteenth century. Other notable early civilizations include the Nok people (1000 BCE–300 CE) of Nigeria, the ancestors of several modern groups including Hausa and Kanuri people, and the Igbo Nri Kingdom (1043–1911 CE) made up of a people who did not believe in violence.

In the sixteenth century, the Atlantic slave trade began, first with the Portuguese sending slaves to the Americas, and then the English, French, Spanish, and Dutch starting the practice. Colonization by European powers began in the seventeenth century and accelerated in the nineteenth century. In the twentieth century, two world wars were fought on African soil. Former colonies in Sub-Saharan Africa have struggled since independence with the economic dependence, environmental devastation, ethnic conflict, and cultural identity crises that come with colonization. In addition, Sub-Saharan Africa is affected by HIV/AIDS disproportionately to the rest of the world and educating people about and treating HIV/AIDS has become a top priority for activists and community organizers.

YORUBALAND AND WOLE SOYINKA

The earliest settlement of the Yoruba people, the city of Ife, dates back to the fourth century BCE. Several groups of people made up what is called "Yorubaland," but it was Oyo that emerged as a powerful Yoruba kingdom. The first *Alaafin*, or ruler, of the Oyo Empire probably began ruling in the fourteenth century. Each *Alaafin* was selected by the Oyo Mesi, a legislative body that represented the will of the people, and the power of the *Alaafin* could be checked by the Ogboni, a religious society with enormous power. Briefly, the Oyo Empire was conquered by the neighboring Nupe in 1550. However, the Oyo nobles were wealthy from trade and established an impressive cavalry and army. Over the next two centuries, the Oyo continued to expand the kingdom and increase the wealth of the state. Historians believe that struggles for political control at the end of the eighteenth century and neglect of military matters in order to focus on economic expansion led to the eventual decline of the kingdom. Oyo was attacked by Fulani Muslims and the empire fell in 1836.

Out of the Yoruba tradition come several relevant performance practices. The *egungun*, masquerades to honor the ancestors, began some time before the Oya Empire, and continue in Nigeria today. In Yoruba cosmology, the presence of the ancestors' spirits is essential to the good health of the community. The *egungun* masquerades accompany major festivals, especially the festivals to honor the ancestors. There are many variations in *egungun* in each community, but there are many distinctive common elements. The dancer wears an elaborate costume made up of layers and layers of fabric. The body is completely hidden from the spectators. The under-layer represents the burial shroud. Netting masks the dancer's face. Flaps of fabric are hung off the under-layer in rings around the body so that when the dancer whirls, the fabric flies and creates a "breeze of blessing." The name "*egungun*" is thought to mean "supernatural power concealed." Some of the maskers may represent the actual spirit of the ancestor, but this is not always the case. But because they honor the ancestors, their power is considerable. Often people with sticks or whips come ahead of the dancers to move people out of the way so that they will not come into contact with this power. The dancers are often accompanied by people singing praise songs, and the festival, which may last several days, involves feasting and celebration.

Alarinjo, a performance form separate from the ritual, but still in conjunction with the *egungun* festival, also developed during this time. According to Joel Adedeji, the form involved an opening *glee*, a salute to certain deities, and a pronouncement of what is to come. There were then dances, and then the performance of a drama, both a spectacle to honor divine beings and a sketch to address current happenings in the community.

In 1884 and 1885, the Berlin Conference enabled the major European powers to agree on the geographic areas where each had a claim to territory in Africa. Great Britain was given sole domain over south central Africa, a swath of eastern Africa including what is now Kenya and Sudan, and territories in western Africa, including Nigeria. Much of the slave trade came through Lagos, which by this time was of great concern to British politicians. The British parliament banned participation in the slave trade in 1807 (but not slavery), but there were traders from other countries who were happy to fill the void. Other capitalists were attracted to Nigeria for the palm oil. The growing commerce prompted the British to establish oversight in Nigeria in the form of consuls and a mediator for trade disputes. The British took control of Lagos and the surrounding area in 1861. After the Berlin Conference, Britain established control of the Niger River Delta through the Oil Rivers Protectorate in order to protect its interests in palm oil production.

Much of the business conducted in Nigeria was through the National African Company, later called the Royal Niger Company. The company had its own army and had negotiated trade with several of the inland peoples. This pre-colonization laid the groundwork for the British military. In the 1890s, the British launched campaigns against the remaining resisters: the Ijeri, the Benin, the Igbo, and the Sokoto Caliphate established by the Fulani in the north. The conquered territories came under the British Crown in 1900 and were consolidated into Nigeria fourteen years later. The British continued to subdue any resistance, but governed by indirect rule, using an administration of Residents and District Officers working together with a Native Administration headed by traditional rulers. The colonial government collected taxes, harvested Nigeria's resources, and conscripted labor.

As the colonial presence in Nigeria increased, traditional performance forms changed to reflect colonial influence. A clear example of this hybridization, the *hauka*, began in 1925 in the French-colonized Filingué District in southwest Niger among the Hausa people and quickly spread among the Hausa and Songhay people in Niger. *Hauka* migrated to Ghana with people looking for work and was even reported in northern Nigeria in the 1940s. *Hauka* involved spirit possession, which had been practiced by the Hausa and Songhay people for centuries. But *hauka* was unique in that it involved possession by European spirits. The possessed people would behave like the colonial administrators and soldiers and speak in a mix of indigenous and European languages. French filmmaker Jean Rouch traveled to Ghana in the early 1950s and filmed the *hauka* ceremonies. He released his film *Les Maîtres fous* in 1955, and it influenced Jean Genet in his writing of *The Blacks* (1958).

Other groups employed their own form of performing the colonizer. In Nigeria, the Igbo people build *mbari* houses. These structures are for Igbo statues of deities and animals in order to win favor by caring for them. They also house European figures such as colonial officers. The Europeans are caricatures of Europeans, wearing hats and having the facial features the Igbo associate with white people. In the Yoruba *egungun*, maskers who are only there to entertain the crowds impersonate a variety of comic figures. These dancers, the *Agbegijo*, wear masks such as the baboon, the prostitute, and the Dahomean warrior. Some of the masks are of Europeans. Ulli Beier describes them: "Europeans with enormous hooked noses and smooth black hair made from Colobus Monkey skin. They shake hands, say 'how do you do' and perform a ridiculous ballroom dance" (197).

As Nigerians moved to the cities for work and were uprooted from their ethnic homeland, ethnic organizations formed. Labor and professional organizations flourished. Eventually, elite Nigerians in the south began sending their children to British schools. A youth movement grew as young people returned from study with new ideas about the problems of colonialism and a will to work towards independence. Ethnic and religious differences made progress slow. In 1963, Nigeria was finally fully independent. However, the republic did not last long. The people in the north were largely Muslims of Hausa and Fulani descent. In the south, Igbo and Yoruba people vied for control. Accusations of electoral fraud prompted a bloody coup in 1966, followed by two more coups, followed by a massacre of Igbo people in the north. The ensuing civil war lasted until 1970, but stability was not restored. Several attempts to return to democracy have been thwarted by coup attempts, military dictatorships, and violence. Hope returned in 1999 when Olusegun Obasanjo was elected president. Obasanjo attempted to stem the violence from regional and ethnic conflict.

Death and the King's Horseman – *"forget the dead, forget the living"*

During the era of colonialism, several theatre artists began to expand their craft, blending Nigerian traditions with European forms.

Egungun masker and *alarinjo* artist Hubert Ogunde (1916–1990) created what is now called "Yoruba Opera." In 1944, when he was working as a police officer, he wrote his first play, on Biblical themes, for a Protestant group. *The Garden of Eden and the Throne of God* blends African music and storytelling with stories from the Bible. Ogunde continued writing and formed what is considered to be Nigeria's first theatre company, Ogunde Concert Party. His subsequent plays were political satire that criticized British colonialism. After independence, Ogunde wrote *Yoruba Ronu* (sometimes translated as *Yoruba, Think!* 1964) urging national unity. The government banned it initially, citing Ogunde's harsh criticism of certain factional agitators.

Wole Soyinka (1934–) began writing plays while he was studying English, first in Nigeria and then at Leeds in England. His early work attracted the attention of some of the artists at the Royal Court Theatre in London and some of his plays were produced there. Encouraged by his success, Soyinka returned to Nigeria and sought to blend Yoruba tradition with the realities of the time. Soyinka was vocal in his opposition to the government during the civil war and was imprisoned for nearly two years.

After his release, Soyinka wrote *Madmen and Specialists* (1971), an absurdist piece about Dr. Bero, who left his village to become an interrogator during the war. His father had served human flesh to the officers as a protest of the war. But Bero found that he liked it and has become a cannibal. Now he has locked up his father, claiming that it is for his own protection, because he hopes to get his father to give up the secrets of his cult. The Earth Mothers, who have been watching and commenting on the actions of Bero, destroy their sacred herbs to keep Bero from obtaining them. Soyinka's commentary is a bitter one: that one can be turned from a force of healing into an agent of war and terror. Bero now consumes other human beings without feelings of remorse and extracts what he can use. He is part of a generation bent on destroying the binding power of tradition and the potential advancements brought by colonialism. In the end, the fire signals total destruction, but also the possibility of renewal.

Soyinka wrote what is, arguably, his greatest work in 1975. *Death and the King's Horseman* opens with the drummer and the Praise Singer, much like the *egungun*, in a procession with Elesin Oba, the king's horseman. The king has died and it is time for the horseman to follow him to the afterlife so that he can accompany him on his journey. Elesin, the Praise Singer, and the women of the market sing about Elesin's honor and how to make his last day on earth an enjoyable one. Although Elesin insists he is steadfast, he stalls when he sees a beautiful woman enter the stall of his friend Iyaloja, the matriarch of the market. Although she is betrothed to Iyaloja's son, Elesin wants to have her as his own bride. Iyaloja and the other women agree because no one wants to mar Elesin's last moments.

The play is set during World War II, and the colonial administrator and his wife figure prominently in the action. Simon and Jane Pilkings are getting ready for a costume ball when they are interrupted by the native police officer Amusa. Amusa turns over a flower pot when he sees the white couple in *egungun* costume. While Amusa is a Muslim, the appearance of the *egungun* costume unsettles him and he has difficulty even speaking with the Pilkingses. He relays the fact that Elesin is about to commit ritual suicide. Initially, the Europeans are confused. They think a murder may be taking place, but their servant Joseph explains the nature of the suicide. It turns out that Elesin is the father of Olunde, a young man they helped to send to medical school in England. Joseph hears the drumming outside and notes that there is also the sound of drumming for a wedding. The Pilkingses wonder briefly if they should intervene and finally decide that they should, sending Amusa to detain Elesin.

When Amusa arrives at the market, the women of the marketplace stop him and his officers. They refuse to allow them in to the stall they have set up to be Elesin's marriage tent. They tease them, seize their hats and batons, and threaten to remove Amusa's pants. The officers leave humiliated. Elesin emerges from the tent, now married to his bride. He hears the drums that tell him that the horse and dog of the king are being sacrificed. The Praise Singer sings to him the fearful questions of the king: will Elesin, in fact, join him? Elesin assures him that he will, that he is not weighed down by the heaviness of life and he begins to go into a trance. The Praise Singer notes that Elesin is now rushing ahead to the afterlife and that there is no stopping him.

Amusa reports back to Simon Pilkings at the ball that he has failed to detain Elesin. Pilkings and his men decide to take care of the matter themselves and leave the ball to arrest him. Jane Pilkings, meanwhile, encounters Olunde, who has come to the ball looking for Simon. The two discuss the imminent suicide, which Olunde supports, much to Jane's surprise. Jane had assumed that Olunde would be Westernized and reject Yoruba custom as she would. But Olunde has come to bury his father and expresses his feeling that the suicide is vital to the life of the community. He chastises her for making light of the *egungun* and for making light of the seriousness of the war by holding a costume ball. Olunde has been living in England, which he says gives him a new perspective on his own people, on the English, and on colonialism in general. The drumming in the village stops and Olunde announces that his father is dead. However, he soon hears the commotion of the men dragging Elesin into the building and his father's voice shouting at them as they do. Olunde sees Elesin and announces that he has no father.

The final act of the play takes place in Elesin's cell. Simon Pilkings prevented his suicide, but members of the village place the blame squarely at the feet of Elesin. Iyaloja comes to him in his cell to verbalize the gravity of his failure. It is true that colonial authority intervened in Yoruba custom, but Elesin lingered. While he boasted of his resolve, he delayed preparations. He could not quite let go of the pleasures of life and, ultimately, he is responsible for failing in his duty, a failure certain to upset the cosmic order. Iyaloja brings him the body of Olunde, who had stepped into his father's place in order to ensure the duty is fulfilled. At the sight of his son, the depth of his shame drives Elesin to hang himself. But Iyaloja has a message for the colonizer as well. When Simon Pilkings turns to her accusingly and asks if this is what she wanted, she retorts: "No child, it is what you brought to be, you who play with strangers' lives, who even usurp the vestments of our dead, yet believe that the stain of death, will not cling to you." As the silent young bride closes Elesin's eyes, Iyaloja commands: "Now forget the dead, forget the living. Turn your mind only to the unborn" (76).

Soyinka is critical of a people who have forgotten their traditions, but more importantly, he warns against forgetting duty. On the one hand, colonialism disrupts daily practice and intervenes in a world the colonists fail to understand. Colonial notions of restoring order only upset the order already in place, bringing disaster. More importantly, colonial authority has upset the political and social bonds that keep violence in check. The older generation gives up privilege at the proper time in order to allow the younger generation to flourish. But Elesin becomes greedy and complacent and the colonial intervention allows him to stay. The next generation, the native intellectual who has come to not only value his culture, but see a truth built on the present realities, ends up perishing. The only real hope for the future is the next generation, and only if the community can sort out new notions of individual power and communal duty after colonialism.

KENYA: "THE TRUMPET OF THE WORKERS HAS BEEN BLOWN"

People from all over the world have been visiting the eastern coast of Africa for millennia. The port cities of Kenya, Tanzania, and Mozambique attracted Arab, Persian, Indian, and Chinese traders. The active trade spurred the development of these ports into what are called the Swahili city-states beginning at the end of the first millennium CE. In Kenya, the city of Mombasa flourished. Europeans began to explore the eastern coast in the sixteenth century, beginning with the Portuguese, who were anxious to find a way around the Venetian trade monopoly in the Mediterranean. The Portuguese established a fort on Mombasa Island, but were eventually driven out by the Omani Arabs in the eighteenth century. The Omani were seeking a base from which to run their extensive slave trade. By the Berlin Conference, British and German forces had shut down the slave trade and the British claimed much of Kenya as the East African Protectorate in 1895.

With colonization came settlers from Britain and laborers from India. The British government began reserving the best land in Kenya for white settlers, principally in the Rift Valley and the Highlands (now called the White Highlands for that reason). Europeans were given a monopoly on the lucrative coffee crop which pushed the Maasai herders and Gĩkũyũ farmers off the land. Britain was interested in making Kenya into a profitable exporter of crops and raw materials. The rapid development continued to displace ordinary Kenyans. Gĩkũyũ often found themselves landless and worked as migrant farm laborers. Out of the deplorable conditions, the Gĩkũyũ resistance movement grew. Kenyans pushed for greater political access to the mechanisms of government, and for independence, through organizations such as the Kenya African Union, and then finally in full-fledged armed resistance.

In 1952, Gĩkũyũ revolutionaries took up arms in what is now called the Mau Mau Uprising. Scholars cannot say for sure where the term "Mau Mau" originates. The activists who formed the core of the movement called themselves "Muhimu," which means "Essential." And the members of the movement took sacred "Muma" to the cause, or "oaths." Regardless, "Mau Mau" was a colonial term not used by Kenyans until sometime after the rebellion was long over. The Muhimu began by raiding the farms of settlers, attacking police officers, and stealing guns. The killing of Europeans and loyalist Kenyans prompted the colonial government to declare a state of emergency and wage war against the rebels. The British established a Home Guard of Kenyans loyal to Britain and detained people suspected of being part of the Muhimu. Massacres were committed by both sides and the British made full use of divisions in the Gĩkũyũ community to turn Kenyans against each other. The detentions were brutal and many people were tortured and killed in the detention camps.

While the British effectively quashed the uprising, independence did come by 1963. Kenyans held their first elections and chose Jomo Kenyatta as their first president in 1964. The British had detained Kenyatta during the uprising, although he was actually a political moderate. Kenyatta had grown up in humble circumstances, but received a British education at the London School of Economics, and he had married into an elite family. Not long after the election, Kenyatta began consolidating his power, appointing fellow tribesmen to key positions and outlawing the opposition party. Kenyan politics have been marred by ethnic tensions between Gĩkũyũ and Luo people, political corruption, and human rights abuses.

The Kenyan National Theatre, established by the British Council in 1952 in Nairobi, produced exclusively European plays initially. Ciarunji Chesaina and Evan Mwangi note that the location of the theatre in an exclusive area of Nairobi and the high fee for rental of the space made the theatre inaccessible to most Kenyans (218). Most popular theatre by Kenyans was produced in community centers outside of Nairobi. This is certainly true of the work of Ngũgĩ wa Thiong'o (1938–), who helped to establish the Kamiriithu Community Education and Cultural Centre in his hometown.

Ngũgĩ was given the name James Ngugi when he was born. He attended the English university in Uganda where he produced his first play *The Black Hermit* in 1962 to honor Ugandan independence. He then attended the University of Leeds. Radicalized by reading African nationalist writing, he took his Gĩkũyũ name Ngũgĩ wa Thiong'o. Ngũgĩ met Ngũgĩ wa Mĩriĩ (1952–2008) at the University of Nairobi where they were both working. When they returned to Kamiriithu, they created the Kamiriithu Community Education and Cultural Centre to engage people in the community in discourse and action geared toward social change. Kamiriithu was one of several community-based theatre organizations that engaged in "Theatre for Development." Throughout Africa, missions, schools, and community organizations had used theatre for didactic purposes, to help communities learn new farming methods or to discuss health or social issues. Theatre for Development evolved as an organic form where community members would engage in theatre exercises and present performances to deal with issues important to the group. Many groups in Africa today focus on stemming the HIV/AIDS crisis by providing education and support to communities affected by the epidemic. In Kenya, there are several groups, including the Kenya Institute of Puppet Theatre, formerly the Community Health Awareness Puppeteers (see Riccio), and the Kawuonda Women's Group in Sigoti that develop drama by telling stories and then improvising, often interweaving the improvisation into the labor they are doing that day (see van Erven).

Ngũgĩ began writing in the Gĩkũyũ language and producing theatre that was participatory and improvisational. Together, Ngũgĩ and Ngũgĩ wa Mĩriĩ wrote *Ngaahika Ndeenda* (*I Will Marry When I Want*) and staged it at the center in 1977. The play led to the arrest of both men and to the closing of the center. *Ngaahika Ndeenda* begins with two peasants, Kĩgũũnda and his wife Wangeci, preparing for the arrival of some guests, Ahab Kĩoi wa Kanoru and his wife Jezebel. It is clear from their chatter and their actions that they are nervous. Kĩoi is wealthy and there is no reason for him and his wife to ever visit the humble hut of Kĩgũũnda and Wangeci. The couple struggle to prepare some food, fix a chair so that there is a place to sit, and to tidy up the room. Their daughter Gathoni, an attractive girl in rags, does not offer much help. Instead, she says she is going out, with none other than John Mũhũũni, the son of Kĩoi and Jezebel.

Kĩgũũnda and Wangeci reminisce about songs and dances from the old days and worry over the inflation that is slowly degrading their already meager existence. But, despite their poverty, they do own a small piece of land, and Kĩgũũnda takes great pride in this fact. Songs from the chorus punctuate the text, telling the stories from the Mau Mau Uprising and praising the nationalist cause. After Gathoni has left, two neighbors stop by, the factory worker Gĩcaamba and his wife Njooki. They have heard from Gathoni that Kĩoi and Jezebel are stopping by. Gĩcaamba and Njooki are activists and speak eloquently about the exploitation of workers and peasants by the new postcolonial Kenyan elite. Gĩcaamba advises Kĩgũũnda and Wangeci to reject any overtures from Kĩoi and Jezebel, particularly because Kĩgũũnda and Wangeci mistakenly believe Kĩoi and Jezebel are coming over to announce the marriage of John and Gathoni.

Kĩoi and Jezebel arrive with their friends Samuel and Helen. They are clearly uncomfortable in the home of Kĩoi's poverty-stricken employee and they are reluctant to eat the food Wangeci has prepared. The couples, representing the wealthy and the newly wealthy Africans in postcolonial Kenya act out ridiculous parodies of the elite class. They talk non-stop about Jesus, about how classes are more or less divinely ordained, and how the poor should accept their lot. It turns out that they are visiting to encourage the poor couple to join their church and "stop living in sin." Without a Christian wedding, they explain, Kĩgũũnda and Wangeci aren't really married. Disgusted, Kĩgũũnda finally chases them off with a sword.

Gathoni enters after her date with John wearing new clothes, shoes, and lipstick. She announces that John is taking her to Mombasa for the weekend. Enraged, Kĩgũũnda tells her she should not return. But this announcement also prompts Kĩgũũnda and Wangeci to wonder if their thoughts of marriage for the two children weren't true after all. They resolve to join and have their marriage blessed by the church. They go to Kĩoi and Jezebel to announce their intentions, but also to tell them that they do not have the money for the ceremony – the suit, the dress, the cake, and the fee to pay the church. Kĩoi offers to take Kĩgũũnda to his bank so that he can get a loan, putting his tiny property up as collateral. There is nothing to worry about, he assures him, because he can have his monthly payment deducted from his wages. Kĩgũũnda agrees.

Kĩgũũnda and Wangeci happily plan for their wedding, trying on their clothes and dancing around. Kĩgũũnda has purchased a few things for their home as well, including a table and a radio. While they are lost in their reverie, Gathoni comes home and is distraught. In Mombasa, she told John that she was pregnant with his child. He angrily broke off their relationship and brought her back to the village. Her parents are upset, but believe that Kĩoi will make things right. They head to Kĩoi's home to explain the situation. Instead of agreeing that the children should marry first, Kĩoi accuses Gathoni of lying. Kĩgũũnda becomes enraged and brandishes his sword. He is about to make Kĩoi sign an agreement when Jezebel enters with a gun and shoots at him.

In the final scene, Wangeci relays the events from the evening before to Gĩcaamba and Njooki. She says that Kĩgũũnda was dismissed from his job and received notice from the bank that his loan is being recalled. He now spends his time trying to sell the things they purchased and using the money to drink in the bar. He has kicked out their daughter Gathoni who now works as a barmaid. Their land will almost certainly be used by a foreign chemical company for an insecticide plant, operated by Kĩoi and his business partner. Kĩgũũnda comes home drunk, and he and Wangeci begin fighting. Gĩcaamba reminds them that the sellers of alcohol and the church work hand-in-hand to keep the people down, and that their true enemies are the foreign capitalists and the Kenyan elite who benefit at the expense of their compatriots. Lamenting that colonialism has been continued in this new form, the four agree that only unity will save the country and resolve to keep fighting. Together they sing:

The trumpet of the masses has been blown.
We are tired of being robbed.
We are tired of exploitation.
We are tired of land grabbing.
[...]

Soloist The trumpet
All ... of the workers has been blown.
There are two sides in the struggle,
The side of the exploiters and that of the exploited.
On which side will you be when

Soloist The trumpet
All ... of the workers is finally blown?

The play concludes with this rousing musical number asking people to choose sides. The play ran for six weeks before its message of reform and revolution prompted the police to shut it down and jail the writers.

The work by Ngũgĩ wa Thiong'o and Ngũgĩ wa Mĩriĩ and the community members also urged spectators to think critically about gender and the role of women in Gĩkũyũ society. When Wangeci weeps over the fact that her daughter has "become a whore," Gĩcaamba admonishes her and says that parents should not call their children whores. He explains:

> We the parents have not put much effort
> In the education of our girls.
> Even before colonialism,
> We oppressed women
>   [...]
> Forgetting that a home belongs to man and woman,
> That the country belongs to boys and girls.
> Do you think it was only the men
> Who fought for Kenya's independence?
> How many women died in the forests?
> Today when we face problems
> We take it out on our wives,
> Instead of holding a dialogue
> To find ways and means of removing darkness from the land.
>
> (104–105)

Gĩcaamba and Njooki urge reason and understanding of the hard choices Gathoni must make. The revolution is ultimately about the children and finding a better future for them: men and women.

Both authors were held in prison for a year without a trial. In 1982, the two co-wrote *Maitũ Njugĩra* (*Mother, Sing for Me*). Slated for production at the Kenyan National Theatre, the play was also banned. The Kamiriithu Community Education and Cultural Centre was destroyed, and the two men went into exile. Ngũgĩ wa Thiong'o continued to write novels and political essays.

The theatre is most vibrant in the schools and colleges, which hold regular theatre festivals, and in community groups, much like the Kamiriithu center. The Kenya Cultural Centre and the Kenya National Theatre now regularly produce work by Kenyans. The center also holds a regular "gender forum" for addressing issues of gender and gender inequality.

SOUTH AFRICA: ANTI-APARTHEID THEATRE

The Sangoan people lived in what is now South Africa beginning about 50,000 years ago and are the ancestors of the Khoi and San people living in the Kalahari today. Ancestors of the Khoi likely established Mapungubwe in northern South Africa (on the border with Zimbabwe) in the eleventh century CE. The people of Mapungubwe traded with cities on the eastern coast and there is evidence of great wealth, including a gold rhino that was excavated from the site in the early twentieth century. The kingdom flourished until fourteenth-century climate changes pushed people north.

The Bantu expansion finally reached South Africa in about 300 CE and the Bantu-speaking people eventually outnumbered the Khoisan people. Prominent Bantu ethnic groups include the Zulu, Swazi, Xhosa, Sotho, Tswatha, and Tsonga people. The Zulu consolidated power in the nineteenth century under the leadership of Shaka (c.1787–1828) and the Zulu are now the largest ethnic group in South Africa.

Europeans initially had little interest in South Africa, but the discovery of a sailing route directly to spice sources in the east brought the Dutch East India Company. The Dutch established a port and brought Dutch farmers to insure there would be supplies for the fleet. The company also imported slaves from Mozambique and Indonesia. In skirmishes between the British and the French (and therefore, the Dutch), the British seized the colony several times. The Congress of Vienna in 1814–1815 formally recognized the colony as being a British possession and the British began settling the land. The British also brought laborers from India.

This settlement caused tension with the Dutch *boers*, already unhappy with the authoritarian management of the Dutch East India Company. The British exacerbated the tension by attempting to rid the colony of the Dutch language and outlawing slavery. Many of the Dutch Afrikaners migrated north to escape British rule. These *trekboers* became the subject of nationalistic Afrikaans plays, including *Magrita Prinslo* (1897) by S. J. du Toit and *Adam Tas* (1926) by Jacobus Charel Bender Van Niekerk and Allen E. Thompson.

As Anglo settlement spread and as the trekkers moved east and north, British and Afrikaners engaged in conflict with the people they displaced, with major wars fought with the Zulu, the Ndele, and the Basotho. The Afrikaners established separate independent states, but the discovery of gold and diamonds in those regions caused an influx of Europeans that destabilized the settlements. The Afrikaners were forced to surrender the states to the British after the Second Anglo-Boer War in 1902.

South Africa became a dominion under the British Crown in 1910. Some of the new parliament's first acts were a series of segregation laws that set aside only a tiny portion of land for black South Africans. With the rise of the National Party, a conservative and pro-Afrikaner party, Apartheid was formalized in 1948. The conditions of Apartheid meant that black South Africans lacked basic human rights, were deprived of land, and did not have access to good-paying jobs. The government brutally repressed resistance to Apartheid, and leaders of anti-Apartheid movements were assassinated, tortured, and jailed. Black and white South Africans worked together to end Apartheid and, after mounting international pressure, Apartheid was officially ended in 1991. South Africa became a democratic nation, but continues to struggle with poverty, labor unrest, and the HIV/AIDS epidemic.

Early theatre in South Africa consisted of variety shows and drama from Europe. A few theatres were built and closed. The first South African play in English to be staged was *Love and the Hyphen* by Stephen Black, performed first in 1908 in Johannesburg and then developed over the next two decades. The satire of Cape Town life includes white, black, and mixed-race South Africans. But there was no concerted effort to create a South African national theatre until state funding was appropriated for the National Theatre Organization in 1947. The national effort to promote theatre in both English and Afrikaans led to the establishment of companies in all of the major cities.

Black South Africans began organizing drama societies and clubs in the 1920s. Many of these were in Christian missions, such as the

Bantu Dramatic Society in Johannesburg. One of the early Zulu writers from this group was Herbert Dhlomo (1903–1956) who wrote several plays, including *The Girl who Killed to Save* (1935) about a Xhosa woman who prophesied that white rule would end if all the cattle were slaughtered, which led to mass starvation. He also wrote a series of plays about important tribal leaders such as Shaka Zulu. Dhlomo's views were liberal: he believed in racial equality, but believed in leaving tribal identities behind in the quest for progress.

While the government put a ban on mixed-race theatre companies and collaboration, many artists chose to work together despite the ban. In the late 1950s, white playwright Athol Fugard (1932–) began working with black South African actor Zakes Mokae (1934–2009) on several projects, including *The Blood Knot* (1961). In *The Blood Knot*, brothers Morris and Zachariah are awaiting the arrival of a white girl with whom Zachariah has exchanged letters. The brothers are both black, but Morris is light-skinned and Zachariah is dark. The play explores racism through the relationship of the brothers as Morris, who occasionally passes as white, treats Zachariah as his inferior. The bitter resentment between the two reflects the long-simmering hatred between white and black South Africa. In performance, Fugard played the role of Morris. Fugard is best known for his play *"Master Harold,"* . . . *and the Boys* (1982) about Hally, a young white man from Port Elizabeth, and two black men, Willie and Sam, who work for his family. The play shows the affection the three have for each other, but Hally unleashes his latent racism when he hears his abusive father is coming home. The play opened in the United States with Mokae playing Sam and was initially banned in South Africa.

Musicians and actors began performing in the townships designated for black South Africans. Township music blended Bantu music traditions with modern jazz and utilized all kinds of instruments, from accordions and saxophones to guitars and pennywhistles. Township theatre was largely improvisational, involved social satire, and frequently incorporated township music. Soweto playwright Gibson Kente (1932–2004) wrote several township musicals about life under Apartheid and was jailed for a year in 1976 because of them. His plays, such as *How Long?* (1973) and *Too Late* (1981), were initially banned by the government for being anti-Apartheid. In 1988, Kente wrote *Sekunjao*, which suggested that the power of the black elite needed to be kept in check or a post-Apartheid South Africa would be doomed. The government closed the show and arrested the cast. To make matters worse, black extremists fire-bombed Kente's house. Kente's work fell out of popularity after Apartheid and, in 2003, he announced publicly that he was HIV positive and he died the following year.

Mbongeni Ngema (1956–) and Percy Mtwa (1954–) both worked with Kente, performing in his township musical, *Mama and the Load* (1979). While performing together, they began to conceive and improvise a piece about the Second Coming, where Christ arrives in South Africa during Apartheid. This became *Woza, Albert!* (1980), one of the most well-known pieces of anti-Apartheid theatre. Ngema and Mtwa collaborated with white director Barney Simon (1934–1995) and staged the play at the Market Theatre in Johannesburg, also a space that, since its inception in 1976, flouted the laws forbidding mixed-race collaboration (although they were lifted the next year) and resisted censorship by bringing international attention to their work.

Woza, Albert! was performed by the two actors playing several roles. They begin with a series of character sketches of a wide range of people. The play immediately criticizes many of the policies of Apartheid, including the "pass laws" that forbid the free movement of black South Africans. Eventually, Jesus Christ (now named "Morena") arrives, flying on South African Airways. But due to a series of misunderstandings and the absurdity of the Apartheid laws, Christ is put in jail and his followers are persecuted. However, he is able to simply fly out of the first prison and then walk on water to escape Robben Island.

The white "Christians" who try to stop Christ are laughable, and Ngema and Mtwa wore clown noses when portraying them. Eventually, the actors, with participation from the audience, use the power of resurrection to bring back dead and murdered anti-Apartheid activists; the word "woza" means "rise up." They begin with Albert Lutuli, winner of the Nobel Peace Prize for his work on non-violent political protests against Apartheid and president of the African National Congress until his death in 1967. A number of other people include Lillian Ngoyi, who left South Africa illegally in the 1950s to raise awareness about Apartheid, and Steve Biko, who was murdered in police custody in 1977. Ngema went on to write *Sarafina*

(1986), a wildly successful township musical about the Soweto Uprising. The musical starred Leleti Khumalo (1970–) who went on to be in the Broadway production and in the film.

After Apartheid, the new government needed to deal with the aftermath of the human rights violations. The Department of Justice and Constitutional Development established the Truth and Reconciliation Commission (TRC) in 1996 to investigate the atrocities that had been committed. Victims were invited to testify as were perpetrators, who could request amnesty. There has been much debate about the efficacy of such proceedings. In 1997, Jane Taylor (1956–), working in the Laboratory Theatre space at the Market Theatre and with director William Kentridge (1955–) and the Handspring Puppet Company, created a multimedia puppet play about the hearings, *Ubu and the Truth Commission*.

Based on the grotesque comedy by Alfred Jarry *Ubu Roi* (1896), Taylor's play brings Pa and Ma Ubu into modern-day South Africa. Pa Ubu is still as vulgar, cowardly, greedy, and malicious, but now he faces charges of human rights abuses as Apartheid comes to an end. Pa Ubu complains that he was only doing the work of the state:

> Once I was an agent of the state, and had agency and stature. The country's money was in my safe-keeping, as I had blown up the safe and its keeper. I administered the funds to myself, to save the nation the burden of doing so. Now, after my years of loyal service, I find myself cast aside without thanks. My enemies are everywhere. . . .
>
> (30)

Pa Ubu then praises the work of his loyal dog Brutus, a three-headed dog like Kerberos, the guardian of the gates of Hell. But each head has a job, the attack dog, the general, and the politician. The three coordinate "covert activities" in search of a bone or "cartilaginous morsel, still fragrant and warm" (31).

A projection announces "The Light of Truth." Pa Ubu's advisor, a crocodile named Niles, warns him that a commission is coming "to determine Truths, Distortions, and Proportions" (33). Niles suggests that Pa Ubu should come clean and testify, but Ubu is both cowardly and obstinate. And, although she fears he has been cheating on her, Ma Ubu stands firm in her support. In order to avoid prosecution, however, Pa Ubu must get rid of the incriminating evidence. He begins feeding files to his "shredder," Niles, who eagerly gobbles them up. Some of the pieces are easy to digest, "a bit of skull shattered in pieces" (37), but some are too hard to digest, "A hand up-raised in gesture defiant, a Blood-red heart that would not break" (38). He continues to find more things to eat until finally he has heartburn.

While Pa Ubu is out again in the evening, Ma Ubu worries that he is out philandering and begins looking for evidence of his affairs. She pulls something out of Niles's mouth and it is an account of beating to death and burning a man. Ma Ubu is filled with pride at Pa Ubu's importance. However, wary of her precarious position, she decides to sell his stories in order to put money away for her old age. When Pa Ubu returns, he sees Ma Ubu on television as "Screen Ma," a projected animation by Kentridge, giving an interview about Pa Ubu. Pa Ubu threatens Screen Ma to be quiet, but she continues. She also warns him in Zulu as an aside. He screams back at her in Afrikaans. Finally, he mutes her.

A shadow urges Pa Ubu to testify and to shift the blame to someone else. Pa Ubu continues to say that he was just doing his job, that it was war, and that the victims were communists. As he begins to feel the pressure to testify, Brutus tries to convince him to stay silent. They sing a rousing chorus together about their innocence. While the dog's heads are sleeping after the song, Pa Ubu slips evidence into his belly, which is a suitcase. Brutus is tried and convicted of human rights abuses. In order to continue the cover-up, Pa Ubu takes the dog from jail and hangs him by his three heads. However, because Ma Ubu has sold some of his stories, he must still testify.

The story of Ma and Pa Ubu is broken up by testimony from witnesses given by puppets. The testimony is given in English and Zulu and recounts horrific episodes of parents seeing their children burned, parents trying to identify murdered children, and of people who were tortured. The juxtaposition of these testimonies among scenes of Pa Ubu and his cronies makes the behavior of Ubu seem all the more grotesque and disgusting. And, in the end, his cowardice continues: "These vile stories, they sicken me. When I am told of what happened here, I cannot believe it. These things, they were done by those above me; those below me; those beside me. I too have been betrayed!" (45). As he talks of being tortured with remorse, the chorus begins to sing of redemption. Pa Ubu joins in until finally he is drowned out by the chorus singing "Nkosi Sikelel' iAfrika," a song that is now part of South Africa's national anthem and is sung in Xhosa and Zulu. Pa Ubu, no longer relevant, is wheeled off. As does the first scene, the last scene also quotes Jarry's *Ubu Roi*. Ma and Pa Ubu sail off to the Sargasso Sea, where they encounter Niles who climbs on board.

While they head towards "a new beginning" (46), Taylor hints that the work of the TRC will not heal the wounds of Apartheid, nor will it solve the long-standing results of inequality. But perhaps there will be a moment when the perpetrators become completely irrelevant.

6

THE CARIBBEAN ISLANDS

Before Christopher Columbus "discovered" the islands in the Caribbean Sea, several waves of migration had already taken place. Beginning in roughly 5000 BCE, people came to the islands, divided into the Greater and the Lesser Antilles, made their homes there, and in some cases, returned to the mainland. People came to the islands from the Yucatan, from Central America, and from Venezuela. By the time Columbus reached the islands, the two dominant groups were the Taíno and Caribs, both descended from groups present in the Orinoco River Valley in South America. Columbus's characterization of the indigenous island people became an important discursive point in Caribbean postcolonial writing.

No sooner had Columbus reported what he observed when all the European colonizing powers set sail to claim the land in the Americas by way of the Antilles. While the continents of North and South America offered what seemed like limitless resources, the islands were strategically important as ports for traders and as military outposts for colonial domination. It is no accident that the islands gained independence so many decades after independence swept through the colonies on the mainland.

Spain was far and away the most dominant European power at the beginning of the colonial period. By 1600, virtually all Caribbean islands and surrounding land (Florida, Central America, parts of northern South America), were claimed under the Spanish Crown. The indigenous populations of the islands were quickly decimated by violent subjugation and European diseases, making the sparsely populated territories increasingly hard to defend. Ships from England, France, the Netherlands, and Denmark all succeeded in chipping away at the Spanish islands during the seventeenth and into the eighteenth centuries. The Spanish were only able to hang on to Cuba, Puerto Rico, and part of Hispaniola.

The Europeans saw the Antilles as an ideal region for the cultivation of sugar, which was in high demand in Europe. Because so many indigenous people had perished, the colonizers needed to import a labor force. As a result, the operations in the Caribbean relied heavily on the African slave trade, and millions of Africans were brought to the islands and to the Caribbean coasts of the Americas. Additionally, European settlers and indentured laborers from other parts of the world, including India and China, came to the islands. Most of the colonies in the Americas fought for and achieved independence by the early part of the nineteenth century. While there were dozens of slave uprisings, most of the Caribbean islands did not gain independence until after World War II.

A notable exception is Haiti and the Dominican Republic. The French had claimed the western part of the island of Hispaniola from the Spanish, and it became, very quickly, a prosperous French colony. The French Revolution put the future of Haiti, then called "Saint-Domingue," in doubt. Some wealthy European colonists began discussing independence. Free black Haitians and mulattoes, and black slaves were nervous about an independent Haiti under white rule, but were also inspired by the Enlightenment ideals of equality. Fighting escalated soon after 1791, and resistance among slaves, free people of color, and Spanish from the east side of the island coalesced under the leadership of the educated freed slave François-Dominique Toussaint "Louverture." France abolished slavery in 1794, and Toussaint began fighting to keep Haiti under French rule. Toussaint's forces succeeded in taking control of the French part of the island. Although Haiti was to remain under French colonial control, Toussaint, going against the orders from France, attacked the eastern Spanish-controlled part of the island to free the slaves there as well. Toussaint began to resist French rule immediately, but was quickly arrested by the French and taken back to Europe, where he died. Napoleon wanted to reinstate slavery on the island, but because the French were busy with conflicts back in Europe, he was unable to hang onto the colony, and Haiti became fully independent in 1804.

Even outside of the Caribbean, Toussaint became a legend, prompting several dramas about his role in the Haitian Revolution.

In 1893, a German play with allegorical characters was published: *Toussaint, der schwarze Rebelle Amerikas* (*Toussaint: The Black American Rebel*) by Hans Schambeck. And in the United States, African American writers Leslie Pinckney Hill (1880–1960) and Lorraine Hansberry (1930–1965) both penned dramatic projects on Toussaint. Côte d'Ivoire writer Bernard Binlin Dadié wrote *Îles de tempête* (*Islands of Storm*) in 1973. In the Caribbean, Trinidadian C.L.R. James wrote the epic *Toussaint Louverture: The Story of the Only Successful Slave Revolt in History* (1934).

But the aftermath of the revolution was chaos. In the absence of Toussaint, other generals vied for power. Henri Christophe (1767–1820) declared himself king of the northern side of Haiti. Christophe took extreme measures to try to bolster Haiti's economy after war had left it in ruins. He had lofty ideas of elevating Haiti by creating an education system and legal code but, like his colonial predecessors, he was despotic. His increasingly unpopular policies of forced labor created instability and, fearing an uprising, he shot himself in 1820. Caribbean plays on the aftermath of independence take a more critical lens to the Haitian Revolution, including one by Saint Lucien writer Derek Walcott (1930–) *Henri Cristophe* (1950), and two from Martinican writers: *Monsieur Toussaint* (1961) by Édouard Glissant (1928–2011) and *La Tragédie du roi Christophe* (*The Tragedy of King Christophe*, 1963) by Aimé Césaire (1913–2008).

From the 1960s and into the 1980s, several of the British colonies either became fully independent or independent members of the British Commonwealth. The remaining French islands of Guadeloupe and Martinique are still French overseas regions. The United Kingdom and the United States maintain control over several of the islands. The Caribbean islands are a unique blend of cultures and languages from the Americas, Europe, Africa, and Asia. Additionally, many people from the islands have migrated to North America and Europe. These migrations, along with growing tourism to the islands, make the Caribbean islands a site of continuous cultural exchange.

AIMÉ CÉSAIRE: RECLAIMING CALIBAN

Aimé Césaire is credited with beginning the *Négritude* movement, an intellectual, political, and cultural movement dedicated to uniting people of African descent all over the world, celebrating African traditions, recovering African history, and fighting colonialism and its effects on black people. Césaire met several African intellectuals when he studied in Paris. Fellow Martinican Paulette Nardal (1896–1985) had been translating the work of African American writers involved in the Harlem Renaissance and introduced their writing to the Caribbean and African intellectuals in their salons.

When Césaire returned to Martinique, he continued writing poetry, novels, and plays on Caribbean historical themes and several essays on colonialism. Initially a member of the Communist Party, Césaire was elected mayor of Fort-de-France. However, he abandoned Communism when the Soviet regime proved to be repressive. He is probably best known for his critical reworking of Shakespeare's *The Tempest* (c.1611), titled simply *Une Tempête* (*A Tempest*) in 1969. Césaire examines the politics and problems of colonialism through Caliban and Ariel, now a field slave and a mulatto on a Caribbean island.

The Caribbean framing of Shakespeare's play was not new to Césaire. Ngũgĩ wa Thiong'o had already suggested this connection in his novel *A Grain of Wheat* (1967), in which a colonial administrator compares Prospero to the British Empire. In 1971, Cuban writer Roberto Fernández Retamar published a careful analysis of Shakespeare's text and its apparent source material, observations of the indigenous people of the New World. Caliban, Fernández Retamar argues, is a grotesque caricature of the Caribe, considered by Columbus in his diaries to be a subhuman cannibal. Ariel represents the Taíno, described as being peaceful and meek.

In Césaire's play, Prospero explains to his daughter Miranda that he was on the verge of launching an empire from his newly discovered lands when he was betrayed and abandoned on the island. He summons his two slaves: Ariel, who complains that the promised freedom has again been delayed, and Caliban, whom he reviles. Caliban greets him with "Uhuru!" the Swahili word for "Freedom," and Prospero commands him to cease speaking his native language. Prospero remarks on Caliban's ugliness and stupidity, but Caliban retorts: "You haven't taught me anything at all! Except of course to jabber away in your language so as to understand your orders. . . . As for your knowledge, did you ever impart any of that to me? You took care not to. You selfishly keep all your knowledge for yourself alone" (13). In fact, it was Caliban, as the native informant, who taught Prospero to survive.

Prospero imagines that Caliban would not survive without him. He also expresses his fear that Caliban will rape Miranda, echoing the fear of miscegenation already present in Shakespeare's text, and citing that as his reason for forcing Caliban to live in a ghetto. He threatens Caliban with whipping, saying that beating is the only language he understands, and Caliban responds by rejecting European language altogether: "Call me X. That's best. Like a man without a name. Or, more precisely, a man whose name was stolen. You speak of history. Well that's history, known far and wide! Every time you'll call me that will remind me of the fundamental truth, that you stole everything from me, even my identity! Uhuru!" (16).

The relationship between Caliban and Ariel is more complex. On the one hand, they bond over their shared oppression by Prospero. But they also disagree over the strategy to work for liberation. Ariel, the intellectual and pacifist, wants to appeal to Prospero's conscience. He believes that Prospero needs liberation as well and that it is up to Ariel and Caliban to help him change. Caliban feels that such an appeal would fail because Prospero is driven to colonize. He accuses Ariel of being an "Uncle Tom," a slave complicit in his own oppression. Both feel the other's strategy is doomed.

Caliban temporarily finds allies in the sailors Stephano and Trinculo, representing the lower-class Europeans in the colonies. Stephano and Trinculo extol the virtues of democracy in one breath and then drunkenly declare themselves kings of the island in the next. Their first glimpse of Caliban prompts them to imagine the fortune they could make putting him on display for crowds in Europe. The display in carnival shows of indigenous people from the colonies was common practice in the nineteenth century. When they discover that he can speak, they agree to join him against Prospero.

The war between Prospero and Caliban is a war of culture. Prospero prepares a dance of gods and goddess for his daughter and her new lover Ferdinand. But they are interrupted by Eshu, the west African trickster spirit. Eshu sings of his ability to cause chaos and offends the European spirits with his risqué performance. Prospero attempts to send stinging and biting animals after Caliban, but Caliban gentles them. He reminds them that the colonizer is their common enemy because the colonizer is the enemy of nature. In the end, Stephano and Trinculo are ineffective allies, easily distracted by the mirage of material gain, and fighting amongst themselves.

Finally, Caliban and Prospero are alone. Prospero pleads with Caliban for a peaceful resolution, but Caliban rejects anything less than freedom. Prospero fails to understand Caliban's hatred and refuses to be convinced of his own oppressive actions. And although he has the opportunity to leave the island and return home, he is unable to go, feeling that it is his destiny to suppress the growing rebellion. By the end, however, Prospero is feeble against the forces of nature and in need of Caliban, who is nowhere to be found. In the distance, we hear the sound of Caliban singing "LIBERTY, OH-AY! LIBERTY!" (63).

DREAM ON MONKEY MOUNTAIN: DECOLONIZING THE MIND

Like Martinique, Saint Lucia was occupied by French and British colonizers at different times. Unlike Martinique, however, the official language in Saint Lucia is English. While state business is conducted in English, most of the people on the island speak *patois*, a creole French dialect from its French colonial history. This conflicted colonial history is the backdrop of Derek Walcott's play *Dream on Monkey Mountain* (1967).

Walcott was born in Saint Lucia, but moved to Trinidad as a young man. There, he met influential dancer and folklorist Beryl McBurnie (1913–2000), a Martha Graham dancer dedicated to promoting Trinidad and Tobago's culture. In 1948 McBurnie started the Little Caribe Theatre where Walcott staged many of his plays. Walcott and some of the people from the Little Caribe Theatre started the Trinidad Theatre Workshop in 1959. Walcott is a poet and several of his dramas are verse dramas, such as *Ti-Jean and His Brothers* (first produced at the Little Caribe Theatre in 1958) a story told by forest creatures with musical numbers. His best-known play *Dream on Monkey Mountain* addresses some of the complex problems of colonialism in a series of poetic and provocative allegories.

Dream on Monkey Mountain begins with Makak, an old man who makes and sells charcoal for a living, in jail for drunkenly wrecking a café and generally causing a disturbance. Two thieves jailed with him, Tigre and Souris, and the mulatto jail keeper Corporal Lestrade mock him as he relays the story of an apparition of a white woman. The scene shifts to several days earlier, when Makak's friend Moustique comes to get him so they can go to market and sell their charcoal. As they prepare, a white spider crawls over Moustique's hand, which is a bad omen. On the way to the market, they encounter a party of mourners and Basil, the undertaker. They carry a man who has been bitten by a snake. He is not yet dead, but they expect he will be soon. Moustique convinces them to give him some food and, in exchange, he fetches Makak who heals the dying man. The mourners are so grateful, they give the two men money and gifts, which gives Moustique the idea that Makak's abilities could be profitable. Moustique demands Basil's hat. Basil surrenders it, but promises Moustique that he will get it back. They are, after all, at a crossroads, another bad omen.

Many days later, at the market, word has gotten out about Makak's abilities, and people are hopeful that he will come and help them. Makak enters, but it is Moustique dressed as Makak and healing people for a price. Basil, however, is at the market and recognizes Moustique. He exposes him for a fraud, causing the people of the market to turn on Moustique. Lestrade and a market inspector are nearby, but Lestrade refuses to stop the angry mob from killing Moustique.

The flashback ends and we are back in the cell, where the two thieves plot an escape from jail. Makak has been talking about returning to Africa, and the thieves begin to play along to manipulate him. They see that Makak has a knife and convince him to stab Lestrade. The three of them flee into the forest together. Tigre wants to kill Makak because he heard Makak try to bribe Lestrade and thinks that he has money. But, Souris decides that he believes Makak's fantastic musings about returning to Africa and refuses to go along. Meanwhile, Lestrade, still alive but bleeding, catches up with them. He is dying from his wound, but he is reborn when he embraces his blackness. He strips off the police uniform and picks up a spear to defend Makak. He kills Tigre and leads the new movement onward.

Walcott named the final scene "Apotheosis," the moment when a human being rises to the level of the divine. A chorus of women and warriors sings praises for Makak, now king of the new society. Lestrade leads a tribunal to punish the traitors. The list, read by Basil, is extensive: Plato, Shakespeare, Robert E. Lee, Tarzan, Dante, Al Jolson, to name only a few. All are to be banished from the historical record. After the list, Basil reads appeals, which are all rejected by Makak and the chorus: An invitation to be president of the US, an apology from South Africa, flowers from the KKK, the Nobel Peace Prize, and an offer from Hollywood. But when Lestrade announces the prisoners, Moustique is brought in. He pleads for an explanation, but Makak refuses to look at him. Makak only balks when Lestrade instructs him to kill the apparition of the white woman. This all turns out to have been a dream, however, and when he awakens in jail, Moustique has come to take him home.

Walcott's play is a complex parable. First, many of the characters have animal names: *makak* means monkey, *moustique* is a mosquito, *tigre* and *souris* are tiger and mouse. This only changes when Makak becomes a lion, a symbol of the greatness of Africa, in his dreams. Several biblical references are spread throughout the text, especially an allusion to the story of the Penitent Thief. Tigre sees eternal damnation for himself, but Souris, who believes in Makak, ascends with him in the apotheosis.

But the parable also examines the psychological and spiritual violence of colonization and the impossibility of decolonization. In jail, Makak struggles with language, unable to even remember his own name. Lestrade ridicules him for speaking French and insists he speak English: "For we are observing the Roman law, and Roman law is English law" (218–219). He also states that the color of English is white. English is the language of the colonizer. But *patois*, the language of the people, is still derived from French. Makak is a descendant of forced immigration, forced to speak the language of colonial authority, with the language of a distant colonial authority as his own language. According to Ngũgĩ wa Thiong'o in *Decolonising the Mind*, our language reflects who we are: "Language carries culture, and culture carries, particularly through orature and literature, the entire body of values by which we come to perceive ourselves and our place in the world" (16). Makak's being is doubly colonized.

The events of the play mirror the paradox of overthrowing the colonizer. Moustique becomes a leader of the people, but he is a charlatan seeking to profit from the fervent convictions of his followers. When they discover his trickery, they turn on him. The colonial authority, in the form of Corporal Lestrade, does nothing to intervene, preferring instead to safely wait out the violence before enforcing order.

As a mulatto, Lestrade represents the black man who has internalized colonialism, and the character does indeed treat the black

characters as inferior savages. It is only by embracing his blackness
that he is saved. When he sheds his uniform, he undergoes a transformation: "I return to this earth, my mother. Naked, trying very hard
not to weep in the dust. I was what I am, but now I am myself. . . .
I have become what I mocked. I always was, I always was. Makak!
Makak! Forgive me, old father" (299–300). Lestrade then leads the
movement and pushes for purging of whiteness from the kingdom.
The road to apotheosis has already been rocky. Makak notes, after
their jailbreak, that the colonized peoples have turned on each other
already: "Fighting, squabbling among yourselves. I have brought a
dream to my people, and they rejected me. Now they must be taught,
even tortured, killed. Their skulls will hang from my palaces. I will
break up their tribes" (301).

When Moustique is brought before him at the tribunal, he tries to
get Makak to see what he has done:

Moustique All this blood, all this killing, all this revenge. So go ahead,
   kill me. Go ahead. Is for the cause? Go ahead then.
Makak I will be different.
Moustique No, you will be no different. Every man is the same. Now
   you are really mad. Mad, old man, and blind. Once you loved the
   moon, now a night will come when, because it white, from your
   deep hatred you will want it destroyed.

(315)

Moustique is taken away, but then the apparition, the woman for
whom Makak has longed, is brought before him to be executed.
Makak feels confused and lonely. He demands to know who she is
before he beheads her. Lestrade explains:

She is the wife of the devil, the white witch. She is the mirror of
the Moon that this ape look into and find himself unbearable.
She is all that is pure, all that he cannot reach. You see her statues
in white stone, and you turn your face away, mixed with
abhorrence and lust, with destruction and desire. . . . She is the
colour of the law, religion, paper, art, and if you want peace, if
you want to discover the beautiful depth of your blackness,
nigger, chop off her head! When you do this, you will kill
Venus, the Virgin, and the Sleeping Beauty. She is the white

light that paralyzed your mind, that led you into this confusion. It is you who created her, so kill her!

(319)

Makak braces himself and then beheads her. But then, his dream ends. The revolution just brings more bloodshed. After ridding themselves of the colonizer, the people turn on each other. And the purging never stops. Makak must destroy the white apparition, the internalized colonization. But Makak longs for her because he is lonely. He has no wife and no children. He has no future and no past. Instead, he talks of waking up and realizing he is old. Anchorless, he idealizes whiteness and so loathes himself.

The epilogue, then, is a relief to Makak, who wakes up to his mundane existence. His friend Moustique, still alive, and eager to help him home, back to the "green beginning of this world" (326). Tigre still demands food and Souris tells Makak to go with God. Makak blesses them both.

MUSTAPHA MATURA: CARNIVAL AS CARIBBEAN IDENTITY

As slavery was outlawed throughout the nineteenth century by different European powers, the islands in the Caribbean faced a labor shortage. The British turned to the Empire for indentured labor and began importing Chinese and Indians to work on the sugar plantations. The conditions were brutal. Many people died during the voyage to the Caribbean, and many more died from the working conditions. Nearly 100,000 Indian laborers came between 1874 and 1917. Today, there are significant Chinese and Indian populations throughout the Antilles, especially Trinidad, Jamaica, and Haiti. The Chinese and the Indians brought with them their unique cultures and religions. Some quickly assimilated, but continue to be part of a distinct community. In Trinidad and Tobago, the Indian population is the largest ethnic group.

Indians in Trinidad observe Hindu, Muslim, and Christian religions, but most of them are Hindu. In the 1960s, Indian artists began establishing performance institutions devoted to Indian culture. The first was the Trinidad School of Indian Dance, established by Rajkumar Krishna Persad in 1967. He had traveled to Madras to study Bharat Natyam under a scholarship issued by the Indian government. Mandira

Balkaransingh established the Nrityanjali Theatre in 1977. Although the Nrityanjali Theatre is primarily dedicated to Odissi classical dance, the space is used for theatre and music. Ralph Maraj, a Trinidadian politician and playwright, has staged some of his plays there.

Perhaps the most well-known Indo-Caribbean playwright is Mustapha Matura, who was born in Trinidad in 1939. Matura wrote several plays about growing up in Trinidad, including *Rum and Coca Cola* (1976), *Independence* (1979), and *The Coup* (1991), and his adaptations set in Trinidad: *Playboy of the West Indies* (1988), based on J. M. Synge's *Playboy of the Western World* (1907), and *Three Sisters* (2006), based on Chekhov's play of the same name (1901).

Matura's drama *Play Mas* (1974) focuses on the events around the independence of Trinidad and Tobago, which came in 1962. Matura is decidedly critical of the party in power, the People's National Movement (PNM), which was instrumental in gaining independence. Trouble came for the party when the Black Power Movement gained momentum and workers began to strike in the late 1960s. A protester was shot and killed by police, which triggered a wave of protests throughout Trinidad and Tobago. Prime Minister Eric Williams, the founder of the PNM, declared a state of emergency, imposed a curfew, forbade public meetings, and detained several political enemies. His strong-arm tactics were hugely unpopular.

In the play, the main character, Indo-Trinidadian RamJohn Gookool, works as a tailor in Trinidad. He dreams of making a suit: "double breasted eight buttoned wit vest an drape trousers" (7). His mother runs the shop, but he talks with Samuel, an Afro-Trinidadian, about movies and about the people around them. RamJohn is saving his money to run the biggest tailor shop in Trinidad, but for now he makes work pants for the workers in the oil fields. Samuel is excited that Carnival is coming and looks forward to "playing mas," the Trinidadian tradition of masquerade brought to the island by the French. RamJohn notes that he isn't interested in Carnival, which makes Samuel question whether he can actually claim to be a Trinidadian. The upcoming political rally highlights the relationship of political affiliation to ethnicity as Samuel asks RamJohn if he belongs to the Democratic Labour Party, the party representing Indo-Trinidadians:

Samuel You is a DLP?
RamJohn I is a businessman.

Samuel But you is a Indian, an DLP is a Indian party.

RamJohn A tell yer I en' no DLP I is a businessman, dat is all, an I en' no Indian, I is a Trinidadian.

Samuel But yer is a Trinidadian Indian.

RamJohn You is a African.

Samuel (*stands up*) No, I do' live in a tree an wear no bush clothes an paint up my face, I is a Trinidadian, I look like a African ter you, I born an bred in Trinidad, you car' call me no African, a do' like dat, a do' like dat at all.

RamJohn All right yer see, de same way you en' an African, I en' a Indian.

Samuel But you is a Indian, you have Indian name, I en' have no African name, my name en' Aba Abadaba.

RamJohn What kinda name yer have?

Samuel I have a Trinidadian name.

RamJohn Yer have a English name.

Samuel Yes, Trinidadian, we does talk English.

RamJohn But you en' English.

Samuel Of course I is English, I does talk English, so I is English, we is English, all a we is English, man.

RamJohn A tought yer was Trinidadian.

Samuel Yes, but Trinidad is English, man.

(46–47)

Being Trinidadian is bound up with speaking English, the language of the current colonial power. RamJohn and Samuel are both immigrants who, under the worst of circumstances, were alienated from the original languages of their cultures. The confusion over identity in the postcolonial Caribbean is compounded by ethnic divisions among the colonized. The struggle is over who gets to claim citizenship versus who continues to be the "other" in the current state.

After an evening of work, Samuel is keen to get to the political rally. RamJohn lets him go, but his mother demands that Samuel finishes sweeping the floor. Finishing the work means missing the last bus, and Samuel feels torn. RamJohn's mother gives him an ultimatum, finish or don't come back. Samuel leaves.

During Carnival, Samuel returns to the shop dressed as a soldier and carrying a machine gun. He says he has been ordered to kill the Gookools. RamJohn and his mother, fearing for their lives, promise

Samuel money. They plead with him. Samuel fires the gun, which turns out to be a toy gun that sprays them with water. Samuel tells them this is part of playing "mas." He wanted to have a good laugh with RamJohn, but the stress kills RamJohn's mother, who is old and has a weak heart. Several other celebrants stop by, the doctor dressed as a stereotypical African, the neighborhood philanderer Frank dressed as a "midnight robber," a woman dressed as a bishop, and two men dressed as undertakers.

The second act is several years later, after independence. Samuel is now an official of the new party, the People's National Movement, the PNM. He summons RamJohn because he believes RamJohn has information on the growing opposition movement in RamJohn's neighborhood. The two catch up and reminisce about old times. RamJohn has no information on his neighbors because he does not mix with them, but Samuel pressures him to find out. Characters from the first act drift in and out of Samuel's office as he attempts to manage the department. Their costumes from Carnival in the first act serve as ironic foreshadowing to their status in the new regime – a woman dressed as a bishop is now married to a bishop, the undertakers are now actually undertakers, and the midnight robber is now the head of the Chamber of Commerce. Samuel has declared a state of emergency and all are concerned about the financial impact it has had on the country. Carnival, once a defining act of Trinidadian identity, has become a tourist attraction, the commodification of that identity. They urge Samuel to lift the emergency for Carnival. He does, but only to use it as a pretext for attacking the organizers of the opposition.

Eric Williams continued to be re-elected until he died in office in 1981. The PNM remained dominant until 1995 when the Indo-Trinidadian Basdeo Panday of the United National Congress was elected prime minister. The first woman prime minster, also an Indo-Trinidadian, Kamla Persad-Bissessar was elected in 2010.

SISTREN: HONORING THE ANCESTORS

When the Spanish began colonizing Jamaica, they enslaved the Taíno people, most of whom quickly perished from abuse and disease. The Spanish brought the first African slaves to Jamaica, but not more than a few thousand, as Jamaica was not the main focus of their colonizing efforts. Sparsely populated, the island was an easy target for the English in the mid-seventeenth century. With the Spanish defeated, the few slaves on the island fled into the forests and formed permanent settlements of their own. The Maroons, as they were called, successfully fended off British attempts to re-enslave them. A full-scale war against the Maroons in the early eighteenth century resulted in a stand-off. However, the resulting negotiations ensured that the Maroons would not interfere with the retention of slaves brought by the British. In fact, the Maroons helped to put down a major slave rebellion a few decades later. A second war with the Maroons resulted in some of the Maroons being transported – first to Canada, and then to Sierra Leone.

There were several slave rebellions and, after emancipation, the rebellions continued, spurred by poor working conditions and economic inequality. Labor unrest throughout the twentieth century fueled the drive for independence from the United Kingdom, which was achieved in 1962. Jamaica still retains the British monarch, however.

The early twentieth century is notable for several other reasons, including the arrival of Marcus Garvey (1887–1940), the famous activist from the United States who founded a movement to empower people of African descent all over the world. He lived in Jamaica briefly after being deported from the US. The second is the Rastafarian movement, a spiritual movement based on the belief that Haile Selassie I, the king of Ethiopia, was the Second Coming of the Messiah. The Rastafarian religion quickly spread through Jamaica and throughout the world. The Rastafarians believe in the religious use of marijuana, which some scholars suggest was imported by the Indo-Jamaican laborers. Because Haile Selassie I spoke of equality, Rastafarian belief possesses a not-always-realized ideal of gender equality. All people are *bredren* and *sistren*, or brothers and sisters. Rastafarians were also key in the creation and promotion of reggae music, the most visible artists of which were Bob Marley, Peter Tosh, and Bunny Wailer.

While there are plenty of records of theatrical activity in Jamaica throughout the colonial period, most of the theatre involved professional tours from Europe. The push for a Jamaican theatre did not begin until the twentieth century, with plays by political activists such as Frank Hill (1910–1980), Una Marson (1905–1965), Archie Lindo (1908–1990), and Roger Mais (1905–1955). With the establishment in 1950 of the College of the West Indies in Jamaica, Jamaican theatre began to flourish. The drama department there, initially headed by Trinidadian Errol Hill (1921–2003), was later run by Jamaican Dennis Scott (1939–1991).

Dennis Scott is perhaps best known for his play *An Echo in the Bone* (1974). Scott used the structure of the "Nine-Nights" ceremony as the framing device of his play about a black gardener who commits suicide after killing his white employer. Without the body, the mourners cannot send the spirit on his way. To make sense of the events they reenact scenes from the history of the oppression of black people. The "echo" refers to the physical memories of racial oppression. Scott's use of Jamaican folk culture influenced many later Jamaican artists, including Sistren, a women's theatre collective that began working in Kingston in 1977.

Sistren's mission was, and still is, to use popular theatre methods to help women in the community address issues of poverty, domestic violence, teenage pregnancy, and other issues important to the poor and working-class women in Jamaica. The original members had no theatre training, but began working on dramatizing stories from their own lives. They later enlisted the help of Honor Ford-Smith, a drama director at the Jamaican School of Drama. Ford-Smith began working with them on dramatic techniques and improvisation. The company would collectively generate ideas and tell stories and then begin improvising scenarios. From this, Ford-Smith would create the final scripts. The first of these dealt with the women workers organizing at a garment factory, *Downpression Get a Blow* (1977). The second piece, *Bellywoman Bangarang* (1978), was created out of stories of teen pregnancy.

In 1980, following a rash of violence between warring political parties, a fire broke out in a wing of the Eventide Home for poor, elderly, mostly women Jamaicans. Some suspected arson. At least 153 women were killed or died from their injuries. The women of Sistren worked with Hertencer Lindsay to create a performance called *QHP* in 1981, honoring the women who died in the fire. Lindsay and Ford-Smith went on to become part of what was later called the Groundwork Theatre Collective.

QHP stands for the main characters: Queenie, Hopie, and Pearlie. Each of the characters begins the play in a coffin. Queenie, still living, is in the hospital recalling the events of the fire. A chorus is singing offstage. As the set changes to flash back to the stories of the women, the chorus surrounds Hopie and a woman "shawls" her. To understand what this means, it is important to understand that the play is framed as an Etu ritual, a ceremony honoring the dead brought to Jamaica from Yoruba tradition. The women are dancing in a circle, when the leader places a shawl around the waist of the dancer and pulls her to the center. The players are all painted with goat blood, and shaved kola nut is put on their tongues. The Etu enables the living to communicate with the dead.

Hopie grew up working as a domestic for a British family. In a flashback scene, we see Sissy, the white woman she has known all her life, announce that they are moving back to England. She ends up begging on the street. The scene shifts to the shawling of Pearlie, who has had a life of privilege. But when she reveals that she is pregnant by the gardener, she is kicked out of her house. In the next scene, she is a prostitute working on the harbor, an alcoholic, and easy prey for thieves. Finally, Queenie is shawled. In her scenario, she gives a sermon in a *pocomania* church, a Christian revivalist church with African elements. Controversy has erupted, however, over her relationship with the Bishop, who has been absent for some weeks. The church elders evict Queenie from the church. Queenie sets out to sell sweets on the street, but gets notice from the government that she must take down her stall so that they can begin building on that lot.

In the second act, the women are together in the Eventide Home, referred to by residents as the "Almshouse." They are taunted by Rastafarian men blasting reggae from a boombox. Then two victims of the Orange Lane tenement fire from 1976 come walking by, lamenting a state where you would work hard all of your life and end up living in poverty. The women spend time exchanging stories and talking about their regrets. They help each other cope. When Pearlie begins drinking again, Queenie confronts her: "Why yuh do dis to yuhself, yuh is woman. Tek care of yuh body" (174). In the final scene, the women enact testimony from the hearings of the Investigative Commission. They recount the circumstances that put them in the home, the events of the fire, and plead with the Commission to make reforms so that such tragedies would not be repeated. The performance ends with more Etu dancing, the sprinkling of rum, and the acknowledgment of the ancestors.

7

THE AMERICAS

For much of the twentieth century, the prevailing scientific consensus was that the first Americans came to Alaska from Siberia in a land bridge region scientists refer to as "Beringia." This is still the consensus today, but with the analysis of DNA, the picture turns out to be much more complex than initially thought. Very generally, it can be said that such a migration occurred over 15,000 years ago. People migrated during the ice age when low sea level made such land travel possible. We know now that more than one such migration happened and that at least one group traveled back from Alaska *to* Siberia. But scientists have found new genetic evidence that links groups in the Amazon to Australasians.

Much of early anthropology in the nineteenth century focused on finding evidence of these migrations but, lacking DNA analysis, early anthropologists relied on physical measurements to classify racial groups. Much of this research was geared toward creating racial hierarchies in order to bolster European racism and justify colonialism. Eventually, these early anthropologists saw a link between language and migration, and began collecting linguistic and cultural inform-ation as well. Anthropologists studying the people of the Americas recorded and preserved indigenous texts. Many did so with the hope of proving the first Americans came from Europe and were, therefore, genetically superior to Asians or Africans.

INDIGENOUS AND HYBRID DRAMA OF LATIN AMERICA

The scant evidence we have of theatre in the Americas before the arrival of European colonists comes from this drive to collect linguistic evidence. In Guatemala, the Abbot Charles Étienne Brasseur de Bourbourg (1814–1874) began collecting Mayan and Aztec texts in the mid-nineteenth century. Like some of the Europeans of his time, he perpetuated the belief that the Mayans came from Atlantis. Europeans had difficulty accepting that the ancient Mayan cities could be constructed by anyone but their own ancestors.

In 1862, Brasseur de Bourbourg saw a Mayan dance-drama. He translated into French the text of the drama *Rabinal Achí*, known also as *Xajoj Tun* (*Dance of the Trumpets*). In the play, the kingdom of Rabinal has just defeated the kingdom of Quiché. The Rabinal court of Lord Five Thunder puts the Quiché warrior Cawek on trial. The dialogue between the Rabinal warrior and the Quiché warrior is made up of a series of repetitive greetings and recounting of past deeds. Cawek knows he will die, but asks to say goodbye to his native land. He accuses the court of thinking he would be a coward and leave, but he bravely faces his death. The other characters are the king's virgin daughter, Mother of Green Feathers, a slave, and the thirteen eagles and thirteen jaguars which serve as totems in the great hall.

The text Brasseur de Bourbourg used came from a Rabinal man, Bartolo Sis, who originally transcribed *Rabinal Achí* in 1850 in order to preserve the text for his descendants. Scholars imagine the drama dates back as far as the fifteenth century, not long after the events alluded to in the text originally occurred. However, it is extremely difficult to put a date on such a text as it has emerged from an oral tradition that is always changing. In the Spanish colonies, authorities forbade native storytelling, songs, or rituals and employed native people instead in staging Spanish *autosacramentales*, pageants based on Christian doctrine or stories from the Bible. Dennis Tedlock suggests that the performance necessarily had to change under colonialism as the Spanish repressed expressions of Mayan culture:

> Events in the history of royal lineages provided subjects for dramas long before the Spanish arrived, but the dialogues were sung or chanted by choruses while the actors danced silently. . . .
> The dramatists who scripted and produced ancestral versions of *Rabinal Achí* worked under the constant threat of censorship. Their solution to the problem of keeping the memory of Mayan court drama alive was to separate the words from the music and

remove all but the outlines of the original religious content from public view. To this day the dialogue is spoken by actors rather than sung by a chorus, and the dance music is purely instrumental.

(2)

The surviving text represents what Brasseur de Bourbourg witnessed and transcribed over a century and a half ago. It is probably not what the performance has been over the centuries and also is not what the performance will be as long as it is performed.

A similar puzzle is presented by the Inca text *Ollantay*, transcribed in Peru in the eighteenth century. The most well-known copy was transcribed by the priest Antonio Valdez. The drama tells the story of the rebellion by Ollantay, a warrior in the kingdom ruled by Pachacuti. He wishes to wed the king's daughter Coyllur, who is pregnant with his child, but he is a commoner. The king banishes him and imprisons his daughter. The king's general Rumiñahui battles Ollantay, but loses. Years pass. The daughter of Ollantay and Coyllur, Yma Sumac, has grown up not knowing her parents. Coyllur is still locked away. Pachacuti has died and his son Túpac-Yupanqui vows to capture Ollantay once and for all. Rumiñahui tells Ollantay that he wants to join him. After Ollantay opens his gates to his enemy Rumiñahui's army defeats him and brings him back to Túpac-Yupanqui. Initially, Ollantay and his men are to be executed, but are eventually forgiven. Ollantay is reunited with his family and allowed to marry Coyllur.

The presence of the elements of Spanish drama, especially with regard to the scene of forgiveness, resolution, and marriage at the end, caused some early scholars to suggest that Antonio Valdez wrote the play himself. However, the drama is in the native language Quechua, and would have been inaccessible to Spanish audiences. John Beverly makes the astute observation that *Ollantay*, regardless of its possible precolonial origin, may have changed during colonial times. If the sudden stay of the execution is uncharacteristic of Incan justice, it may reflect the thinking of a new Inca ruling class considering Incan statehood (54–55).

The Nicaraguan text *El Güegüence* provides a clear example of the hybridized indigenous–colonial text. The dance-drama dates back to the seventeenth century. It was transcribed by a Nicaraguan linguist in the mid-nineteenth century, copied by a German explorer, and passed on to a US anthropologist who published it in 1882. *El*

Güegüence serves as the only example of a text written entirely in a hybrid Nahuatl–Spanish language.

El Güegüence has distinctly colonial characters, including a colonial governor named "Gobernador Tastuanes," which means "Governor Governor" in Spanish and Nahuatl. The title character (Güegüence means "old man") makes his living trading wares along the road to the northern Central American countries. He travels with his two sons, Don Forcico and Don Ambrosio, and scratches out an existence stealing and swindling.

The governor and his constable lament their poverty in the royal court. They have no gold ink wells or pens. They have no embroidered table cloth or even nice paper with the royal seal with which to carry out their business. The governor tells the constable to summon Güegüence to pay taxes. When the constable finds Güegüence, Güegüence pretends to be deaf and not very clever in order to confound him. When Güegüence says he does not know the etiquette for appearing at the court, the constable offers to teach him for a fee. Using the "short count" con, Güegüence gets the better end of the deal.

During his appearance, Güegüence uses word play based on the hybrid language to insult the members of the court. He also makes a series of crude sexual jokes and brags about his sexual prowess. He allows the governor to think he is indeed wealthy and should pay his share of taxes in order to lure him into a deal. He has his sons show the members of the court his goods. Don Forcico supports his father's claims, listing his father's treasures: "chests of gold, chests of silver, cloth of Spain." But Don Ambrosio refuses to go along. He calls his father a liar and notes that the items he lists are mostly trash that he has stolen. Güegüence, angered by Don Ambrosio's impertinence, says that he is a "bad seed" and that he is not his son. He tells the governor that his wife cheated on him while he was traveling and became pregnant with Don Ambrosio.

Güegüence begins to brag about Don Forcico. He lists his accomplishments and the jobs that he has had: sculptor, metalworker, grinder, and pilot. But all of these words in Nahautl sound like words for "scoundrel," "thief," "sloth," and "garbage collector." Finally, Güegüence convinces the governor to allow the marriage of his daughter to Don Forcico. Since the governor believes Güegüence is wealthy, this seems like a better deal than just having Güegüence pay taxes. He summons the women and Güegüence and Don Forcico begin to evaluate them. It appears that several of the women are already pregnant by Don Ambrosio. When Güegüence asks Don Ambrosio where he learned to do that, he replies: "From sleeping with you."

After the marriage, the governor requests payment in the form of bottles of Spanish wine. Don Forcico tells Güegüence that he need not bother to look for wine as he has procured some already, from "a friend." Indeed, he has stolen it from the governor's own cellar. The characters begin a procession with the mules. Güegüence makes a series of sexual jokes about the mules' genitals and, drinking the wine, the party rides from the court. Throughout the play, the action is broken up with several dances. All of the characters wear masks with blue eyes and elaborate costumes that look vaguely like Spanish colonial dress. Musicians play a drum, guitar, and violin while a line of men in black mule masks encircles the human characters making braying noises. In the twenty-first century, the communities where the tradition of *El Güegüence* originates present the dance-drama as part of St. Sebastian's Day festivities. Usually, the performers do not speak the text, as no one understands the archaic hybrid language. Usually, the performers just do the dance and the music as part of an event that involves several folk dance traditions and a procession of the saints through the streets of the town.

Spanish colonization of the Americas was swift and brutal. Beginning in the early part of the sixteenth century, the Spanish gained control of much of North and South America within the half-century. This territory included the entire southwest of what is now the United States and Florida. Colonial authority was administered through *encomiendas*, a feudal system of fiefdom whereby the people are required to work and pay tribute to a feudal lord. The system was used to enforce labor in mines and on large plantations throughout the Americas. The conditions were tantamount to and as brutal as slavery. The Crown ordered the Conquistadors to convert the indigenous people to Catholicism. Early on, Bartolomé de las Casas (c.1484–1566), the Bishop of Chiapas, pushed for an end to the mistreatment of indigenous people based on his belief that they could be converted to Christianity and were fully human. This resulted in the New Laws of the Indies for the Good Treatment and Preservation of the Indians in 1542, which decreed that labor was to be handled directly by the Crown to prevent abuse. To replace labor lost, Las Casas suggested importing slaves from Africa.

The Spanish colonies in the New World developed a complex racial hierarchy based on birthplace and percentage of European blood. Purely indigenous and African people occupied the bottom of the hierarchy. People of mixed blood, *mestizos* and mulattos, began to make up most of the population. *Criollos*, white people born in the Americas, made up the aristocratic and administrative classes, with the Spanish-born Spaniard at the top. Europeans believed that being born someplace other than Europe made you essentially inferior even if you were of European descent. This separation of *criollos* from the Spanish-born put into motion an idea that Americans (meaning people born in North or South America) were distinct from Europeans and the push for independence in the colonies began.

By the nineteenth century, Spain began to lose its grip on its colonies in the Americas and, one by one, each nation declared independence. The Spanish colonies in the Caribbean, however, re-mained under Spanish control until the twentieth century. Cuba remained a colony until the Spanish–American War put it under control of the United States officially until 1902, and practically until the Revolution in 1959. Puerto Rico continues to be a United States territory. The Dominican Republic was freed from Spain, then became part of Haiti, was then controlled by Spain again, and was then controlled by the United States until 1924.

The feudal structure of colonialism came into direct conflict with modern development in Latin America, and several of the resulting civil wars, coups, and rebellions have been fought along the lines of those competing interests. Conservatives tended to favor the status quo of monoculture exports grown on large plantations. Liberals sought foreign investment to develop urban infrastructure and industry. But each nation developed a distinct character, depending on the racial demographics, the national resources, and the international relationships each fostered.

The growing urban bourgeoisie at the turn of the twentieth century were keen to create a Latin American theatre tradition. There were already theatres that produced European drama and variety shows. But at the beginning of the twentieth century, several writers began to write comedies and sketches based on the foibles of recognizable Latin American characters. Uruguayan Florencio Sánchez (1875–1910) wrote over twenty plays that firmly established the *costumbrista* tradition (culture that includes caricatures of local customs and idiosyncrasies). His play *M'hijo el dotor* (*My Son the Doctor*) premiered in Buenos Aires in 1903. The play features a young man returning to his family in the country after studying medicine in the city. He is appalled at the backward behavior and beliefs of his family and they are, in turn, aghast at his new attitudes. Through a series of heart-wrenching events, he comes to appreciate his family and the values with which they raised him. *M'hijo el dotor* inspired several other dramas throughout Latin America.

Immigrants from other parts of the world began to arrive in Latin America. Most Germans and Italians settled in the Southern Cone – Argentina, Chile, and Uruguay – but migrated to several other places as well. Jewish people fleeing pogroms came to the Americas. Workers came from China to build railroads. Japanese, with assistance from the Japanese government, also began to immigrate to Latin America after the turn of the century in order to work on and purchase farms. Latin America is also home to several sizable Arab communities. The cosmopolitan cities of Latin America were home to people who brought performance traditions from all over the world and who were continuously exposed to innovations in the performing arts.

As the twentieth century progressed, many artists in Latin America read and saw the work of the European avant-garde. The Italian Futurist Filippo Marinetti visited South America in the 1920s and 1930s. Many of the wealthy elite sent their children to universities in Europe, often in Paris, one of the epicenters of the avant-garde. Futurism, Dadaism, Expressionism, and Surrealism all had an impact on theatre throughout the Americas. Writer Carlos Solórzano has referred to this period as the "universalist" period in Latin American theatre. In Argentina, the writer Roberto Arlt (1900–1942) wrote *La isla deserta* (*The Desert Island*) in 1937 about the alienation of workers in an office. Xavier Villaurrutia (1903–1950) wrote *Invitación a la muerte* (*Invitation to Death*) in 1943, using Shakespeare's *Hamlet* as a springboard to explore the existential crisis of a young man in contemporary Mexico.

GRISELDA GAMBARO: A TOUR OF TORTURE

At the same time, the twentieth century ushered in a new era of intervention from the United States. Virtually unopposed as an imperialist power, the US government and US-based companies enacted policy that affected Latin American governments all the way to the Southern Cone. As Cold War tensions and fear of communism grew, the US took an active role in attempting to thwart communism in Latin America. The Alliance for Progress in 1961 ensured US aid to "friendly," often repressive, regimes in Latin America. Those regimes that were anti-communist could count on the United States for military intervention and financial support to prop up their regimes or help topple democratically elected governments. Many Latin Americans endured censorship, curfews, and the "disappearances" of political dissidents. Theatre artists creating work critical of these regimes were forced into exile.

Many plays of the post-World War II period often reflect on life under dictatorship. Manuel Galich (1913–1984) wrote *El tren amarillo* (*The Banana Train*) in 1955 after a US-funded coup toppled the government of Jacobo Arbenz in Guatemala. The play chronicles the history of the United Fruit Company and the dire economic and social consequences of US intervention. Cuban José Triana (1931–) wrote *La noche del los asesinos* (*Night of the Assassins*) in 1965 about children replaying the murder of their parents. After Augusto Pinochet stepped down as president in Chile (he remained as Commander-in-Chief of the Chilean Army), Ariel Dorfman (1942–) wrote *La muerte y la doncella* (*Death and the Maiden*) in 1990. The play focuses on the aftermath of state violence when a woman thinks she recognizes the voice of an unexpected guest as the doctor who aided in her torture.

The Argentine playwright Griselda Gambaro (1928–) wrote several plays before and during Argentina's *Guerra Sucia* or Dirty War (1976–1983). In 1966, her play *Las paredes* (*The Walls*) premiered at the Teatro Agón in Buenos Aires. In the play, a Young Man waits in a room that seems perfectly comfortable. The Functionary and the Usher treat him well enough, but he cannot leave. Worried about missing work, he hopes that his cooperation will bring a swift end to his "detention." As the play progresses, the Functionary and the Usher become menacing. The Young Man hears screams and realizes the curtain only reveals more wall and not the window he expected. Arbitrary actions by his captors torment him until, by the end, he believes the walls are caving in on him. Finally, when the Functionary leaves the door open, the Young Man is too paralyzed to flee.

Gambaro followed *Las paredes* with *El campo* in 1967. *El campo* follows a similar formula: Martin, an accountant who has come to work for a school, doesn't recognize that he is in a concentration camp. He reports to Frank, who proceeds to invade his space. He has an "elegant" guest play the piano for him at a small concert, but it is clear she is an abused prisoner, as are the other audience members. Much of Gambaro's early work takes a complacent Argentine public to task for inaction. The victims of Argentina's oppressive regime are complicit in their own victimization.

Gambaro wrote *Información para los extranjeros* (*Information for Foreigners*) in 1973 based on accounts of disappearances. She structured the play in twenty episodes to be played in different parts of a large house or other playing space that has stairs and a variety of rooms. Tour guides lead groups of participants through the space and take them from room to room. Gambaro leaves it up to each director to decide the order of the scenes for each small group, but she specifies that everyone should end up in the last room for the last episode together. Guides will preface scenes with an "explanation for foreigners," reports from newspapers on disappearances. The episodes themselves are absurdist, actions that allude to things that happen in detention presented in a purely abstract way. The spectator feels the sense of menace and violence, but Gambaro does not present realistic scenes of torture.

In one scene, a guard hands a girl his pistol. He asks if she wants the gun and suggests that shooting the head or the heart is a "sure thing." She is soaking wet and he suggests that they are filling the tub again. In another scene, Gambaro recreates the Max Planck Institute and Milgram experiments on obedience, making one of the word association questions "Nation: prison, bars, Germany, torture." The student replies "Argentina," and the teacher shocks him. Repression relies on obedience from the actors who execute it and from a complacent public that ignores it. Another episode presents a court scene where a man faces various criminal charges. However, he could not have committed them because he was in prison. The judge keeps ruling that he is not guilty and the guards keep saying he can go, but then they push him down into his chair again and read another charge. Gambaro bases this scene on the case of Robert Quieto, who evaded kidnapping and called the police only to discover the kidnappers *were* the police. He was detained and then charged with subversive acts that were supposed to have happened while he was detained.

Gambaro mixes spectatorship and action, sometimes instructing that characters come out of the audience to murder a woman and then rejoin the audience. The episodes mix children's games with poems by Federico García Lorca (1898–1936), the Spanish poet murdered by fascists. They also include lines from Shakespeare's *Othello*, and quotations of scenes from fairy tales. In the final episode, a group of prostitutes watches some men play a deadly game of Blind Man's Bluff with a prisoner who is already feverish. They torment and injure the man until they finally take him behind a screen. The spectators see the man being strapped to a table. The prisoner screams as music is turned up on stage. Two men come out to coerce the prostitutes into singing and clapping. When it is clear that the prisoner is dead, the action stops abruptly and the actors, including the one playing the prisoner, begin taking down the set. The Guide urges people to clap and then begins ushering them out of the room. As police sirens sound outside, the Guide recites a line from the poem "Límites" by Juan Gelman (1930–2014) whose son and daughter-in-law were disappeared and murdered: "Who once said: man here, and here not?" People in the audience who know the poem would know that it ends with "Only hope has unstained knees. They bleed."

Forced to flee Argentina in 1977, Gambaro continued to write plays that turned a critical lens on the government. At the end of the Dirty War, Gambaro wrote *Antígona furiosa* as an indictment of the inaction of the new government in 1986. Based on *Antigone* by Sophocles, the play begins with Antigone hanging. During the course of the play, she awakens, removes the noose, and confronts Creon. The play expressed the frustration of the victims of the Dirty War who were waiting for justice.

THEATRE OF THE OPPRESSED

Augusto Boal (1931–2009) also emerged during this time as a theatre maker and social justice activist. After studying about Bertolt Brecht (1898–1956) and his Epic Theatre in New York, Boal returned to

Brazil to create theatre in the countryside with Brazilian peasants. The German director and playwright Brecht theorized about a kind of theatre that did not allow spectators to submit uncritically to any performance. He wanted spectators to consider the consequences of the events they witnessed and to spur them to political action. Boal wanted to take Brecht's ideas further and make the spectators the authors of their own kind of political theatre. This kind of "community-based" political theatre, called Nuevo Teatro Popular (New Popular Theatre) was spreading through Latin America along with the grassroots political organizing of revolutionaries. Teatro Escambray formed in Havana in 1969, and other groups followed.

After being tortured and exiled in 1971, Boal formulated his ideas for the Theatre of the Oppressed in a book by that title. Using the pedagogical theories of Paolo Freire (1921–1997), Boal outlined strategies to engage community members, encourage critical thinking about actions on stage, and allow spectators – he called them "spec-actors" – to intervene and troubleshoot in order to solve problems. The scenarios, generated by the spectators, revolve around moments when a spectator feels oppressed. The creation and intervention into these scenarios is called "Forum Theatre." Forum Theatre enables community members to discover oppression in their lives and consider effective ways to confront it. Boal's methods influenced generations of theatre practitioners all over the world.

CANADIAN SOVEREIGNTIES

The receding of the glacial ice shelf as global temperatures rose 10,000 years ago, allowed people to move from Beringia inland. People began to settle in areas throughout North America, including the Iroquois and the Algonquin-speaking people. By the time Europeans arrived, Algonquin-speaking people occupied the entire eastern half of what is now Canada.

While evidence exists that Norse explorers visited and even settled in North America, there was no significant contact with Europeans until the fifteenth and sixteenth centuries. At that time, English, French, Portuguese, and Spanish explorers all laid some claim to Canadian territories. French fishing vessels and fur traders successfully negotiated with indigenous people in eastern Canada and soon the French had established a significant presence there. The explorer and geographer Samuel de Champlain (1574–1635) founded Nouvelle-France, with Ville de Québec as the capital, under the auspices of the Compagnie de la Nouvelle France; it was later ruled directly by the Crown.

By the eighteenth century, the French colonies extended to Fort Niagara and the British had established some settlements in Newfoundland and a firm foothold on the east coast of the United States. The British Hudson Bay Company made inroads around Hudson Bay, but there had already been a few skirmishes there with the French. Several major conflicts known as the "Intercolonial Wars" between the British and the French throughout the eighteenth century resulted in the British taking control of French-held Canadian territories, including Québec and Nova Scotia.

In Nova Scotia, French colonists continued to resist British rule until they were deported to France and to French colonies in Louisiana and the Caribbean. While the British gained control over colonized territories in Canada, the British colonial government recognized the right of French Canadians to continue speaking French and practicing Catholicism. The colony was initially divided between "Upper" and "Lower" Canada, with Upper Canada situated in what is now southern Ontario (the upper part of the St. Lawrence River) and Lower Canada containing everything to the east of that. English-speaking people lived mostly in Upper Canada and French-speakers in Lower Canada. They were united in 1840 as the United Province of Canada. As a result of their separate colonial history, Québec has its own unique French culture resulting in a movement that has pushed several times for Québec to secede from Canada.

Immigrants from the United States and northern Europe began to settle throughout the Canadian colony. Most of the immigrants in the nineteenth century were English-speaking people, from England, Ireland, and Scotland. This tipped the balance of power in Canada toward Anglos. As Great Britain began to establish colonies on the west coast of Canada, the need for greater cooperation between colonies and centralization of economic control resulted in the formation of the Dominion of Canada in 1871. When the new Canadian government commissioned the building of the Canadian Pacific Railway, the company hired thousands of Chinese immigrants to do some of the most dangerous labor. In 1976, parliament passed the Immigration Act, which essentially allowed people to immigrate from all over the world. As a result, today about 20 percent of Canadians are foreign-born, making Canada one of the top five immigrant destinations in the world. Canada was not fully independent from Britain until 1982, and even then they have retained Queen Elizabeth II as their monarch.

TOMSON HIGHWAY: FIRST NATIONS

Soon after Upper and Lower Canada were united into the United Province of Canada, the Canadian parliament passed several acts that had a profound impact on the First People, or First Nations. The Gradual Civilization Act 1857 and Indian Act 1867 both served the white Canadians' project for assimilating indigenous people into white culture. The acts, and later emendations to them outlawed the speaking of indigenous languages, the observation of indigenous religious practices, traditional dress, and other cultural practices such as the *potlatch*, songs, and dances. The Indian Act stipulated that Native people had to move to reservations where hunting and fishing were restricted, and the administration of the nations' affairs was put in the hands of the Minister of Indian Affairs and Northern Development.

Perhaps the most devastating program to emerge from the Indian Act was the employment of the residential school system to forcibly assimilate children from First Nations. The Canadian government removed children from their homes to be sent to Catholic-run boarding schools where they were forbidden to speak their languages or to practice their traditions. Parliament modified the Indian Act in 1951 to allow for indigenous religious and social practices, but the policy of removing children from their homes to send to boarding school remained in force until the last school closed in 1996.

Native people began creating networks in order to collectively negotiate treaties and address other pressing issues in the late nineteenth century. Several provincial organizations formed and, in 1961, organizers created the National Indian Brotherhood. Initially, the organization represented the interests of Native people who were registered (had the official government status as a Native person), people who were not officially registered, and the *métis* or people who had mixed heritage, usually, but not always, descendants of French trappers and Native people from the Hudson Bay area. The organization did not include the Inuit people in the far north who had their own set of issues to address and their own activist groups. Eventually, the *métis* people and non-status Native people split from the Brotherhood as their political needs were different.

In 1969, the Minister of Indian Affairs Jean Chrétien issued a White Paper calling for the complete assimilation of indigenous people, granting them full citizenship and rights, but stripping them of the official status of Native people, the meager reserve land, and any sovereignty they still possessed. The National Indian Brotherhood responded with a "Red Paper," rejecting the measures outlined by Chrétien and convinced Prime Minister Pierre Trudeau not to implement them. The Brotherhood expanded to include more tribal leaders in 1982 and became the Assembly of First Nations.

The Cree playwright Tomson Highway (1951–) spent his youth in a Las Pas boarding school nearly 300 miles from the reserve where he was born in Manitoba. His critically acclaimed book *Kiss of the Fur Queen* (1998) was a somewhat autobiographical account of the time he and his brother René spent there. In the novel, two boys were sent to the school, their names were changed, they were forbidden to speak Cree, and they were sexually abused by priests. On the other hand, Highway has positive things to say about his time at school, given that there were no schools in northern Manitoba:

> There are many very successful people today that went to those schools and have brilliant careers and are very functional people, very happy people like myself. I have a thriving international career, and it wouldn't have happened without that school.
>
> (Highway quoted in Ostroff)

In the boarding school, Highway channeled his creative energy into learning the piano, and he mastered the work of eighteenth- and nineteenth-century classical composers. Highway noted: "How many white boys can get to do that? And they grew up with grand pianos in their living rooms!" (ibid.).

After high school, Tomson Highway studied piano and English at the University of Western Ontario. Afterward, he began a career as a social worker serving Native children from dysfunctional families, Native people in prison, elders, and politicians. This broad perspective on Native life in Manitoba and Ontario inspired Highway to write plays that reflected the problems Native people faced, but also their hopes and dreams.

Highway began writing plays and working in the theatre in Toronto in the early 1980s. At the same time, Dennis Lacroix and Bunny Sicard established a theatre company in the Native Canadian Centre in Toronto, the Native Earth Performing Arts in 1982. The small group survived by getting project grants for each production. Several prominent Native Canadian artists began working there, including Highway, Drew Hayden Taylor (1962–), Monique Mojica, Barry Karp, and Tomson Highway's brother René, then a dancer and choreographer. The group performed pieces written collectively, and they also brought in Native performers and directors from other companies. Most notably, Native Earth hosted artists from the Spiderwoman Theatre in New York, Gloria and Muriel Miguel. Then, in 1986, Native Earth received five-year core funding from the Native Community Branch of the Ministry of Citizenship and Culture. This launched a new phase for the group and much-needed stability. It was the beginning of a cultural boom of Native playwrights in Canada. As Taylor noted:

> it seems that theatre, for one reason or another, has become the predominant expressive vehicle for Canada's Native people. I believe the reason is that theatre is just a logical extension of storytelling. To look back at the roots and origins of traditional storytelling – not just Native storytelling but storytelling in general – it's about taking your audience on a journey through the use of your voice, your body, and the spoken word. And going from that onto the stage is just the next logical progression.
>
> (140)

It was at that point that Tomson Highway became the artistic director of Native Earth, and they began rehearsals for Highway's play *The Rez Sisters* (1986), the first fully scripted piece written by a solo playwright to be performed there. Highway had spent time at the Wikwemikong Indian Reserve on Manitoulin Island and had done some work with the De-ba-jeh-mu-jig Theatre Group there. Highway set the play in the fictional Wasaychigan Hill Indian Reserve on Manitoulin, but with much of the character of Highway's home reserve, the Barren Lands Indian Reserve. In addition to English, the characters occasionally speak Ojibwa and Cree, reflecting the fact that people from different nations often live together on reserves, but also the close relationship of the two languages, which are both in the Algonquin language family.

Highway uses the play *Les Belles-soeurs* (*The Sisters-in-Law*, 1968) by Québec writer Michel Tremblay as a jumping off place for the premise of *The Rez Sisters*. As in *Les Belles-soeurs*, *The Rez Sisters* features a group of women, related by blood, marriage, or adoption, dreaming about what they will do with the winnings from a contest. In *Les Belles-soeurs*, the women are working-class Québécois women gathering at the home of Germaine, winner of a million trading stamps. She has enlisted their help pasting the stamps into the stamp books. In *The Rez Sisters*,Veronique has heard about "THE BIGGEST BINGO IN THE WORLD" happening in Toronto.Tired of the small bingo game in Espanola, the largest town in the area, and even more tired of the very small bingo game on the island, the group of women begin planning and raising money for a road trip to Toronto.

The women are each haunted by demons and the long history they have with each other is punctuated by trauma. Highway weaves the women's stories throughout the play, paying homage to Tremblay's use of individual monologues addressed directly to the audience. Occasionally, the group breaks into long-simmering conflict. Veronique, a Catholic woman who has adopted a mentally disabled girl, hears about the game first, but refuses to go ask Gazelle, the woman who first mentioned it to her, about the date. Gazelle is at the home of her lover Big Joey: "there's all kinds of women who come streaming out of that house at all hours of the day and night. I might be considered one of them" (400). But Annie is the first to question her self-righteousness, calling her a gossip and snoop. The other women quickly jump into the fray and we learn that Emily thinks Philomena is pushy, that Philomena hates that Pelajia wears pants, thatVeronique thinks Emily is a pervert who should have stayed in San Francisco "where all the other perverts are" (403), and that Marie-Adele thinks that Veronique only adopted Zhaboonigan to get the disability check.The conflict finally abates when people see that Marie-Adele, who has cancer, is reeling from pain and exhaustion. Annie gets news of the bingo game from a package from her daughter "who lives with this white guy in Sudbury" as she is fond of reminding everyone.

Highway then presents the fundraising activities of the women in a series of scenes in a long montage. The activity is slow at first, but then gradually picks up speed until the women are frantically working: baking, collecting bottles, cleaning windows, doing laundry. Finally, after the "World's Biggest Garage Sale" and a concert by Emily, the women have raised enough money to take the van to Toronto. In the van, they share stories as they travel, reflecting on the tragedy in their lives and the choices they have made, and the people they have loved.

When the scene fades to the bingo palace, the lights come up in the theatre and the audience becomes part of the bingo action. Everyone has a bingo card and gets to play in the first round until someone in the audience wins. The final round, for the half-million-dollar jackpot, is played only by the actors. The women at the table resemble the image of the Last Supper. The scene becomes frantic until the women finally storm the bingo machine, frustrated that it isn't producing the number B14. They haul it through the audience and out of the theatre.

In addition to the seven women, Highway includes an eighth character, Nanabush. Nanabush is the trickster figure prominent in Ojibwe, Cree, and other Anishinaabe storytelling. Nanabush can be both heroic and crafty, clever and simple. The trickster figure exists to teach humankind and helped with the creation of the world. In *The Rez Sisters,* Nanabush appears as a seagull in the first act, a nighthawk in the second, and then finally as the elegant and mysterious bingo master. Only Zhaboonigan and Marie-Adele, who is dying, can see him for who he really is. At times when Marie-Adele's health is failing her, she imagines Nanabush is attacking her. Finally, at the end, when all the women run out of the bingo hall with the machine, the chaos abates and the bingo master waltzes with Marie-Adele, leading her to the spirit world. Zhaboonigan, who witnesses this, tries to follow, but is stopped by Emily. The remaining women dance and chant to honor their dead sister.

In the end, life on the reservation does not change much. Emily finds out that she is pregnant. Veronique spends her days cooking for Marie-Adele's family and complaining about the burden of her charity, and the play finally ends where it began, back on the roof of Pelajia's house where she was fixing broken shingles. Nanabush again is the seagull and dances to the sound of Pelajia's hammer. Highway makes a point of reminding people that the trickster character is a celebration of life. His brother René danced the role of Nanabush in the first production. Sadly, René died from AIDS just a few years later.

Highway wrote several more plays, including a follow-up piece to *The Rez Sisters*, *Dry Lips Oughta Move to Kapuskasing* (1989). In this, Highway focuses on seven men, most of whom are mentioned by the women in *The Rez Sisters*, in the fictional reservation on Manitoulin Island. The women are starting a women's hockey team, which becomes the subject of much of the discussion by the men who feel resentful at the women appropriating something they feel belongs to them. Nanabush, an entity that has no distinct gender, appears in the second play as a woman, but wearing exaggerated feminine attributes – big breasts as Gazelle and a large rump as another character, Patsy – as a reflection of objectification by the men. In this play, violence against women only hinted at in *The Rez Sisters* is fully realized. A boy with fetal alcohol syndrome rapes the Nanabush character with a crucifix, a reaction to the violence of colonial missionary zeal. While the play was harshly criticized for the portrayal of women and the graphic violence against women, Highway thought that it was important to show social problems as they are in order to address them.

JOUAL AS DRAMATIC LANGUAGE: *LES BELLES-SOEURS*

The people of Canada must constantly address the question of national identity as it is made up of several First Nations in addition to the European settlers, the *métis* people, and the new immigrants that make up the Canadian population. A serious challenge comes in the form of the movement for Québec sovereignty. As we discussed earlier, the French-speaking people of Lower Canada were permitted by the English to practice Catholicism and continue to speak French. However, the assimilationist impulse of colonialism has been keenly felt by the people of Québec, many of whom see their province as a distinct nation. Also, the political reality is that Canadian government business is conducted in English and many French-speaking Canadians have a lower standard of living compared to English-speaking Canadians.

The constitutional coherence of Canada survived two referendums on Québec sovereignty, once in 1980 and again in 1995. To address the movement, Prime Minister Brian Mulroney helped to facilitate an agreement in 1987 between the people of Québec and the people of the other provinces in Canada to decentralize some of the Canadian government. The Meech Lake Accord, however, was never ratified. While the accord had been altered to address the concerns of some of the provincial leaders, the First Nations were never consulted. In the Manitoba Assembly, a lone minister named Elijah Harper, a college classmate of Tomson Highway, held up an eagle feather to stop the rules from being waived to speed debate. He did so despite the enormous pressure from Mulroney and other Canadians who felt the accord was important for the French–English relationship. But this moment highlights the complexity of living in the postcolonial world, where groups of people with different cultures, religions, languages, and history try to imagine themselves as citizens together in the modern nation.

The theatre in Québec has developed along with Québec's political consciousness. Early theatre, of course, consisted of a few productions of French plays, but only for the elite. The Theatre Royal opened its doors in Montreal in 1825 and then moved three times before it closed in 1913. The offerings usually consisted of European opera and other musical entertainments. A few Québec writers in the nineteenth century wrote plays on Québec nationalism, including Louis-Honoré Fréchette (1839–1908). Much of his writing focused on the events of the 1838 Rebellion against British rule. His first play *Felix Poutré* (1862) he based on the account of a man who had escaped from prison after being incarcerated for his role in the rebellion, although it has since come to light that Poutré was a spy for the British. Initially, Fréchette's work was not well received, but his two later plays packed the house: *Papineau,* which is about the rebellion leader Louis-Joseph Papineau, who fled to Paris after orders were issued for his arrest, and the less controversial *Le retour de l'exile* (*Return of the Exile*), both staged in Montreal in 1880. One of Montreal's theatre critics writing for *Le Nouveau Monde* stated that Fréchette's plays marked the beginning of the Canadian National Theatre.

As global travel became easier, companies and actors traveling from Europe came to Montreal and Ville de Québec including stars like Sarah Bernhardt (1844–1923). The Catholic clergy were vocal in their opposition to the theatre, particularly during Bernhardt's numerous visits, which certainly slowed the growth of theatre.

However, they were unable to prevent Bernhardt's performances from being sold out each night.

In 1894, the very large (1500 seats) Monument National opened in Montréal. At the same time, the French-speakers in Québec felt alarmed at the rate of French attendance at English-language theatre, mostly at the Theatre Royal, which presented theatre the Catholic clergy considered scandalous. The Société Saint-Jean-Baptist, a Québec cultural association formed in 1834, together with civic leaders, agreed to fund an amateur French-language troupe to be housed in the Monument National. Under the direction of Elzéar Roy (1855–1939), the group began presenting *les Soirées de famille* (Family Evenings) in the Monument National in 1898. Roy noted that the purpose of the *Soirées* was to present "lovely shows" that would "amuse, instruct, and edify." He also stated that he hoped the French–Canadian repertoire would cause Montreal audiences to forget: "the road to some English theaters where art is replaced by immorality" (Beaulieu 60). Despite official support, the company only lasted until 1901. However, Théâtre National, a professional company started by Julien Daoust (1866–1943) in 1900, still exists today.

By the mid-twentieth century, French-language Québec theatre flourished. Several theatres dedicated to producing work by Québécois playwrights opened their doors, including the Théâtre du Rideau Vert in 1947, Le Théâtre de la Comédie-Canadienne in 1957, and the Théâtre d'Aujourd'hui in 1968. In 1965, a group of playwrights combined efforts to create a workshop for playwrights, the Centre d'Essai des Auteurs Dramatiques. This enabled writers to develop plays through staged readings and get feedback from peers. One of the first plays to be workshopped there was *Les Belles-soeurs* (1968) by Michel Tremblay.

Tremblay came from a working-class family in Montreal. He received a scholarship to attend the university, but disliked the culture and the curriculum and left for a smaller college. He began writing both fiction and drama and had already received awards for his work before he wrote *Les Belles-soeurs*. Because he wrote in the *joual* dialect, the slang spoken by working-class people in Québec, and because he created characters who were a realistic portrayal of working-class life, many people thought the play was not fit for the stage. At the reading at the playwrights' center, however, the play was well received by young theatre artists, including the acclaimed actor Denise Filiatreau. She contacted friends at the Théâtre du Rideau Vert and convinced them to produce the play. It was directed by André Brassard.

Les Belles-soeurs centers around Germaine Lauzon, who has just won one million trading stamps in a contest. She has invited her sisters Rose and Gabrielle, and several other women from their parish to help stick the stamps into the stamp booklets so that Germaine can send them in for household items. She dreams of redoing the entire house and continually talks about the kitchenware and linens she has seen in the product catalogue. Germaine has told her daughter Linda to be there as well, but Linda sneaks out in the beginning of the play and doesn't return until much later. Included in the group is her sister-in-law Thérèse and Thérèse's mother-in-law, who has dementia and is bound to a wheelchair. Other women arrive alone or in small groups: Marie-Ange, beside herself with jealousy over Germaine's good fortune, complains bitterly about how unfair contests are. Lisette enters and drops endless hints about her trips to Europe and her wealth. Des-Neiges laments how lonely she is and tells risqué jokes she hears from a salesman who visits her house from time to time. Eventually, there are fifteen women in Germaine's kitchen.

The pace of the play varies, from monologues of the individual women talking about their hopes or complaining about their hardships or passing judgment on the people in their lives, to scenes of just a few of the women talking, to bursts of chaotic cacophony when controversy arises. Although they only have each other, they express continual disappointment with each other's behavior. When Yvette mentions her daughter's honeymoon, Germaine reminds her, in the guise of congratulations, that she was not invited to the wedding. When Lisette offers to give her old mink stole to Yvette because she is getting a new one, Rose criticizes her for lying about how much money she has: "We know goddamn well your husband's up to his ass in debt because of your mink stoles and your trips to Europe. You're not fooling us with that shit about being rich. You've got no more money that the rest of us" (44). They all tease Des-Neiges mercilessly because of the salesman who visits, something they see as scandalous, although the visits are completely innocent. Everyone compliments Thérèse for her patience in dealing with her mother-in-law, but her "care" for the elderly woman involves smacking her on the head when she does something that inconveniences Thérèse. However, when Rose suggests chucking the old woman off the balcony, Thérèse becomes enraged.

Isolated by class and language, the women also fear any foreign influence – Europeans are dirty, their Italian neighbors are shameless, and anyone who strays from normative behavior is immoral. They talk of Germaine's youngest sister Pierrette as if she were a prostitute, when the fact is that she merely works in a nightclub. Germaine did not invite Pierrette to the stamp-sticking party, but she has heard about it and arrives anyway. The others instantly shun Pierrette, but when Pierrette reveals that she sees one of them in the club every week, the group is beyond scandalized, and the outed woman is mortified, even though she does not drink or behave in any other way the women might judge as inappropriate.

The women continually bring up different contests they have entered and spend some time discussing their love for bingo at the church. But any time anyone mentions a contest they have entered, and then are faced with the inevitable question, "Did you win anything?" the answer is always the same: "Do I look like somebody who's ever won anything?" As Germaine criticizes her guests and brags endlessly about the things she will get, the other women become increasingly resentful. They begin taking stamps – just a few at first, but eventually all of the women are stuffing stamps into their purses. When Germaine realizes the stamps are missing and accuses them, they are all incensed. She makes them open their purses and she sees how much they have taken. At this point, the women rush her and take all the stamps they can before running out, feeling justified because contests aren't fair. The only person who tries to help Germaine is Pierrette, but Germaine continues to reject Pierrette vehemently.

Tremblay hints at change in Québec society through the younger characters. When Linda arrives back home, she brings her friends Lise and Ginette. Germaine and the others continue to be scandalized by Linda's behavior and choice of friends and they warn her: "you will end up like your Aunt Pierrette." When Pierrette does arrive, the younger women bond over mutual problems. Lise is pregnant and desperate for an abortion. Pierrette gets her the name of a doctor she knows. Meanwhile, Pierrette has just been dumped by Johnny, the club owner, now that she's 30, and has nothing to turn to except alcohol. They discuss their limited options, but it isn't long before the young women begin judging each other as well.

Montreal theatre critics were outraged by the play. Michèle Martin's comprehensive analysis of the reviews of *Les Belles-soeurs* reveals the ambivalence of some critics – those who felt that the use of *joual* was necessary to accurately portray the working-class Montreal community or those who felt the play could be instructive for such a community to reform – but many critics were vehemently opposed to the language, the characters, and the subject. Martin cites one critic who noted that the use of *joual* was: "a necessary tool to make people aware of their nauseating cultural condition so they can vomit it up once and for all" (121).

On the other hand, Tremblay's play was ideally situated in the cultural shift known as the *"Révolution tranquille,"* or the Quiet Revolution. Beginning in the 1960s, government reforms put education and social welfare under government control instead of in the hands of the Church. The Liberal governments of Jean Lesage and Robert Bourassa expanded social welfare programs and created a social security pension system. They poured money into public education and nationalized utilities. The movement away from Church control and expansion of the government helped to alleviate poverty and the social problems that come with it. And because of the changes happening throughout the world, women could finally address the repressive culture in which they lived. This new willingness to face social realities head on meant that the work of playwrights like Tremblay would be accepted in time. And now *Les Belles-soeurs* is considered to be the single most important play to come out of the Québécois theatrical scene. It has been translated into several languages and now runs in Montreal as an English-language musical. Tremblay says he has seen it in Scotland, Italy, and the US, and so often, in fact, that he said, jokingly, in 2014: "I can't say I hate that play, but I can't suffer it anymore" (Kenney, 2014).

Tremblay continued to write about women and LGBT characters. Several women made important contributions to the Québécois theatre in the 1970s and 1980s. In 1976, a group of seven women presented the collective creation *La Nef des sorcières* (*A Gathering of Witches*) at the Théâtre du Nouveau Monde. The play presented the monologues of six women, all discussing the most intimate issues in their lives in ways that were both touching and disturbing. Jovette Marchessault (1938–2012) worked in a textile factory as a young woman, then began her career as a painter and sculptor before becoming a writer. Her work focuses on strong women and lesbians, such as Gertrude Stein, painter Emily Carr, Violette Leduc, and Helena Blatavsky. Her play *Chronique lesbienne du moyen-âge Québécois* (*Lesbian Chronicle of a Middle-Aged Québécois*) was published in *Triptyque lesbien* in 1980, and she began to see her work staged at major theatres such as the Théâtre du Nouveau Monde and the Théâtre d'Aujourd'hui. The door had been opened for the next generation to explore what it meant to be Québécois and what it meant to be Canadian.

8

COLLABORATIONS

Not many of the people reading this text now remember a time before the Internet became widely available. And very few people alive now would remember a time before television or before commercial flight shortened the time of intercontinental travel from days to mere hours. But those who lived through much of the twentieth century can attest to the blinding speed at which the world shrank for people in the industrialized world. Technological advances have made communication and information sharing so easy that the world is available at the swipe of a smart phone. This has necessitated a new focus toward understanding the world in which we live and has inspired theatre artists around the globe to collaborate.

Theatre artists have always traveled and have always shared their work outside of their respective communities. From the first wandering troupes or disciples who came to train with known masters, traditions have spread from one place to the next, have been altered, and have sparked new traditions. Actors have moved from one country to another in search of work on the stage. Writers have gone into exile. But in the last sixty years, theatre artists have sought out opportunities to work with groups that have traditions that are vastly different from their own. This type of international collaboration is beneficial, but also potentially harmful. While collaborative projects are to be applauded for bridging gaps and promoting cultural understanding, it is important to understand the politics at work surrounding every encounter.

IMPORT: PETER BROOK'S *THE MAHABHARATA*

Perhaps, one of the most celebrated collaborations was between British director Peter Brook (1925–) teamed up with French writer Jean-Claude Carrière (1931–), designers Chloé Obolensky (1942–) and Jean Kalman (1945–), and composer Toshi Tsuchitori (1950–) to stage a nine-hour version of the Indian epic the *Mahabharata*. The production employed an international cast of performers and was staged at the Avignon theatre festival in France in 1985. Obolensky's set made use of a limestone quarry, putting spectators on scaffolding, with a canal running by them into a pond.

While most theatrical productions that take their stories from the Hindu epics – such as *kutiyattam, kathakali,* and *wayang* – focus on just one episode, Brook decided to mount the entire *Mahabharata* in one comprehensive performance. Following the story within a story structure of the original poem, the playwright Carrière framed the epic as a story being told by Vyasa, the author to whom the story has been credited, to a small boy and being written by Ganesha. To make it wholly theatrical, the three characters discuss at length the nature of the story, how it is the great story of humankind. They frequently break up the action, commenting upon it as a representation, with the boy's mother even stepping in to play a role. Carrière worked to keep as much of the story intact as possible, beginning with Vyasa, Ganesha, and the beginning genealogy of the heroes, the Pandavas, and their cousins, the Kauravas. The play then follows the dice game that causes the Pandavas to lose their kingdom, their exile, the great battle to regain the kingdom, the final end of the Kauravas, and the final journey of the Pandavas into the Himalayas and the spiritual realm.

Brook and his company toured *The Mahabharata*, first to Paris, then to other cities in Europe and the United States. The response of critics from Europe and the US was rather favorable. *The New York Times* critic Margaret Croyden noted that:

> [Brook's] production of the Indian epic represents a culmination of a lifelong search for theatrical expression of mankind's greatest dramas and deepest dilemmas. In his colossal French-language adaptation, of "The Mahabharata," Mr. Brook, synthesizing all his previous theatrical inventions, did nothing less than attempt

to transform Hindu myth into universalized art, accessible to any culture.

Croyden discusses the staging in Avignon and the production elements and also talks about how the members of the company actually traveled to India to better understand the context of the epic. She also noted how successfully Brook had made the production something that the European and US audiences could recognize: "In translating this to the stage, Mr. Brook and his company make it meaningful to us through the creation of real characters and highly dramatic action rooted in Hindu culture and religion but at the same time archetypical and symbolic" (Croyden). Indeed, universality provided much of the driving impulse behind the project of *The Mahabharata*. Brook said in his "Foreword" to the published English translation (he translated it himself from Carrière's French text) that upon first hearing the epic poem, read to him and to Carrière over a series of evenings by a friend who was a French scholar, he understood that "like all great works, it is both far from us and very near" (xiv) and he wanted to "celebrate a work that only India could have created but which carries echoes for all mankind" (xvi).

The ideal of universality in European thought dates back to Aristotle's assertion that poetry deals with universal truths, but took hold in the popular imagination with the Enlightenment, a philosophical paradigm that frames the seventeenth and eighteenth centuries in Europe and fueled many of the independence movements in the Americas. The idea that we are all born with the same potential, we are all essentially good, and that we all worship the same God gave rise to religious tolerance and a trend toward equal rights. However, the "universal" has always been based on a Eurocentric notion of what is right, good, and aesthetically pleasing. This way of seeing the world has persisted in Europe and the United States through the twentieth century. On one hand, the view that we are all the same laid the foundation for the push for an end to slavery, for civil rights, and for equality for women. On the other hand, the notion of universality allowed for colonialism in that Europeans could say they were merely "helping" the uncivilized. It often forms the humanist rhetoric we still see in economic imperialism and military intervention from the United States. A Eurocentric universalism flattens and invalidates the ideals, customs, and aesthetic senses found in other cultures.

Peter Brook writes at length in his "Foreword" about how he decided against using Indian performance forms in order to tell the story of *The Mahabharata*:

> The day I first saw a demonstration of Kathakali, I heard a word completely new to me—The Mahabharata. A dancer was presenting a scene from this work and his sudden first appearance from behind a curtain was an unforgettable shock. His costume was red and gold, his face was red and green, his nose was like a white billiard ball, his fingernails were like knives; in place of beard and mustache, two white crescent moons thrust forward from his lips, his eyebrows shot up and down like drumsticks and his fingers spelled out strange coded messages. Through the magnificent ferocity of the movements, I could see that a story was unfolding. But what story? I could only guess at something mythical and remote, from another culture, nothing to do with my life. Gradually, sadly, I realized that my interest was lessening, the visual shock was wearing off.
>
> However, after the interval, the dancer returned without his makeup, no longer a demigod, just a likable Indian in shirt and jeans. He described the scene he had been playing and repeated the dance. The hieratic gestures passed through the man of today. The superb, but impenetrable image had given way to an ordinary, more accessible one and I realized that I preferred it this way.
>
> (xiii)

Brook carried this impression through his shaping of the project, that the "strange coded messages" had "nothing to do with my life." And so he opted to "suggest the flavor of India" (xvi) in order to make the performance engaging.

Critics familiar with Indian performance forms immediately pointed out that Brook's play had "no recognizable Asian style" (Long 233) or that without the Hindu religious context, the play was unintelligible, with "no framework of reference in Brook's production that provides a Hindu perspective of action in the larger, cosmic context" (Bharucha, "Peter Brook's 'Mahabharata'" 1643) and as an "empty shell" (Dasgupta 11). However, many of the criticisms leveled at Brook and his company were much more serious.

With the best of intentions, but misguided all the same, Brook, Carrière, and the international company of actors visited India to learn more about the epic and about Indian performance. They did so, it seems, on their own terms, without making a significant investment in building relationships and learning about the artists they used, the people they met, or the culture they elected to borrow. In an interview with Phillip Zarrilli, Probir Guha of the Living Theatre of West Bengal recounts several situations where the actions of company members put him in an awkward position. Members of Brook's staff haggled over fees that were really very modest or, in some cases, protested having to pay at all. They showed up late to performances set up for them or left early. There were many instances where they did not recognize local customs and people often felt as if they were not getting anything in return.

The most egregious example of this cultural blindness happened when Brook, after witnessing a performance arranged by Guha of the Chhau dance of western Bengal, invited Guha to come to Paris. He also singled out a dancer, a young man who was about 16, to come as well. But months went by, and Brook never contacted them. After a period of about two years, he finally contacted Guha and invited him only, saying he no longer needed the dancer, and then even that fell through. Brook made casual promises that suited him with little regard for the impact they would have on the people to whom they were made. As Guha states: "When I come to your place or you come to our place, there should be respect. I am going to learn, and if I have something to share, I will share it – from this exchange things develop. This should be the attitude. But with some foreigners they just come here and grab something. They grab it and take it and go" (Zarrilli, "The Aftermath" 96).

Stories such as these prompted scholars such as Rustom Bharucha to state: "Peter Brook's *Mahabharata* exemplifies one of the most blatant (and accomplished) appropriations of Indian culture in recent years. . . . in its appropriation of non-western material within an ori-entalist framework of thought and action, which has been specifically designed for the international market" (1642). For Indians, the pro-duction evoked a colonial dynamic, where Europeans come to take the products from the "uncivilized" in order to sell them elsewhere. The colonized get nothing in return. Una Chaudhuri suggested there was a "glass-beads-for-land" exchange in play, bringing to mind the practice of taking valuable property from the natives and giving them useless trinkets in return.

Gautam Dasgupta had kinder things to say about the production and Brook's work overall, but he warned that such projects can be guilty of *Orientalism*. "Orientalism" is a term coined by postcolonial scholar Edward Said to define the paradigm used by people in the "West" (or in Western Europe) to represent the people of all of Asia – including the vastly different cultures of the Middle East, South Asia, Southeast Asia, and East Asia. Said contends that Europeans have viewed and portrayed the "Orient" as mysterious and exotic and a territory that needed to be dominated by European power. Dasgupta also noted that in the minds of Europeans, the "Orient" could only be represented *by* the "West" and in a way intelligible to the European ideas of the "Orient." He suggests such a mindset is at work behind Brook's play and its reception in Europe and the US. But Dasgupta holds out hope for something better when he states:

> nor am I suggesting that we do away with all cross-cultural artistic endeavors. What concerns me is that the representation of another culture's artistic product address the lived, sensate fabric of that borrowed cloth. And more, that such expressions of cultural give and take not descend to banal generalities about the foreign culture, but seek to uncover its specificities, its actual, and not merely perceived, links with its own society.
>
> (11)

Long echoes this thought: "this Mahabharata brings me no closer to understanding how Asian and Western theatre can be successfully fused while retaining the essence of both" (235). What then constitutes an ethical and meaningful way to collaborate across cultures?

Practitioners must consider who benefits from artistic collaboration. An artist must be conscious of any imbalance of power and privilege, and contemplate appropriate ways to acknowledge what someone has given in an exchange. It should involve developing an awareness of the philosophies that govern the practices of other cultures, not imposing a philosophy because of an unshakable belief in universal truths.

EXPORT: SHAKESPEARE AND *KATHAKALI KING LEAR*

After seeing that his foreign guests recognize his reference to "the undiscovered country" as being a quote from the play *Hamlet* (1602), the chancellor tells them: "You have not experienced Shakespeare until you have read him in the original Klingon." This line, spoken by the Klingon character Gorkon in the movie *Star Trek VI: The Undiscovered Country*, highlights the prevailing notion that cultures throughout the galaxy feel an ownership of the works of William Shakespeare (1564–1616). When counting the number of performances of Shakespeare's work and the number of times his plays have been translated and adapted to the performance conventions of other cultures, this idea has a ring of truth to it.

Although Shakespeare was highly regarded, sometimes begrudgingly, by many of his contemporaries, his work did not initially translate well to other countries in Europe. In criticizing attempts by fellow French writers to adapt Shakespeare to the prevailing French aesthetic of neo-classicism, François-Marie Arouet (1694–1778), also known as "Voltaire," referred to Shakespeare's plays as "shining monsters," beautiful in many respects, but otherwise constructed by a barbarian. While many historians cite Romanticism as the beginning of the European passion for Shakespeare, Gauri Viswanathan notes that the British used Shakespeare as a colonial tool to instruct natives in proper English attitudes and morals. Viswanathan suggests that colonial authorities were uncomfortable using an overtly religious text such as the Bible, and saw their national literature as an effective substitute. Hence, the first departments of English were established in British colonies.

For both of these reasons, many cross-cultural collaborations use the plays of Shakespeare. Tadashi Suzuki (1939–) of Toga, Japan, collaborated with four theatres in the United States for his *The Tale of Lear* in 1984. Yukio Ninagawa directed several Japanese versions of Shakespeare's plays for the Royal Shakespeare Company. While devotees of Shakespeare will say this is a testament to the "universal themes" in Shakespeare, we can at least say, whether we like it or not, that this is evidence of how much Shakespeare has become a lingua franca in Europe and the postcolonial world.

French dancer and director Annette Leday studied *kathakali* dance-drama beginning in 1978 at the Sadanam school in Kerala and then at Kerala Kalamandalam under a fellowship from the Indian government. She has continued performing with both groups and speaks Malayalam, the local language of Kerala. In 1989, she and the other dancers at Kerala Kalamandalam collaborated with Australian director David McRuvie to create a *kathakali* version of Shakespeare's *King Lear* (1605). Because practitioners of *kathakali* approached the text in terms of what would be appropriate to *kathakali*, the project represents a deeper approach to cross-cultural collaboration than something like Brook's *The Mahabharata*. As Zarrilli notes: "If Brook erases distinctive cultural codes in his attempt to be universal, Leday and McRuvie chose to challenge their European audiences by maintaining as much of *kathakali*'s structure and technique as possible" ("For Whom Is the King a King?" 26).

To make the text work for a *kathakali* performance, McRuvie had to limit the action to the relationship of Lear to his three daughters: Goneril, Regan, and Cordelia. The only other characters were the Fool, Mad Tom, and the King of France. The company then had to put the roles into appropriate categories – as the makeup and costumes, the movement, and the music all had to conform to that role type. The King of France was configured a *pacca* character. Cordelia followed the *minukku* type. They chose the *teppu* type for Mad Tom, and Goneril and Regan were cast as the *kari* demoness roles. The company chose to have two actors play King Lear. One was dressed as the *knife* character to convey his dual kingly and troubled nature. The second actor played Lear in only part of a costume to represent a mad King Lear. Because the Fool did not fit into any of the role types, the creators of the piece borrowed the Brahmin clown character from *kutiyattam*. Both McRuvie and the Indian dancers insisted that Leday play the role of Cordelia.

McRuvie streamlined the text to work as a *kathakali* text. The scene where the King of France chooses Cordelia involves dances by Goneril and Regan to win his hand. The dances are vulgar and somewhat risqué. The remaining dialogue of the scene is boiled down to its essence in the lines sung on the part of the King of France:

> She is the richest who has no dowry.
> I take up what has been cast away.
> Your dowerless daughter shall be my queen.

The sung dialogue, translated into Malayalam, takes up only a very few pages, with most of the story represented in the dance of the *kathakali* form.

The reception of the *Kathakali King Lear* varied from place to place and from critic to critic. The play was performed in cities in Europe and in Kerala, but also toured to international theatre festivals at Edinburgh and Singapore. As Zarrilli observes, the different groups of spectators:

> brought to the production not only their own native cultural assumptions but also an increasingly global flow of ideas, images, and information all of which affected their expectations about what they would experience, their perceptions and categories for understanding that experience, and therefore how they received and responded to *Kathakali King Lear*.
>
> ("For Whom Is the King a King?" 22–23)

The *kathakali* elements did challenge the European spectators and this is reflected in the reviews. Some European reviewers rejected the foreignness of the production altogether, dismissing it as "two fellows with skirts" or "somewhere between mime and a sign language conversation." Others were willing to go along with what they could not understand: "You can, without any training, be subjugated, letting the music intoxicate you." But many European critics thought that *kathakali* proved to be an able vehicle for communicating the emotional depth of Shakespeare's text, particularly in the final scene where Lear laments the death of Cordelia.

But, as Zarrilli points out, many critics in Kerala and, indeed, several of the practitioners who worked on the production had difficulty reading Lear as a proper *kathakali* character. European audiences find the story poignant, that of an aged king who would foolishly reject his daughter because she honestly suggests that her love would be divided between her father and her husband. People of Kerala thought this odd for a couple of reasons that Zarrilli outlines: that a daughter would naturally give her love to her husband, and that it was so unlikely that an elder man and a king would believe the likes of Goneril and Regan. In an epic paradigm that views kings as a heroic element in the cosmic order, Lear's behavior is unintelligible. Lear does not translate into the *kathakali* idea of a king, although the attempt to use the British text in a codified Indian form sparked an interesting discussion about the nature of collaborating through the narrative and practice of other cultures.

THE PENDULUM: ONG KENG SEN AND CROSS-CULTURAL SYNTHESIS

Many cross-cultural collaborations involve generating new work or creating theatre out of contemporary literature. I have called this section "The Pendulum" to evoke Rustom Bharucha's idea from his book *Theatre and the World* that the cultural exchange inherent in working across cultures involves swinging back and forth in a cultural negotiation. The movement in the space between cultures generates disagreement, misreading, and also representation, discourse, and a questioning of assumptions. Complicite, a company in London under the direction of Simon McBurney (1957–), and the Setagaya Public Theatre of Tokyo have collaborated a couple of times in the creation of new work. They first collaborated on *An Elephant Vanishes* in 2003, a series of plays based on the short stories by Haruki Murakami (1949–). They came together again in 2008 to create *Shun-kin*, a play based on the stories of Jun'ichirō Tanizaki (1886–1965).

While *An Elephant Vanishes* used contemporary performance elements, such as digitally produced animation, video screens, and lighting that evokes trains and cars, *Shun-kin* employed techniques from *bunraku*. The title character in *Shun-kin* studies the *shamisen*, a three-stringed instrument used in the music for *bunraku* and *kabuki*. She is blind and her older servant Sasuke waits on her patiently. He loves her and will do anything to be around her. Sasuke begins learning the *shamisen* on his own, and Shun-kin agrees to be his teacher. But she is cruel and ridicules him. As their relationship develops, the two become embroiled in a sadomasochistic erotic dynamic. Framing the play is the reading of the story for a recording by a middle-aged radio actor. She occasionally interrupts the reading with her own commentary about Shun-kin and Sasuke, or the reading is interrupted by calls from her lover, a man who is younger than she is. Their relationship offers a contrast to the relationship in Tanizaki's story. The use of puppetry created a stunning visual layer in the performance. For instance, Shun-kin's body literally flies apart with the ecstasy of love making. But it also added layers to the narrative, which was a play within a play, a representation with objects of a story being read by an actor within a play. But it also added a through-line with a storytelling tradition, modern fiction, and postmodern theatre.

Many international theatre collaborations, and certainly nearly all of the international collaborations that receive acclaim in the international press, spring from companies based in Western Europe and the United States. The reason for this is simple: these projects cost a great deal of money, and the US and many European countries have the kind of funds needed for such projects available at their disposal. The exception to this is Japan. The Japan Foundation provides funding for individual artists and theatre companies to collaborate abroad. The list of projects is long, including avant-garde performer/writer/director Kara Jūrō (1940–) who has collaborated with colleagues in South Korea, Hirata Oriza (1962–) who has collaborated with playwrights in South Korea and China, and Satoshi Miyagi (1959–) who collaborated with Korean Jung Yang Ung on a production of *The Trojan Women* in 2005. In 1999 Noda Hideki mounted a Thai-language play *Akaoni* at the Setagaya Public Theatre with Thai actors. For companies based in the global south, the costs involved are prohibitive.

There have been several projects featuring companies from all over Asia. Meng Jinghui (1966–), an avant-garde director from the National Theatre of China, collaborated with Felix Ching Ching Ho at the Malthouse Theatre in Melbourne to stage Bertolt Brecht's (1898–1956) *Der gute Mensch von Sezuan* (*The Good Person of Szechwan*, 1943) in 2014, featuring burlesque entertainer Moira Finucane. Zuni Icosahedron, a company based in Hong Kong, frequently collaborates with artists from Shanghai and Taipei. Zuni Icosahedron's director Danny Yung (1943–) invited artists from Bangkok, Jakarta, Taipei, and Nanjing to create *The Book of Ghosts* in 2009, a performance that involved dance and theatre forms from each of the different cultures on the theme of ghosts.

Groups in Africa have also collaborated with each other, most notably the Handspring Puppet Company from South Africa and the Sogolon Puppet Company from Mali. We discussed Handspring's work on *Ubu and the Truth Commission* in Chapter 5. In 2004, the two companies collaborated on *Tall Horse*, the story of the journey of the giraffe from Sudan given to the King of France by the Viceroy of Egypt in 1827.

Theatre groups have found common political goals such as the Jana Natya Manch company in New Delhi and the Freedom Theatre in West Bank, Palestine. The directors of the two companies, Sudhanva Deshpande (1967–) and Faisal Abu Alhayjaa, respectively, collaborated on the street performance *Hamesha Sameida* (*Forever Steadfast*) in 2015. The play featured scenes in Arabic and Hindi on the theme of Palestinian identity. The two groups found common cause in addressing political oppression; as Alhayjaa noted: "We, Palestinians, have a special relationship with India. People here know what it means to live under oppression, especially the older generation. We are fighting for freedom just like you did. We have learnt about Gandhi and his resistance" (Modi).

Perhaps one of the most fascinating international collaborators is director Ong Keng Sen (1963–) from Singapore. Singapore has a fascinating history as a multicultural city-state in South Asia. Initially settled by Sumatran people, the island of Temasek became a refuge for fleeing princes of the Srivijaya empire after being overrun by Singhasari forces from Java. The Srivijaya prince Sang Nila Utama renamed Temasek the Kingdom of Singapura (Lion City) in the fourteenth century. Although it became an important port for trade in medieval times, fighting over the territory caused a decline in population after the fourteenth century and the island remained relatively obscure. It was absorbed into the Johor Sultanate (now Malaysia) to the north.

In the nineteenth century, Thomas Stanford Raffles negotiated with Johor on behalf of the British East India Company for the island. Singapore became one of the Straits Settlements, along with other coastal cities on the Malay Peninsula under the administration of British India. Raffles had made Singapore a free port where trade duties were not collected, and trade on the island soon reached a brisk pace. This drew people from the South Asian islands including ethnic Chinese who had immigrated to Malaysia centuries before and were assimilated into Malaysian culture. It also drew traders from China, India, and the Arab countries. Singapore continued to grow in importance on the world map as steamships quickened the pace of transoceanic trade.

The Japanese occupied Singapore during World War II. The British had been unable to defend the island. The Japanese renamed the island *Shōnan-tō*, which means "Light of the South Island," and massacred thousands of Chinese people. After World War II, Singapore began pushing for self-rule. It was made a Crown Colony in 1947, and then achieved self-governance partially in 1955 and fully in 1959. Many in Singapore initially thought being part of Malaysia would be ideal since Singapore is so small and lacks its own natural resources. Singapore citizens elected to merge in 1963. However, by this time the population in Singapore had a majority of Chinese citizens who resented the Malaysian government's preferential treatment of ethnic Malay. The ethnic tension and resulting riots in Singapore prompted the Malaysian government to formally expel Singapore in 1965.

The People's Action Party dominate the political scene in Singapore. The government has a long history of persecuting anyone suspected of communist sympathies and policing culture against "indecency." However, the center-left Worker's Party made significant gains in the 2011 general election. The strict rules about political protest and indecency mean ongoing censorship in the Singapore theatre. And although the government subsidizes the arts, the funding tends to go to groups that promote the government ideal of the Singapore nation.

Melissa Wensin Wong outlines a few instances where the government has directly stifled innovative theatre in the last forty years. In 1993, Alvin Tan and Haresh Sharma (1965–) returned from a Brecht Forum in New York and created a piece using Augusto Boal's Forum Theatre techniques. Joseph Ng created a performance art piece called *Brother Cane* to protest homophobic press coverage of a criminal case involving gay men entrapped by police and then caned as punishment. The government shut down both and Ng was arrested. The ministries of Home Affairs and of Information and the Arts put out a joint statement restricting improvisational theatre. The *Straits Times* reported that the government ministers were concerned that:

> new art forms such as "performance art" and "forum theatre" which have no script and encourage spontaneous audience participation pose dangers to public order, security and decency, and much greater difficulty to the licensing authority. "The performances may be exploited to agitate the audience on volatile social issues, or to propagate the beliefs and messages of deviant social or religious groups, or as a means of subversion," the [Ministries'] statement said.
>
> (*Straits Times*, 22 January 1994)

The ministries ruled that the National Arts Council of Singapore could not fund improvisational work such as Forum Theatre or Performance Art and Ng was barred from ever performing again. Censorship and self-censorship continues to stifle the arts in Singapore.

Ong Keng Sen creates pieces that reflect the ethnically and linguistically diverse landscape of Singapore. Together with his company TheatreWorks, Sen has explored *King Lear* twice. In 1997, Sen collaborated with Japanese playwright and director Rio Kishida (1946–2003) to mount *Lear*. Kishida is best known for her plays that focus on women struggling within a patriarchal system, an issue both artists wanted to address in the Lear story. In *Lear*, Kishida combined *noh* theatre, *Jīngjù*, Burmese puppets, Thai dance, Indonesian martial art, and Korean music interspersed with *gamelan*. The script was in Japanese, Thai, English, Chinese, and Indonesian and the piece toured to Hong Kong, Australia, Japan, Indonesia, and Europe. Sen revisited Lear again in 2012 with *Lear Dreaming*, changing some of the components, but with the same *noh* actor Umewaka Naohiko in the role of Lear.

In 2003, Sen collaborated with performers from Japan and Australia to create *Sandakan Threnody* about the Sandakan Death Marches of Australian and British prisoners of war by the Japanese in World War II. The piece used digital media, dance, and theatre and was based on the war crimes trial records and survivor accounts. Sen also participated in Zuni Icosahedron's *One Table, Two Chairs* festival in Hong Kong in 1998 with his performance of *Eat Me*, a meditation on world hunger.

That Sen often relies on Asian traditional performance and occasionally uses it to reconfigure European classics such as *King Lear*, has raised many questions for Sen. In his 2001 article "Encounters," Sen ponders:

> I wonder: Am I using traditional arts only to gain personal recognition for my own projects? Am I buying "Asian art" just like Europeans and Americans before, fascinated by otherness? Am I the new colonizer in Asian disguise, vested with the financial strength and confidence of Singapore? Are *Lear* and *Desdemona* the new Peter Brook *Mahabharata*? Who owns the work? Does it belong to the persons who paid for it or the persons who created it? But who created it? Do I appropriate the work of other artists? So many questions with no answers.

(129)

Sen feels he is in danger of appropriating traditions and constantly examines the ethics of using forms that he feels are not his own. However, I would argue that his self-aware use of form, his conscious employment of tradition, and his sensitive collaboration with artists from those traditions make his work truly reflective of the dynamic of cultural exchange and cultural change.

One of Sen's more recent projects, *Fear of Writing* (2011) written by Tan Tarn How, focuses on the absurdity of doing theatre under Singapore's oppressive censorship. The play continues their earlier collaboration on plays on similar themes, such as *The First Emperor's Last Days* (1998), which features four writers who are assigned the task of writing a biography of a country's first ruler; however, they are writing while imprisoned and under continual surveillance.

CITY DIONYSIA: INTERNATIONAL THEATRE FESTIVALS AND NETWORKS

I think it is worth mentioning here the role played by international theatre festivals in the exchange of practices and ideas. Theatre festivals occur all over the world and have often brought people from different cultures together throughout history. Huge theatre ruins throughout the Middle East, the Mediterranean, and Europe are a testament to the crowds that would come to watch days of dramatic competition. In the twenty-first century, theatre festivals continue to provide opportunities to learn about the theatrical forms practiced in other countries.

Although festivals tend to draw artists regionally, since traveling overseas is often too expensive for companies from poorer countries, some do successfully draw people from other continents. The Festival Internacional de Teatro that happens each September in Nicaragua principally hosts artists from Latin America, but sometimes draws groups from Europe and the United States. The Centro Latinoamericano de Creación e Investigación Teatral (Latin American Center for Theatre Creation and Research) has produced the festival for over fifteen years.

The International Arts Carnival in Hong Kong brings together practitioners of theatre for young audiences every year. It has hosted companies from China, Taiwan, Korea, Australia, the UK, countries from continental Europe, Canada, Peru, and the US. The Israeli group the Train Theatre hosts the International Festival of Puppet Theatre every year in Jerusalem. Puppet practitioners come from all over Europe and from countries like India and China. European countries host dozens of street theatre festivals such as the well-known festival at Avignon (where Peter Brook's *The Mahabharata* had its premiere), but there are street theatre festivals in other parts of the world as well. One of the largest festivals outside of Europe is the HI Seoul Festival in South Korea. Along with Korean street theatre companies, recent festival events have drawn groups from Spain, France, the Netherlands, Vietnam, and Brazil.

The Internet has made communicating between groups and individual artists easier than ever, and digital tools such as streaming and video calls have given rise to unprecedented real-time collaboration across the globe. One organization that has expanded with the digital age is the Magdalena Project, an international network of women theatre practitioners. Originally conceived by women in Italy and Wales in the 1980s, the network's regular gatherings "jumped the pond" (crossed the Atlantic) for the first time in 1988 with a gathering featuring women from Peru, Colombia, and Uruguay. By the end of the century, the Magdalena Project had three official subgroups in Wales, Argentina, and Aotearoa/New Zealand. The network continues to grow, with subgroups forming in other countries in Europe, Brazil, Peru, Cuba, Colombia, and Australia, and events being hosted in Singapore and India. The network also includes individual artists from places like Egypt, Mali, Algeria, Turkey, Israel, South Korea, China, Taiwan, and Indonesia. The Magdalena Project continues to generate dialogue about issues important to women in the theatre with regular gatherings happening several times a year.

CONCLUSION: THE UNDISCOVERED COUNTRY

The digital age has made the world smaller in terms of time and distance, but it has also made the world richer in terms of the potential for deeper understanding. In the twentieth century, people in the industrialized world had television and newspapers for current events and sets of encyclopedias for more comprehensive information about the world. You could send letters, and the people with ample resources could travel. The Internet connected people in the 1980s, but it was not until the birth of the World Wide Web in 1989 that the Internet became a meaningful tool for people who were not necessarily tech literate. Even in developing nations, the tech boom has changed the lives of millions of people. Tech companies have established several organizations to aid schools and civic groups through gifts of computers and "smart" mobile phones in order to allow children in the developing world to have access to information. Wireless technology has allowed many places to "skip" the infrastructure that was necessary for old telephone and computer modem technology.

The end of the Cold War between communist countries such as the Soviet Union and China and the capitalist countries of Western Europe and the United States has allowed many travel barriers to come down. Trade agreements have led to freer commercial activity between countries, although globalization has had many negative consequences for working people and the environment. It has also spurred the migration of people to find work. Clashes with extremists and civil war between ethnic groups have pushed people to flee and find refuge in other countries. Migration, economic globalization, and technology will continue to alter the landscape of the theatre throughout the world. The future of world theatre then involves questions about the very nature of theatre and about the use and preservation of unique cultural practices.

We began this textbook by defining "theatre." And while theatre takes many forms, scholars and practitioners agree that theatre involves a narrative performed live for spectators by live actors in a given space. Recall Peter Brook's famous statement: "A man walks across this empty space whilst someone else is watching him, and this is all that is needed for an act of theatre to be engaged" (*The Empty Space* 9). And many people agree that people using objects such as puppets is also live theatre. Mediated forms such as television and cinema have much in common with theatre, in fact they can be filmed or televised theatre performances, but they are not, in and of themselves, theatre. Experiments in using technology on stage challenge the idea of liveness.

Motion-capture animation has already stirred controversy in the film industry; Anthony Serkis has played several roles where animation was added to his motion-captured acting. In each instance, adjudicators have been confused or divided on whether he was eligible for acting awards. Motion-capture animation has been used to create characters manipulated by actors moving on stage such as Mocomotion's Theatre of Animation in Brisbane in Australia.

The use of robots will continue to raise questions about the nature of acting. In 2009, the Seinendan Theater Company in Tokyo began collaborating with the Osaka University Robot Theater Project to create *Sayonara* and *I, Worker* which they performed until 2013. In 2014, they collaborated again using French actors for *La Metamorphose Version Androide*, a version of Franz Kafka's *Metamorphosis,* but with the main character turning into a robot instead of a cockroach. The last play was especially interesting to critics in that a robot played the main character and not just an incidental role.

Holograms, too, have made stage appearances. Initially, they have been used in music acts, such as the hologram of the deceased Tupac Shakur performing "live" with Snoop Dogg and Dr. Dre at the Coachella music festival in California in 2012. Even fictional holographic characters have become pop stars, such as Hatsune Miku in Japan. The character had released songs beginning in 2007, but appeared as a hologram for a concert in 2010. In the theatre, the

South African director and composer Adam Donen created *Symphony to a Lost Generation* in 2016 in the UK to memorialize World War I. The opera contained over 400 holograms of performers from around the world.

It makes sense that some would fear that theatre might disappear completely. However, people thought cinema and television would replace theatre, and they have not. Certainly, attendance at the so-called legitimate theatre has declined as people find other forms of narrative entertainment. But, in most parts of the world, the desire for human beings to gather never ceases. People seek each other out to celebrate, to protest, and to memorialize, and these acts often produce narrative performances by actors for spectators.

Technology will not erase theatre. It will be employed in the theatre to varying degrees for a wide range of reasons. Oriza Hirata (1962–), the director of the Seinendan Theater Company, hopes to find a "contemporary colloquial theatre," a new theatre not modeled on European forms and styles:

> Our strategy is to critically reconsider existing theatrical theories and to reconstruct delicate and dramatic space on stage. We believe that we can create such a space by basing our theater on the Japanese language and life style, while at the same time creating a new theatrical language which is a unified form of both written and spoken language.
>
> ("About Seinendan")

Hirata is not attempting to replace theatre or even to replace actors, but to make something new rooted in what is Japanese, and what is Japanese right now, and that means finding and combining new tools.

THE REVOLUTION WILL BE TELEVISED: SOCIAL MEDIA AND THE ARAB SPRING

Another digital revolution has come to us in the form of social media. There are few places in the world social media has not touched, with users in China, India, Brazil, Turkey, Saudi Arabia, and even islands like Fiji and remote villages in Nunavut above the Arctic Circle. Research already shows that social media does not replace live contact, but actually enhances and complements face-to-face interaction. In the theatre world, Facebook has become a dominant player in advertising performances, announcing auditions, and posting photographs of events. Social media has also played a role in political activism and the theatre that springs from the push for social change.

Much has been made of the use of social media in what has been called the Arab Spring. Political upheaval escalated in the Arab world beginning in 2010 in Tunisia. Oppressive dictatorships, economic problems, and a new generation of educated young people inspired by popular uprisings throughout history all contributed to the uprisings throughout the Middle East and North Africa. However, in the aftermath, only Tunisia has successfully transitioned to a democratic government. Protesters managed to cause the government to be overthrown in Egypt, Yemen, and Libya, but three nations – Syria, Iraq, and Libya – were plunged into civil war. In other countries, the protests were either quickly put down by the government, or the government made a few key political changes that satisfied enough people to neutralize the movement.

In both Tunisia and Egypt, many of the activists were active on social media. The regimes of both countries were rather ineffectual at monitoring social media. Witnesses posted images and videos of atrocities and demonstrations, and used social media to organize and publicize events. Social media also gave a window to the world on what was happening on the ground. Social media did not cause the political movements, but it acted as a platform to quickly disseminate information and enabled public expression that was otherwise forbidden in the other public spheres.

Certainly, there are aspects of any protest that are theatrical or have elements of a theatre performance. However, being mindful of the tendency to reduce everything to theatre or to dismiss the complexity of the Middle East political crisis of this decade by viewing it as theatre, I want to turn to two examples analyzed in the *Theatre Research International* special issue from 2013 edited by Egyptian scholar Hazem Azmy and US scholar Marvin Carlson. In politically repressive regimes where theatre is heavily censored, performers use private spaces for small performances, or they perform outside of the country, or they use digital platforms and social media to disseminate their work.

Edward Ziter chronicles the work of Ahmed and Mohammad Malas, twins who are clown performers and were active members of the resistance in Syria. The twins already had a large following on YouTube and Facebook where they posted several webisodes, but their work turned decidedly anti-Assad as opposition to the regime mounted in 2011. They began performing their short play *Tomorrow's Revolution Postponed to Yesterday*, about a conversation between a police officer and a jailed protester, in private homes and abroad. The brothers were arrested with other writers and artists (including their uncle Mohammad Malas, a celebrated filmmaker) after participating in a march against the regime. They performed *Tomorrow's Revolution Postponed to Yesterday* twice in the prison for their fellow prisoners. But the guards and officers supportive of the regime also watched the play. Of one of the officers, the brothers noted: "The police officer objected, saying that our criticisms of the regime were too harsh, but we asked him to try to take it lightly and continue watching" (interview quoted in Elali).

The Malas twins developed a new piece using two characters from their earlier piece *Melodrama* (2009). *Najim and Abu Hamlet in the Shadow of the Revolution* features two characters, Najim and Abu, who were extras in a production of *Hamlet*. They posted the play in three webisodes. In the reworking, the actors are stuck in their tiny apartment, relegated to insignificance by their circumstances. But their existential isolation becomes a real isolation as the appearance of tanks to put down the uprising makes leaving physically impossible as well. Not long after the brothers posted the webisodes, they were forced to flee, first to Egypt, then France, for fear of being detained or killed. When the threat of bodily harm prevented them from performing their work publicly, the brothers used social media to share revolutionary theatre with fellow activists at home and around the world.

In activist theatre, people put their bodies on the line, both on stage and on the stage of the public square. They tell their stories, they mourn those who have perished, they voice their demand for justice. Theatre can also serve the function of reflecting on revolutions in the aftermath. During the actions in the Arab world, protesters compiled hours of video footage and hundreds of thousands of images. These images were not just posted to social media, but have returned to real time in theatre pieces that examine the events they depict.

For Egyptian writer and performer Dalia Basiouny, images of Tahrir Square and the events leading up to the revolution spark her search for her identity in *Solitaire* (2011). The work was performed initially as part of *Tahrir Stories*, a series of monologues to document the Egyptian revolution through testimonies of the demonstrators, and to honor those who had died in a community ritual. The story follows Basiouny's autobiographical character Nora. The images move from her life in New York, where she is faced with anti-Arab sentiment before and after the attacks of 9/11, to her decision to return to Cairo to take part in the protests. The images include offensive caricatures of Arabs, the destruction of the World Trade Center and the photos of missing people on the walls in New York, the Israeli siege of Ramallah, the bombs falling on Baghdad, and then images of the protests in Tahrir Square.

Basiouny's Nora, initially depressed over the events in the new millennium, finds inspiration in the events she witnesses on television and decides to join her fellow Egyptians. The protests in Tahrir Square transform the space from city landmark to a communal reconfiguration and contestation of the nation:

> Tahrir Square is a spiritual place.
> Where the most positive energy on the planet exists at the moment.
> Just as coal is purified under intense pressure,
> And becomes a diamond.
> Now, Tahrir is sparkling more than any diamond ring. A Solitaire!
> With the light of the revolution, the energy of change, the souls
>   of the martyrs.

Basiouny's solitaire diamond stands for temperance under pressure, a pressure that creates nations, but also transforms human beings. She continues to recount the actions of the people, but also the brutal repression that resulted. She gives the audience a vision of people united, recognizing each other as actors of change in bringing about a new Egypt.

Even then, Basiouny did not have any illusions that the social transition will be easy. Nora says at the end of the play:

> Unfortunately, the Arab Spring turned into a nightmare in many
>   places.
> And I wonder, who wants to keep all these people in the dark
>   ages?

Who benefits from that?
But that's another long story.
What I know is that the change has already started,
And no power can stop it.
We don't live in the same world anymore.
2011 was just the beginning,
The revolution is NOT over.
It is just starting.

And so is the discussion taking place in the forum of the theatre.

Not only did Basiouny use images from television and from the Internet for this performance, but during the protests Basiouny gathered images and video. She posted on blogs to report the events in Tahrir Square. At one point, she live-streamed the events of the protest. These images were then projected onto actors at CultureHub in Greenwich Village in New York. Basiouny's role in her own play, then, is that of the balladeer, memorializing the events of the revolution, but also that of the provocateur, pushing people to think and act beyond what has happened, urging them to follow through to the next step. As she stated in an interview: "For me, art and expression are an integral part of the revolutionary process, not just in mobilizing, but reflecting" (interview quoted in El Nabawi). The feedback loop between digital media and performance, protest and the Internet allows them to feed each other in the movement toward social change.

In the face of such turbulent change, what is the future of world theatre? Amid social unrest, mass migration, the importation of foreign culture through the Internet, and globalization, are there theatrical traditions that are in danger? The answer is always "yes." And in some ways that is the beauty of theatre. It happens and it is gone, and even the record of it on social media does not last forever, quickly covered with an avalanche of other images, messages, and performances. Should we do something about it? We cannot.

I am reminded of a walk I took through the ruins of the theatre at Epidaurus in Greece. I was struck not just by the palimpsest of cultures that had built onto the facility there, which was a place of healing, a spa dedicated to the god Asklepios, but by attempts to preserve what was there. The spa, built by Greeks before the fourth century BCE and then used by the Romans, sat next to the ancient theatre of Epidaurus, built in the fourth century BCE and then doubled in size over the next five hundred years. It sits next to the ruins of a fourth century CE Christian basilica, by the modern town of Ligurio. The theatre was forgotten for centuries, until archaeologists uncovered it in 1881 and then began to renovate it. In the twenty-first century, renovations continue, sometimes to rectify the damage done by earlier renovations done incorrectly. A balance is struck – let the ruin be a ruin, or try to restore what we think it might have been.

It is the same problem when we think about culture in general, and about theatre specifically, partly because we have so much less evidence, no actual *ruins* to help us reconstruct a tradition. Regardless, recreating a tradition means *re*-creating it – making something in the current moment that says more about who we are now than it does about who we might have been then. Ong Keng Sen muses in the program for his first production of *Lear*:

> Time constantly forces us to recontextualize. Ultimately, we need to recognize that there may be no such dichotomy of tradition and modern. We simply journey on this time-line . . . . Tradition has continued to include change, in order to sustain its relevance. Change is not to be feared. It is only the societies that have mythicized tradition into a stable phenomenon. Tradition is perhaps best seen as a continuum rather than as a monolith. The rigid meaning of tradition has little significance in the world of the twenty-first century where walls are breaking down.
>
> ("Director's Message")

World theatre is a lived tradition. It changes, it grows, it disappears. It incites, it entertains, and it tells us something about who we are and where we hope we are going.

GLOSSARY

Abhinaya   In classical Indian dance-drama, it is the performance, which is made up of gestures, words, costume and makeup, and the representation of emotion or states.

Abydos Passion Play   The title given to the ritual at Abydos, Egypt, about Horus recapturing the throne from Seth after resurrecting his father Osiris whom Seth had killed and dismembered. The practice dates from around 2600 up to the fifth century BCE, and was long thought to be the first known instance of theatre.

Aesthetics   The underlying set of ideas about art and beauty in each culture.

Alarinjo   Yoruba performance in western Africa that evolved out of the *egungun* festivals of the Oyo kingdom. It involved musicians and masked performers and eventually influenced the development of Yoruba Opera.

Aniconism   A prohibition, usually religious, against creating images of humans and other living things.

Antagonist   The character in a story that works against the main character, sometimes called the "villain."

Aragoto   The "rough style" acting used in *kabuki* with energetic movement, exaggerated and colorful makeup, and enlarged costumes.

Atoza   The rear part of the stage in Japanese *noh* theatre where the musicians sit.

Autos sacramentales   Spanish plays on religious themes written during medieval times and into the seventeenth century.

Avant-garde   Anything that is new to the point that it changes the way people behave toward or think differently about how things have been done in the past. Meaning "the front guard," like the first row of soldiers in combat, it usually means art that breaks the rules of that art form and challenges the given aesthetics of the time.

Balladeer A storyteller who conveys a narrative through music.

Bashira The corner post on the stage in the Japanese *noh* theatre.

Bhava The emotional state, either dominant or transitory, the actor seeks to convey through performance in classical Indian dance-drama, in order to elicit a specific *rasa* or "taste" in the spectator.

Blocking Prescribed movement of the actors on the stage.

Bunraku The Japanese puppet theatre that began in the seventeenth century and shares many elements (such as plays and music) with the *kabuki* theatre.

Burlesque Originally pertaining to comic performances with exaggerated caricatures that satirized well-known art or public figures, the modern meaning includes variety show entertainers of various kinds, bawdy humor, and occasionally, striptease acts.

Butoh Avant-garde Japanese dance created in the late 1950s in order to resist the traditional Japanese aesthetic of refinement and to incorporate the movement of ordinary people into dance.

Catharsis A Greek word to denote the purging of undesirable emotion or impulses, to be experienced after watching the downfall of the protagonist in classical Greek tragedy.

Character Usually the person that an actor pretends to be on stage for the benefit of an audience, however, the role played by an actor may be based on a real person (Marsinah in *Marsinah Accuses*), a mythical or fictional person (Pa Ubu in *Ubu and the Truth Commission*), a non-human being (Monkey or Nanabush in *The Rez Sisters*), or any concept (Death or Fire).

Chŏu The clown roles, such as Sūn Wùkōng the Monkey, in Jīngjù (Beijing Opera) performance.

Community-based theatre Performance that is done using community members as actors and writers, often to help the community address issues that matter to them.

Corroboree An Australian Aboriginal gathering for music and dance that may take the form of a ritual or a celebration.

Costumbrista A form of theatre created in Latin America at the beginning of the twentieth century that features, and often lampooned the foibles of, typical middle-class, and recognizably Latin American characters.

Cycle plays   Performances that cover loosely related chapters of an epic, often used to refer to the drama of stories in the Bible performed during medieval times in Europe.

Dalang   The puppeteer of various *wayang* traditions in Indonesia who controls every aspect of the *wayang* performance.

Dàn   The female roles, usually played by male actors, in Jīngjù (Beijing Opera) performance.

Dance-drama   A form of theatre that involves choreographed movement (dance), a narrative (drama), and music.

Deigan   In Japanese *noh* drama, the mask of a female character who is turning evil through her repressed jealousy.

Dengaku   Harvest dances from rural Japan that influence Japanese *noh* drama.

Didjerridu   The name given by Europeans to the wooden wind instrument used by Aboriginal Australians that was created between 1000 and 1500 years ago. Today, Aboriginal people use the word along with their own various native words for it.

Dreaming   Also called "Dreamtime," the creation of the world, according to Aboriginal Australian cosmology, and the formless space of the spirit world to which we all return.

Egungun   The Yoruba ritual honoring the ancestors where otherworldly spirits communicate with us through untouchable masked dancers and send a breeze of blessing through the twirling of the flaps of the dancers' costumes.

Etu ritual   A Yoruba ceremony to honor the ancestors that continues to tie Yoruba people of western Africa with Yoruba people of the African diaspora, in particular Nigeria and Jamaica. The word "etu" comes from the Yoruba word "etutu," meaning atonement.

Forum Theatre   A kind of participatory drama devised by Brazilian Augusto Boal to help community members work through pressing problems and to empower them to make changes in their circumstances.

Fuebashira   The "flute pillar," or the stage pillar closest to the flute player, in Japanese *noh* drama.

Gamelan   An ensemble made up of a variety of mostly percussion instruments that play traditional Indonesian music. This music accompanies the *wayang* traditions as well as traditional Indonesian dance-drama.

Genzai   A type of *noh* drama that involves characters and situations in the real world.

Glee   Songs that accompany the *alarinjo* performance, in particular the "opening glee," which introduces the actors and the performance, and the "closing glee," a triumphant finale.

Guójù   The Chinese word for "national theatre," usually referring to the *Jīngjù* (Beijing Opera) as it is performed in Taiwan.

Hakawati   The Arabic word for "storyteller," someone who narrates stories using different voices for characters and dramatic gestures.

Hamartia   A Greek word that literally means "missing the mark," used to describe an excessive trait of the protagonist (such as pride) that brings about his or her downfall. Used in analyzing classical Greek tragedy, but also used to analyze character and plot in contemporary drama as well.

Hana   The Japanese word for "flower," used to describe a *noh* actor of exquisite skill, an ability that is not immediately apparent, but excites the spectator because of the actor's concentration, spirit, and artistry to create a sense of novelty rooted in tradition.

Hanamichi   The Japanese word for "flower path," and the name of the bridge that extends out into the audience in *kabuki* theatre.

Hannya   A mask in Japanese *noh* theatre used for a woman who has been transformed into a vengeful demon after repressing her jealousy.

Hashigakari   In Japanese *noh* theatre, the bridge from the actors' preparation room to the stage, figuratively connecting the supernatural world with the mundane.

Hauka   An African ritual involving spirit possession practiced by the Hausa and Songhay people, unique in that it involves possession by European spirits. The possessed people would behave like the colonial administrators and soldiers and speak in a mix of indigenous and European languages.

Hubris   A Greek work meaning excessive pride, which often leads to the downfall of the protagonist.

Ikhernofret Stela   The stone that contains the account by Ikhernofret of his participation in the ritual drama at Abydos, previously thought to be the first account of a theatrical event.

Jidaimono   A type of *kabuki* or *bunraku* play dealing with historical events and characters.

Jìng   Roles in *Jīngjù* (Beijing Opera) of warriors and demons that have elaborate makeup.

Jīngjù   The Chinese word meaning "capital theatre," which English speakers call "Beijing Opera." It is a form of performance that involves elaborate costume and makeup and often features acrobatics from the *chǒu* characters such as Sūn Wùkōng, the Monkey.

Jiutaiza   The part of the stage in Japanese *noh* theatre where the chorus, or *jiutai*, sits on stage left (the left as the actor faces the audience).

Jōruri   Japanese storytelling song accompanied by the *shamisen* (a stringed instrument). The puppet theatre *bunraku* is narrated with *jōruri*.

Kalarippayattu   A form of martial art from the Indian state of Kerala. Many *kathakali* actors train in this form.

Kata   The Japanese word for "movement." *Kata* is a series of movements performed by actors in both *noh* and *kabuki*.

Kathakali   A form of ritual dance-drama from Kerala in India, begun in the seventeenth century, that focuses on the epic stories from the *Ramayana* and the *Mahabharata*.

Kayon   The "tree-of-life" puppet used in the shadow puppet *wayang kulit* tradition in Indonesia. The *kayon* is used to open the performance, to indicate scene changes, and to represent buildings, forces of nature, or war.

Kazuramono   A category of Japanese *noh* plays about female spirits and graceful women and which usually involve a graceful dance.

Kiri No   The fast-paced ending plays in Japanese *noh* theatre, often involving demons and animals.

Krishnattam   A form of ritual dance-drama from Kerala in India, begun in the seventeenth century, similar to *kathakali*, but dealing specifically with the life of Krishna.

Kuchipudi   A form of ritual dance-drama from Andhra Pradesh, India, begun during the fourteenth through sixteenth centuries as a devotion to Krishna, and marked by energetic dancing.

Kusemai   A Japanese dance form popular from the fourteenth through the sixteenth centuries involving a dancer who recites the narrative while dancing to musical accompaniment. The music of *kusemai* influenced the music for *noh* theatre.

Kutiyattam One of the earliest forms of Sanskrit dance-drama from Kerala in India and one of the principal influences of *kathakali.*

Kyōgen The name of short comic plays featuring common characters in the Japanese *noh* theatre.

Marae The meeting house in the Māori culture where important ritual and civic gatherings take place.

Mawari-butai The revolving stage on the Japanese *kabuki* stage.

Metsukebashira The "sight" pillar on the Japanese *noh* stage, or the pillar that serves as a landmark for *noh* actors.

Mie The Japanese word for "appearance," a freeze after the vigorous movement of the *kata* in *kubuki*, used to highlight the moment on stage.

Mise-en-scène The way in which the creative team, usually a director, stages a particular play, including the design elements, the place, and the time period.

Monogurui No A category in Japanese *noh* theatre involving characters who are driven mad, usually by grief.

Monomane The Japanese word for "imitation," used by Zeami to specify the extent to which an actor should imitate a person depending on the particular kind of character.

Mugen "Fantasy" plays in Japanese *noh* theatre that involve supernatural characters.

Natyasastra The text written sometime between 200 BCE and 200 CE attributed to the master Bharata Muni, dictating the performance of and training for Sanskrit dance-drama.

Nine-Nights ceremony A Caribbean celebration of the life of someone recently deceased, as in a "wake." On the ninth night, the spirit of the deceased gathers food from the party and says goodbye to the living.

Ningyō Jōruri Another way of saying *bunraku,* the Japanese puppet theatre. *Jōruri* refers to the song that tells the story, and *ningyō* means "puppet."

Nirvahanam In classical Indian dance-drama, a solo performance, as in *kutiyattam,* that tells the audience the story up to the point that the drama begins.

Noh The Japanese theatre form begun in the fourteenth century by Kan'ami (1333–1384) as a fusion of several forms, including the music of *kusemai*, the theatre of *sarugaku*, and the harvest dances of *dengaku*.

Nohgaku The tradition of Japanese *noh* and *kyōgen* passed down for generations.

Nuevo Teatro Popular Political theatre in Latin America to organize workers and push for social change using popular theatre forms such as circus, street theatre, and musical performance.

Okina The blessing that begins a night of *noh* theatre entertainment in Japan.

Omote Wooden masks worn by actors in Japanese *noh* theatre.

Onnagata Female roles in Japanese *kabuki* theatre played by male actors.

Oshiroi The white makeup used as a base in Japanese *kabuki* theatre but also denoting high class, noble spirit, and femininity.

Plot The part of a story that is taken up in a play.

Poorvangam Originally a ritual to pay homage to the gods before a performance in classical Indian dance-drama; a prologue to introduce the play.

Presentational A style of theatre not attempting to imitate life, rather the actors often address the audience and involve the audience in the action, or otherwise acknowledge that they are part of a performance.

Proscenium A kind of theatre where the audience sits on only one side of a stage and often separated from the stage by a framing arch.

Protagonist The main character whose struggles are the main focus of a drama.

Punakawan The clown servant characters in Javanese *wayang kulit*. Similar characters appear in other *wayang* traditions under different names.

Puranas The Hindu stories that are older than the classical epics of the *Ramayana* and the *Mahabharata*, but contain many stories that are later included in those epics.

Ramlila The Sanskrit word for "play about Rama," it is the festival of dramatic performance about the lives of Rama from the epic the *Ramayana*.

Rasa Literally meaning "taste," it is the sensation the performer seeks to arouse in the spectator of Indian classical dance-drama.

Ravana Chhaya Meaning "the Shadow of Ravana," who is the enemy of Rama, it is a form of shadow puppetry from the state of Odisha, in India, dating back over a thousand years and focusing on stories from the *Ramayana*.

Realism Popularized at the end of the nineteenth century in Europe, theatre where the artists are attempting to imitate real life, with realistic settings, characters, and events, as well as actions that reflect the psychological depth of the character.

Regional theatre A professional theatre company, usually non-profit, that generally draws an audience, funding, and talent from a region, or that operates independently of touring productions from a theatrical center, such as New York. In the United States, many regional companies are part of the League of Resident Theatres and are located in cities such as Cleveland, Denver, Atlanta, and Seattle.

Ritual drama Theatrical presentations that are traditionally part of a religious rite or celebration, such as *egungun* or *Rabinal Achí*.

Ritual-to-theatre model An outdated historical paradigm popularized in the early twentieth century that suggested theatre evolved from ritual, that such evolution was inherent in all cultures and was linear, and that European civilization was the pinnacle of such an evolution.

Sanskrit drama The earliest theatrical presentations in India based on the classical Indian epics the *Ramayana* and the *Mahabharata*, or using contemporary characters and situations. The aesthetic ideals for training and performance for Sanskrit drama are laid out in the *Natyasastra* and the performance of it influenced the development of classical Indian dance-drama, such as *kathakali*.

Sarugaku A Japanese comic theatre tradition from the eleventh through fourteenth centuries that included acrobatics, which later influenced the *noh* drama and, especially, *kyōgen*.

Sewamono A genre of Japanese *kabuki* and *bunraku* drama based on contemporary characters and situations.

Shamisen A Japanese three-stringed musical instrument used to accompany the Japanese *bunraku* theatre.

Shēng The male roles in *Jīngjù* (Beijing Opera).

Shichisan The "seven-three" position on the *hanamichi* in Japanese *kabuki* theatre, the spot seven-tenths on the way to the stage, where actors may pause to show their great skill.

Shingeki A contemporary Japanese theatre, started by *kabuki* actors at the beginning of the twentieth century to break out of the strictures of classical theatre and incorporate more European styles into productions, such as realism.

Shite The main character in Japanese *noh* theatre.

Shitebashira The pillar on the Japanese *noh* theatre stage associated with the main character.

Shosagoto The genre of dance plays in Japanese *kabuki* theatre.

Shozoku The outer robe worn by the actor in Japanese *noh* theatre, woven of a thick silk with elaborate embroidery.

Shura No The genre of plays about warriors and battles in the Japanese *noh* theatre.

Staged reading Where actors read a play aloud for an audience and include as much of the movement and technical elements (such as properties and costumes) as possible to give the spectator an idea of what the play would be like if it were fully staged. This is usually a part of the development of a new play, which involves little cost to the theatre company, but an opportunity for a playwright to test new material.

Stagehand Someone who assists backstage during a performance in moving properties and scenery and otherwise facilitates the smooth operation of the technical elements in the theatre.

Sthayi Bhava In Sanskrit dance-drama, it is the dominant state that the actor seeks to convey and that elicits a particular *rasa* or "taste" in the spectator.

Strike (the set) To dismantle the playing space, removing all partitions, furniture, properties, and costumes, in order to travel or to make room for different performance.

Suriashi The subtle sliding of the feet by the actor in Japanese *noh* theatre.

Ta'ziyeh The ritual mourning and reenactment of the martyrdom of Hussein by Shia Muslims, particularly in Iran.

Tabi The slippers worn on the feet of Japanese *noh* actors.

Theatre for Development Performance used to instruct community members about new issues or practices, or used to engage community members to talk about things that are important to them at the time.

Theatre-in-Education The use of theatre or theatrical elements in a classroom or with young spectators to teach them about various topics or help them develop certain skills.

Theatron The Greek word for "seeing place" and the name of the area where spectators sit in the classical Greek theatre (fifth and fourth centuries BCE).

Theme An idea that is central to a story (i.e. revenge, loyalty, injustice).

Township theatre Performances of plays written and acted by black South African residents of "townships" or reservations created by Apartheid policy. The performances involved *township music* and stories of life under Apartheid.

Waki The secondary character in Japanese *noh* theatre.

Wakibashira The pillar on the Japanese *noh* theatre stage associated with the secondary character.

Wayang Golek The puppet theatre of West Java in Indonesia, based on traditional Indian epics, but rooted in the Muslim religion.

Wayang Kulit The shadow puppet tradition in Indonesia, with puppets made of water buffalo hide, elaborately painted, and with articulated limbs, based on stories from the Indian epics.

Wayang Wong Meaning "person *wayang*," it is the Javanese dance-drama based on stories from the Indian epics, with variant forms in Bali.

Yugen The idea in Zeami's writing about Japanese *noh* theatre of the actor's grace or spiritual depth.

BIBLIOGRAPHY

"About Seinendan." Seinendan Theater Company 2010. www.seinendan.org/eng/about/. June 28, 2016.

Abramson, Glenda. *Encyclopedia of Modern Jewish Culture*. New ed. 2 vols. London: Routledge, 2005.

Adedeji, Joel. "'Alarinjo': The Traditional Yoruba Travelling Theatre." In Yemi Ogunbiyi, Ed. *Drama and Theatre in Nigeria: A Critical Source Book*. Lagos: Nigeria Magazine Publications, 1981.

Akhter, Afreen. "Sistren: The Vanguard of Popular Theater in Jamaica." *Signs* 33, no. 2 (2008): 431–436.

Amine, Khalid. "Re-Enacting Revolution and the New Public Sphere in Tunisia, Egypt and Morocco." *Theatre Research International* 38, Special Issue 02 (2013): 87–103.

Assmann, Jan. *Death and Salvation in Ancient Egypt*. Ithaca, NY: Cornell University Press, 2005.

Awasthi, Suresh. "The Intercultural Experience and the Kathakali King Lear." *New Theatre Quarterly* 9, no. 34 (1993): 72–78.

Azmy, Hazem, and Marvin Carlson. Eds. Special Issue "Theatre and the Arab Spring." *Theatre Research International* 38, no. 02 (2013).

Badawī, Muḥammad Muṣṭafá. *Early Arabic Drama*. New York: Cambridge University Press, 1988.

Banham, Martin. Ed. *A History of Theatre in Africa*. Cambridge: Cambridge University Press, 2004.

Banham, Martin, Errol Hill, and George William Woodyard. *The Cambridge Guide to African and Caribbean Theatre*. 1st pbk ed. Cambridge: Cambridge University Press, 2004.

Basiouny, Dalia. Solitaire. Arab Stages, 1:1 (Fall 2014). http://arabstages.org/2014/12/solitaire-an-egyptian-multimedia-performance/

Beaulieu, Germain. "Les Soirées de famille." *L'Annuaire théâtral*, Montréal, Geo. H. Robert éditeur, 1908–1909, pp. 59–60.

Beeman, William O. and Mohammad B. Ghaffari, "Acting Styles and Actor Training in Ta'ziyeh." *TDR* 49, no. 4, Special Issue on Ta'ziyeh (2005): 48–60.

Behrend, Heike, and Ute Luig. *Spirit Possession, Modernity and Power in Africa.* Madison: University of Wisconsin Press, 1999.

Beier, Ulli. "The Agbegijo Masqueraders." *Nigeria Magazine* 82 (1964): 188–199.

Bell, John. "Puppets, Masks, and Performing Objects at the End of the Century." in *Puppets, Masks, and Performing Objects.* Ed. John Bell. Cambridge: MIT Press, 1999.

Bell, John. "Islamic Performance and the Problem of Drama." *TDR* 49, no. 4, Special Issue on Ta'ziyeh (2005): 5–10.

Beverley, John. *Subalternity and Representation: Arguments in Cultural Theory.* Durham, NC: Duke University Press, 1999.

Bharata, Muni, and Manomohan Ghosh. *The Nāṭyasāstra: A Treatise on Ancient Indian Dramaturgy and Histrionics, Ascribed to Bharata Muni.* Bibliotheca Indica. 2 vols. Calcutta: Manisha Granthalaya, 1961.

Bharucha, Rustom. "Peter Brook's 'Mahabharata': A View from India." *Economic and Political Weekly* 23, no. 32 (1988): 1642–1647. www.jstor.org.proxy.lib.umich.edu/stable/4378860.

Bharucha, Rustom. *Theatre and the World: Performance and the Politics of Culture.* London: Routledge, 1993.

Brook, Peter. *The Empty Space.* London: MacGibbon & Kee, 1968.

Brook, Peter. "Foreword." In Jean-Claude Carrière and Peter Brook. *The Mahabharata: A Play Based Upon the Indian Classic Epic.* 1st ed. New York: Harper & Row, 1987: xiii–xvi.

Campbell, I. C. *A History of the Pacific Islands.* Berkeley: University of California Press, 1989.

Carnegie, David. "Review of *Nga Tangata Toa: The Warrior People.*" *Theatre Journal* 47, no. 2 (1995): 310–311.

Carrière, Jean-Claude, and Peter Brook. *The Mahabharata: A Play Based Upon the Indian Classic Epic.* 1st ed. New York: Harper & Row, 1987.

Carson, Margaret, Diana Taylor, and Sarah J. Townsend. *Stages of Conflict: A Critical Anthology of Latin American Theater and Performance.* Ann Arbor: University of Michigan Press, 2008.

Casey, Maryrose. *Creating Frames: Contemporary Indigenous Theatre 1967–1990.* St. Lucia: University of Queensland Press, 2004.

Césaire, Aimé. *The Tragedy of King Christophe; a Play.* Evergreen Original, E-547. New York: Grove Press, 1970.

Césaire, Aimé Fernand. *A Tempest.* Electronic Edition by Alexander Street Press, 2016.

Chang, Donald, John D. Mitchell, and Roger Yeu. "How the Chinese Actor Trains: Interviews with Two Peking Opera Performers." *Educational Theatre Journal* 26, no. 2 (1974): 183–191.

Chaudhuri, Una. "The Future of the Hyphen: Interculturalism, Textuality, and the Difference Within." In Bonnie Marranca and Gautam Dasgupta, Eds. *Interculturalism and Performance: Writings from PAJ.* New York: PAJ, 1991:192–207.

Chelkowski, Peter J. *Ta'ziyeh, Ritual and Drama in Iran.* New York University Studies in Near Eastern Civilization No. 7. New York: New York University Press, 1979.

Chesaina, Ciarunji and Evan Mwangi." Kenya." In Martin Banham. Ed. *A History of Theatre in Africa.* Cambridge: Cambridge University Press, 2004.

Chi, Jimmy, and Kuckles. *Bran Nue Dae.* In Helen Gilbert. *Postcolonial Plays: An Anthology.* London: Routledge, 2001: 324–347.

Conteh-Morgan, John, and Tejumola Olaniyan. *African Drama and Performance.* Bloomington: Indiana University Press, 2004.

Crane, Diana, Nobuko Kawashima, and Kenichi Kawasaki. *Global Culture: Media, Arts, Policy, and Globalization.* New York: Routledge, 2002.

Cronin, Stephanie. *Iranian–Russian Encounters: Empires and Revolutions since 1800.* New York: Routledge, 2013.

Croyden, Margaret. "Peter Brook Transforms an Indian Epic for the Stage." *The New York Times* August 25, 1985, sec. Arts. www.nytimes.com/1985/08/25/arts/peter-brook-transforms-an-indian-epic-for-the-stage.html. June 28, 2016.

Dasgupta, Gautam. "'The Mahabharata': Peter Brook's 'Orientalism.'" *Performing Arts Journal* 10, no. 3 (1987): 9–16.

Daugherty, Diane. "The Pendulum of Intercultural Performance: 'Kathakali King Lear' at Shakespeare's Globe." *Asian Theatre Journal* 22, no. 1 (2005): 52–72. www.jstor.org/stable/4137075.

Davis, Jack Leonard. *The Dreamers.* Electronic Edition by Alexander Street Press, L.L.C., 2016 [1981]. Also published in *Kullark and The Dreamers.* Sydney: Currency Press, 1982. http://solomon.bld2.alexanderstreet.com.proxy.lib.umich.edu/cgi-bin/asp/philo/navigate.pl?bld2.676. June 28, 2016.

Doniger, Wendy. "Hanuman (Hindu mythology)". *Encyclopædia Britannica.* Updated October 14, 2014. Retrieved February, 2, 2016. https://www.britannica.com/topic/Hanuman.

Drewal, Henry John. "The Arts of Egungun among Yoruba Peoples". *African Arts* 11, no. 3 (1978): 18–98.

El Nabawi, Maha. "Playwright Reflects on Role of Independent Theater in Egyptian Revolution." *Egypt Independent.* 3 October 2013.

Elali, Nadine. "Sentient Solidarity." *NOW News.* September 16, 2011. https://now.mmedia.me/lb/en/reportsfeatures/sentient_solidarity. June 28, 2016.

Eldar, Shlomi. "East Jerusalem Theater Fights to Keep Doors Open." *Al-Monitor* December 22, 2015. www.al-monitor.com/pulse/originals/2015/12/palestinian-national-theatre-el-hakawati-east-jerusalem.html#ixzz44nm6wG7v. June 28, 2016.

Enoch, Wesley, and Griffin Theatre Company. *The Story of the Miracles at Cookie's Table*. Sydney: Currency Press; in association with Griffin Theatre Company, 2007.

Ernst, Earle. "Notes on the Form of Kabuki, I." *Educational Theatre Journal* 6, no. 3 (1954): 201–209.

Fernández Retamar, Roberto. "Caliban: Notes towards a Discussion of Culture in Our America." Trans. Lynn Garafola, David Arthur McMurray, and Robert Márquez. *Massachusetts Review* 15, no. 1/2 (1974): 7–72. www.jstor.org/stable/ 25088398. Originally published as *Calibán; apuntes sobre la cultura en nuestra América*. Mexico: Editorial Diógenes, 1971.

Fitzgerald, Mary Ann, Henry J. Drewal, and Moyo Okediji. "Transformation through Cloth: An Egungun Costume of the Yoruba". *African Arts* 28, no. 2 (1995): 55–57.

Foley, Kathy. "Shakespeare–Asian Theatre Fusions: Globe-'alization' of Naked Masks (Bangkok), Shadowlight (San Francisco), and Setagaya Public Theatre (Tokyo)". *Asian Theatre Journal* 28, no. 1 (2011): 7–43. www.jstor.org.proxy.lib. umich.edu/stable/41306469.

Gambaro, Griselda, and Marguerite Feitlowitz. *Information for Foreigners: Three Plays*. Evanston, IL: Northwestern University Press, 1992.

Gassner, John, and Edward Quinn. *The Reader's Encyclopedia of World Drama*. New York: Crowell, 1969.

Gerould, Daniel Charles. *Theatre, Theory, Theatre: The Major Critical Texts from Aristotle and Zeami to Soyinka and Havel*. New York: Applause Theatre and Cinema Books, 2000.

Gilbert, Helen. *Postcolonial Plays: An Anthology*. New York: Routledge, 2001.

Goodlander, Jennifer. "Gender, Power, and Puppets: Two Early Women 'Dalangs' in Bali". *Asian Theatre Journal* 29, no. 1 (2012): 54–77. www.jstor.org.proxy.lib. umich.edu/stable/23359544.

Guy, Nancy A. "Peking Opera as 'National Opera' in Taiwan: What's in a Name?" *Asian Theatre Journal* 12, no. 1 (1995): 85–103.

Hatley, Barbara. "Women in Contemporary Indonesian Theatre: Issues of Representation and Participation". *Bijdragen Tot De Taal-, Land- En Volkenkunde* 151, no. 4 (1995): 570–601. www.jstor.org.proxy.lib.umich.edu/stable/ 27864704.

Hatley, Barbara. "Ratna Accused, and Defiant." *Inside Indonesia* Edition 55, July–September 1998. www.insideindonesia.org/ratna-accused-and-defiant. June 28, 2016.

Hellwig, Tineke, and Eric Tagliacozzo. *The Indonesia Reader: History, Culture, Politics*. Durham, NC: Duke University Press, 2009.

Hereniko, Vilsoni. *The Monster & Other Plays*. Suva, Fiji: Mana Publications, 1989.

Hereniko, Vilsoni. "'The Monster (A Fantasy).' A One-Act Play, with an Interview with the Playwright." *Pacific Studies* 15, no. 4 (1992): 177.

Herrick, Linda. "Home Fires Rekindled." *New Zealand Herald* October 13, 2002, Lifestyle. www.nzherald.co.nz/lifestyle/news/article.cfm?c_id=6&objectid= 2998920 June 28, 2016.

Heywood, Christopher. *A History of South African Literature.* New York: Cambridge University Press, 2004.

Highway, Tomson. *The Rez Sisters: A Play in Two Acts.* Saskatoon: Fifth House, 1988.

Hijikata, Tatsumi, Michael Blackwood, Bonnie S. Stein, Lynn Piasecki, and Russell Connor. *Butoh: Body on the Edge of Crisis.* Northvale, NJ: Michael Blackwood Productions, 2006. DVD Video.

Holledge, Julie and Joanne Tompkins. *Women's Intercultural Performance.* New York: Routledge, 2000.

Hughes-Tafen, Denise. "Women, Theatre and Calypso in the English-Speaking Caribbean." *Feminist Review* no. 84 (2006): 48–66. www.jstor.org.proxy.lib. umich.edu/stable/30232739.

Hutchins, William M. *Tawfiq Al-Hakim: A Reader's Guide.* Boulder, CO: Lynne Rienner, 2003.

Hutchison, Yvette. "South African Theatre." In Martin Banham. *A History of Theatre in Africa.* Cambridge: Cambridge University Press, 2004: 312–379.

Jess, Allison. "I Don't Wanna Play House: Raising Awareness on Domestic and Child Abuse." *ABC Goulburn Murray* July 9, 2010. www.abc.net.au/local/ audio/2010/07/09/2949459.htm. June 28, 2016.

Johansson, Ola. "The Limits of Community-based Theatre: Performance and HIV Prevention in Tanzania." *TDR (1988–)* 54, no. 1 (2010): 59–75. www. jstor.org.proxy.lib.umich.edu/stable/40650522.

Karnis, Michael V. "Surviving Pre-Columbian Drama." *Educational Theatre Journal* 4, no. 1 (1952): 39–45.

Kaynar, Gad. "National Theatre as Colonized Theatre: The Paradox of Habima." *Theatre Journal* 50, no. 1 (1998): 1–20. www.jstor.org.proxy.lib.umich.edu/ stable/25068480.

Kenney, John. "Belles Soeurs: The Musical." *Montreal Gazette* 24 October 2014. https://www.youtube.com/watch?v=hnq5TqbdmI4 (accessed 15 June 2016).

Kerbel, Sorrel. *The Routledge Encyclopedia of Jewish Writers of the Twentieth Century.* New York: Routledge, 2004.

Klein, Maxine. "Theatre of the Ancient Maya." *Educational Theatre Journal* 23, no. 3 (1971): 269–276.

Korsovitis, Constantine. "Ways of the Wayang." *India International Centre Quarterly* 28, no. 2 (2001): 59–68. www.jstor.org.proxy.lib.umich.edu/stable/23005511.

Kruger, Loren. *The Drama of South Africa: Plays, Pageants, and Publics since 1910.* New York: Routledge, 1999.

Kuniyoshi, Kazuko. "Two Kinjiki: Diametrical Oppositions". *TDR (1988–)* 50, no. 2 (2006): 154–158. www.jstor.org.proxy.lib.umich.edu/stable/4492681.

Kunjunni Raja, K. *Kutiyattam, an Introduction.* 1st ed. New Delhi: Sangeet Natak Akademi, 1964.

Leiter, Samuel L. *Historical Dictionary of Japanese Traditional Theatre.* 2nd ed. Lanham, MD: Rowman & Littlefield, 2014.

Levy, Emanuel. *The Habima, Israel's National Theater, 1917–1977: A Study of Cultural Nationalism.* New York : Columbia University Press, 1979.

Liaw, Yock Fang. *A History of Classical Malay Literature.* Translated by Bahari Razif and Harry Aveling. Singapore: ISEAS, 2013.

Lienhard, Martín. "La épica incaica en tres textos coloniales (Juan de Betanzos, Titu Cusi Yupanqui, el Ollantay)." *Lexis* 9, no. 1 (1985): 61–80.

Liu, Siyuan. *Routledge Handbook of Asian Theatre.* New York: Routledge, 2016.

Long, Roger. "Peter Brook's 'The Mahabharata': A Personal Reaction." *Asian Theatre Journal* 5, no. 2 (1988): 233–235. www.jstor.org.proxy.lib.umich.edu/stable/25161495.

Looser, Diana. *Remaking Pacific Pasts: History, Memory, and Identity in Contemporary Theater from Oceania.* Honolulu: University of Hawai'i Press, 2014.

Mahani, Mahnia A. Nematollahi. *The Holy Drama: Persian Passion Play in Modern Iran.* Leiden: Leiden University Press, 2013.

Martin, Michèle. "Modulating Popular Culture: Cultural Critics on Tremblay's 'Les Belles-Soeurs.'" *Labour/Le Travail* 52 (2003): 109–135. www.jstor.org.proxy.lib.umich.edu/stable/25149385.

Matura, Mustapha. *Play Mas.* Electronic Edition by Alexander Street Press, L.L.C., 2016 [1974]. http://solomon.bld2.alexanderstreet.com.proxy.lib.umich.edu/cgi-bin/asp/philo/navigate.pl?bld2.1214. June 28, 2016.

Meisami, Julie Scott, and Paul Starkey. *Encyclopedia of Arabic Literature.* London: Routledge, 1998.

Melançon, Joseph, and Lisa Gosselin. "The Writing of Difference in Québec." *Yale French Studies* no. 65 (1983): 21–29.

Modi, Chintan Girish. "Making Art in the Time of Occupation." *The Hindu.* 8 January 2016.

Moosa, Matti. *The Origins of Modern Arabic Fiction.* 1st ed. Washington, DC: Three Continents Press, 1983.

Mrázek, Jan. "Javanese Wayang Kulit in the Times of Comedy: Clown Scenes, Innovation, and the Performance's Being in the Present World. Part One". *Indonesia* no. 68 (1999): 38–128.

Mrázek, Jan. "Javanese 'Wayang Kulit' in the Times of Comedy: Clown Scenes, Innovation, and the Performance's Being in the Present World. Part Two". *Indonesia* no. 69 (2000): 107–172.

Mueller, Jacqueline. 1986. "A Chronicle of Great Peace Played Out on a Chessboard: Chikamatsu Monzaemon's Goban Taiheiki". *Harvard Journal of Asiatic Studies* 46, no. 1: 221–267.

Ndlovu, Duma. *Woza Afrika!: An Anthology of South African Plays.* New York: G. Braziller, 1986.

New, William H. *Encyclopedia of Literature in Canada*. Toronto: University of Toronto Press, 2002.

Ngũgĩ wa Thiong'o. *Decolonising the Mind: The Politics of Language in African Literature*. London: J. Currey, 1986.

Ngũgĩ wa Thiong'o, and Ngũgĩ wa Mĩriĩ. *I Will Marry When I Want*. London: Heinemann, 1982.

Okpewho, Isidore. *African Oral Literature: Backgrounds, Character, and Continuity*. Bloomington: Indiana University Press, 1992.

Ostroff, Joshua. "Tomson Highway Has a Surprisingly Positive Take on Residential Schools." *Huffington Post* December 15, 2015, Canada ed., sec. What's Working.

Pemberton, John. "Egungun Masquerades of the Igbomina Yoruba". *African Arts* 11, no. 3 (1978): 41–100.

Performing Arts Network Japan. "Artist Interview: A Glimpse of the 'Total Theater' that Mansai Nomura Envisions as a Kyogen Actor Alive in the Contemporary World." The Japan Foundation July 30, 2007. www.performing arts.jp/E/art_interview/0707/1.html. June 28, 2016.

Pettys, Rebecca Ansary. "The Ta'zieh: Ritual Enactment of Persian Renewal." *Theatre Journal* 33, no. 3 (1981): 341–354.

Powell, Brian. *Japan's Modern Theatre: A Century of Change and Continuity*. Folkestone: Japan Library, 1994.

Prentki, Tim. "From Neocolonial to Postcolonial: Some Implications for the Practice of Theatre for Development." *Caribbean Quarterly* 53, no. 1/2 (2007): 194–204. www.jstor.org.proxy.lib.umich.edu/stable/40654984.

Preston, Jennifer. "Weesageechak Begins to Dance: Native Earth Performing Arts Inc." *TDR (1988–)* 36, no. 1 (1992): 135–159.

Raghavan, V. *Sanskrit Drama Its Aesthetics and Production*. 1st ed. Madras: Sarada Raghavan, 1993.

Ramnath Subbaraman. "Beyond the Question of the Monkey Imposter: Indian Influence on the Chinese Novel *The Journey to the West*." *Sino-Platonic Papers* 114 (March 2002).

Reinelt, Janelle G., and Joseph R. Roach. *Critical Theory and Performance*. Ann Arbor: University of Michigan Press, 1992.

Riccio, Thomas. "Kenya's Community Health Awareness Puppeteers." *PAJ: A Journal of Performance and Art* 26, no. 1 (2004): 1–12. www.jstor.org.proxy.lib.umich.edu/stable/3246435.

Rodríguez, Jesusa. "Arquetipas: A Prehispanic Cabaret (2004)." *Holy Terrors: Latin American Women Perform*. New York: Hemispheric Institute – NYU, 2014. http://scalar.usc.edu/nehvectors/taylor/plays-and-performances-1. June 28, 2016.

Rothstein, Mervyn. "A Playwright Holds a Light to Israel's Soul." *New York Times* October 30, 1988, sec. Theatre. www.nytimes.com/1988/10/30/arts/

theater-a-playwright-holds-a-light-to-israel-s-soul.html?pagewanted=all. June 28, 2016.

Said, Edward W. *Orientalism*. 1st ed. New York: Pantheon Books, 1978.

Salhi, Kamal. *African Theatre for Development: Art for Self-Determination*. Exeter: Intellect, 1998.

Sanders, Vicki. "Dancing and the Dark Soul of Japan: An Aesthetic Analysis of 'Butō.'". *Asian Theatre Journal* 5, no. 2 (1988): 148–163. www.jstor.org.proxy.lib.umich.edu/stable/25161489.

Sarumpaet, Ratna. *Marsinah: A Song from the Underworld*. Canberra: Aberrant Genotype Press, 1998.

Sarumpaet, Ratna. *Marsinah Accuses*. In Tineke Hellwig and Eric Tagliacozzo. Eds. *The Indonesia Reader: History, Culture, Politics*. Durham, NC: Duke University Press, 2009.

Schechner, Richard. "Rasaesthetics." *TDR: The Drama Review* 45, no. 3 (2001): 27–50.

Sen, Ong Keng. "Director's Message." *Lear* Program. TheatreWorks, 1999.

Sen, Ong Keng. "Encounters." *TDR (1988–)* 45, no. 3 (2001): 126–133. www.jstor.org.proxy.lib.umich.edu/stable/1146916.

Sikes, Alan. "Theatre History, Theatrical Mimesis, and the Myth of the Abydos Passion Play." *Theatre History Studies* 34, no. 1 (2015): 3–18.

Sistren Theatre Collective. *QPH*. In Helen Gilbert. *Postcolonial Plays: An Anthology*. London: Routledge, 2001: 157–178.

Snir, Reuven. "The Palestinian Al-Hakawati Theater: A Brief History." *Arab Studies Journal* 6/7, no. 2/1 (1998): 57–71. www.jstor.org.proxy.lib.umich.edu/stable/27933738.

Solórzano, Carlos. *Teatro Latinoamericano del Siglo XX*. Buenos Aires: Ediciones Nueva Visión, 1961.

Soyinka, Wole. *Death and the King's Horseman*. New York: Norton, 2002.

Stoller, Paul. "Embodying Colonial Memories." *American Anthropologist*, New Series, 96, no. 3 (1994): 634–648. www.jstor.org.proxy.lib.umich.edu/stable/682304.

Sudraka and Arthur W. Ryder. *The Little Clay Cart (Mrcchakatika): A Hindu Drama Attributed to King Shudraka*. Cambridge, MA: Harvard University, 1905.

Tarulevicz, Nicole. "Review of 'Theatre and the Politics of Culture in Contemporary Singapore' by William Peterson." *Journal of Southeast Asian Studies* 34, no. 1 (2003): 184–185. www.jstor.org/stable/20072494.

Taylor, Diana. "Scenes of Cognition: Performance and Conquest." *Theatre Journal* 56, no. 3 (2004): 353–372. www.jstor.org.proxy.lib.umich.edu/stable/25069464.

Taylor, Drew Hayden. "Storytelling to Stage: The Growth of Native Theatre in Canada." *TDR (1988–)* 41, no. 3 (1997): 140–152.

Taylor, Jane, and William Kentridge, and Handspring Puppet Company. *Ubu and the Truth Commission*. Cape Town: University of Cape Town Press, 1998.

Tedlock, Dennis. *Rabinal Achi: A Mayan Drama of War and Sacrifice*. Oxford: Oxford University Press, 2003.

Tremblay, Michel. *Les Belles Soeurs*. Vancouver, BC: Talonbooks, 1974.

Van Erven, Eugène. *Community Theatre: Global Perspectives*. New York: Routledge, 2001.

Viswanathan, Gauri. "The Beginnings of English Literary Study in British India." *Oxford Literary Review: Colonialism & Other Essays* 9, no. 1 (1987): 2–26.

Walcott, Derek. *Dream on Monkey Mountain, and Other Plays*. New York: Farrar, 1970.

Walker, Hera S. "Indigenous or Foreign? A Look at the Origins of the Monkey Hero Sun Wukong." *Sino-Platonic Papers* 81 (September 1998). http://sino-platonic.org/complete/spp081_monkey_sun_wukong.pdf.

Winet, Evan Darwin. "Between Umat and Rakyat: Islam and Nationalism in Indonesian Modern Theatre". *Theatre Journal* 61, no. 1 (2009): 43–64. www.jstor.org.proxy.lib.umich.edu/stable/40211157.

Winet, Evan Darwin. *Indonesian Postcolonial Theatre: Spectral Genealogies and Absent Faces*. New York: Palgrave Macmillan, 2010.

Wong, Melissa Wansin. "Negotiating Class, Taste, and Culture via the Arts Scene in Singapore: Postcolonial or Cosmopolitan Global?" *Asian Theatre Journal* 29, no. 1 (2012): 233–254. www.jstor.org/stable/23359553.

Worthen, William B. *The Wadsworth Anthology of Drama*. 5th ed. Boston, MA: Thomson/Wadsworth, 2007.

Xu Chengbei. *Peking Opera: The Performance behind the Painted Faces*. 2nd ed. Beijing: China Intercontinental Press, 2010.

Yousof, Ghulam Sarwar. "Islamic Elements in Traditional Indonesian and Malay Theatre." *Kajian Malaysia* 28, no. 1 (2010): 83–101.

Zarrilli, Phillip. "The Aftermath: When Peter Brook Came to India." *The Drama Review: TDR* 30, no. 1 (1986): 92–99.

Zarrilli, Phillip. "For Whom Is the King a King? Issues of Cross-Cultural Production, Perception, and Reception in a Kathakali King Lear." In Janelle Reinelt and Joseph R. Roach, Eds. *Critical Theory and Performance*. Ann Arbor: University of Michigan Press, 1992: 16–40.

Zarrilli, Phillip B. *Kathakali Dance-Drama: Where Gods and Demons Come to Play*. London: Routledge, 2000.

Zeami. "From 'A Mirror Held to the Flower' (1424)." In William B. Worthen, Ed. *The Wadsworth Anthology of Drama*. 5th ed. Boston, MA: Thomson/Wadsworth, 2007: 182–191.

Ziter, Edward. "Clowns of the Revolution: The Malas Twins and Syrian Oppositional Performance." *Theatre Research International* 38, Special Issue 02 (2013): 137–147.

INDEX